LIVING TOGETHER

ENGLISH FOR HOUSEKEEPING AND SOCIAL CARE

von
Maureen Bamming
Horst Beckmann
Gisela Machunsky
Elsa Toben-Vollmer

6., völlig überarbeitete Auflage

Dr. Felix Büchner – Handwerk und Technik · Hamburg

Vorwort

Living Together ist ein Lehrwerk für das Unterrichtsfach Englisch. Es ermöglicht Schülerinnen und Schülern der Hauswirtschaft und Sozialpflege, in zwei Jahren vom Grundlagenbereich bis hin zum Erwerb des erweiterten Sekundarabschlusses I zu kommen. Es entspricht den Lehrplänen des Faches Englisch in den beruflichen Schulen.

Die Themenbereiche in Living Together wurden so zusammengestellt, dass sie zum einen hauswirtschaftliche und sozialpflegerische Kenntnisse vermitteln, zum anderen die Lebensprobleme der Jugendlichen in diesem Alter ansprechen. Die bereits vorhandenen englischen Grundkenntnisse der Schüler werden durch integrierte **Übungen zur Grammatik** (grün hinterlegt) wiederholt.

Weitere Elemente von Living Together

- **Zahlreiche Aufgaben** und Impulse ermöglichen eine Binnendifferenzierung durch die Lehrkraft.
- **Listening Comprehensions** bieten Aufgaben zum Hörverstehen an. Die Audio-Tracks dazu befinden sich auf der Audio-CD, die Transkripte als Texte im Lösungsheft. Alle Audio-Tracks können auch per TING-Stift abgespielt werden (→ CD-Symbol).
- **Kompetenzen:** Es werden Aufgaben zur Rezeption, Produktion und Interaktion ausgewiesen. Die Mediation (die Fähigkeit, durch Übersetzung/Umschreibung mündlich oder schriftlich zwischen zwei Kommunikationspartnern zu vermitteln) wird im Anschluss an Unit 3, 6 und 9 gesondert aufgegriffen.
- **Tipp-Kasten:** Tipps und Hinweise zum fachlichen oder sprachlichen Unterricht
- **Die Methodenseiten/Activities** im Anhang ermöglichen kommunikationsfördernde Unterrichtsformen wie Planung von Quizveranstaltungen, Feiern oder Diskussionen.
- **Verweise auf die Methodenseiten** schaffen Impulse zur Verknüpfung von Kapiteln und "Activities".
- Nach jedem Kapitel folgt ein **Vokabelverzeichnis** der neuen Wörter inklusive englischsprachiger Umschreibung und Lautschrift. Alle Vokabeln sind im Anhang noch einmal alphabetisch zusammengefasst.
- Ein **grammatikalischer Anhang** stellt grundlegende Regeln der englischen Grammatik zum Nachlesen in deutscher Sprache zusammen.
- Spezielle Kommunikationsspiele ("**Talking Game**") für die Partnerarbeit wiederholen spielerisch Wortschatz und Inhalt.

Das Autorenteam und der Verlag wünschen allen Lernenden und Lehrenden viel Spaß und Erfolg mit Living Together. Learning English is fun!

ISBN 978-3-582-01621-8

Zu diesem Buch erhältlich:
Arbeitsheft "Living Together Workbook" (HT 1623)
Audio-CD (HT 16211)
Lösungsheft (HT 1622)

Verlag Dr. Felix Büchner –
Verlag Handwerk und Technik GmbH,
Lademannbogen 135, 22339 Hamburg;
Postfach 63 05 00, 22331 Hamburg – 2011
E-Mail: info@handwerk-technik.de
Internet: www.handwerk-technik.de

Umschlagsmotiv: Harro Wolter, Hamburg
Satz und Layout: Roman Bold & Black, 50672 Köln
Druck: Offizin Andersen Nexö Leipzig, 04442 Zwenkau

Inhaltsverzeichnis

Unit 1 Starting a Career

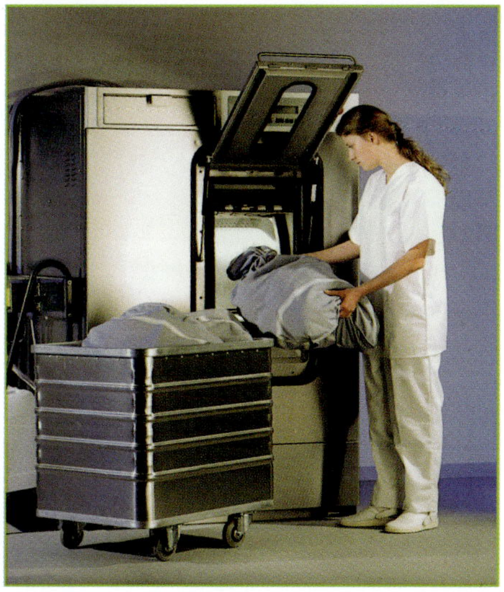

A Do you already have any practical experiences in any kind of work? If so, which ones? Tell your classmates about it.

1.1 Our Practical Training

Carol and Jason attend a vocational school in Manchester. They both like to work with people.
Carol wants to become a housekeeper and Jason would like to become either a male nurse or a geriatric nurse in an old people's home.

At present they are doing some practical training. Carol is working in the kitchen of St. George's Hospital and Jason is working there, too. He works on a surgical ward. Their practical training lasts three weeks.

During their break they meet each other in the canteen. It is their second day in the hospital.

Carol: Hi, Jason, how are things going? Do you like your practical training?

Jason: Hi, Carol, well, I do not really know yet.

Carol: What's wrong? Do you have any problems?

Jason: Well, I feel so insecure. Everything is new to me and I am a bit confused. There is a little boy on the ward who is screaming because he misses his mother so much. I really feel sorry for him. The nurses are running up and down the ward and I do not really know why they are so busy. But I am a little bit proud, too. I already know how to make the beds. After my break I am going to ask the patients what they want to eat next week. I just have to mark it with a cross in the next week's menu.

Carol: Oh, that's not a bad start, is it? I am …

Jason: Bye, Carol, take care. I must hurry back to work. I do not want to be late!

Carol (sighs after Jason has gone):
Why do guys only talk about themselves? He has not asked me how I am doing in the kitchen …

When Carol comes home, it is seven o'clock in the evening. Her mother is already waiting for her.

Mother: Oh, Carol, you look tired!

Carol: I am tired, Mum. You know that I'm on my feet all day and they hurt like hell now.

Mother: Oh, I'm sorry about that but I'm sure that you will get used to it. Do you at least like it in the hospital canteen?

Carol: I really do, I love it. There are so many new things to learn. It's really exciting.

Mother: I am just making some food. Are you hungry?

Carol: No, Mum, not at all. I am working in a kitchen, you see?

It is important that young people get the chance to visit some work placements while they are at school. This helps them to decide which job to choose later on.

A

Carol's little sister Lindsey always likes to listen to Carol. Now Lindsey is telling her girlfriend Kathrin what she has heard. Being so young, she does not understand everything. Help her and correct the sentences.

1. Carol wants to become a nurse.
2. Mark works in the kitchen.
3. When Carol comes home from work she is very hungry.
4. During her work Carol can often sit down.
5. Jason wants to become a housekeeper.
6. Carol's arms and feet hurt a lot.

B

Describe the cartoon. Use either the simple present or the present progressive.
Example:
There **is** a round table in the middle of the room. (simple present)
Two people **are sitting** on this table. (present progressive)

C

This cartoon was printed in a nursing magazine. What do you think does the author want to point out?

Present Progressive

(➜ See also page 166, „Grammatikalischer Anhang" in German)

When do you use the present progressive?

The present progressive describes an activity that is happening right now. You also use the present progressive when an activity continues over a long period (= die Dauer der Handlung soll betont werden).

You use: **am/is/are** + verb + **ing**

Signal words: now, just now, at present, at the moment, all day long, look, listen, but today

Examples:
I **am** work**ing** in a kitchen.
My mother **is** cook**ing** a meal.
Carol and Jason **are** do**ing** a practical training.

Statement Clause (Aussagesatz)			
I	**am**	cook**ing**	a meal.
He She It	**is**		
We You They	**are**		

Negative Clause (Verneinter Satz)			
I	**am**	not work**ing**	in an old people's home.
He She It	**is**		
We You They	**are**		

Question (Fragesatz)			
What	**am**	I	**doing?**
	is	he	
		she	
		it	
	are	we	
		you	
		they	

Spelling Rules:

Verbs that end in -**e**:

mak**e**	➜	**making**
writ**e**	➜	**writing**
driv**e**	➜	**driving**
etc.		

Verbs that end **in a vowel (a, e, i, o, u) with a consonant (p, t, g, m etc.)**:

r**un**	➜	ru**nn**ing
g**et**	➜	ge**tt**ing
sw**im**	➜	swi**mm**ing
etc.		

Verbs that end in -**ie**:

l**ie**	➜	l**y**ing
d**ie**	➜	d**y**ing
etc.		

A What are these people doing right now? Use the verbs in the box to form sentences in the present progressive.

to get – to work – to sweep to go – to relax – to plan to walk around – to wait

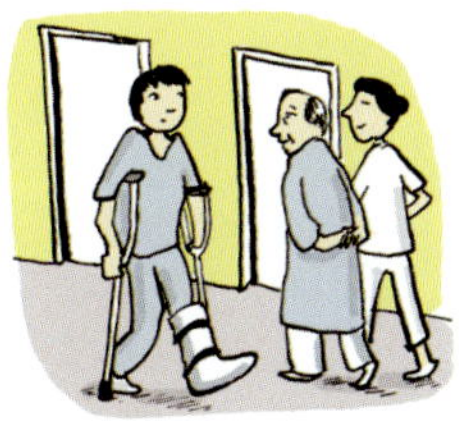

Example:
Carol … ready for work.
- Carol is getting ready for work.

1. Jason ……………..home after work.
2. Carol and her friend……….. on a couch.
3. The kitchen team …………… the menu.
4. Carol and Jason………………… in a hospital.
5. The housecleaners…………… the floor.
6. Some patients ……………….. on the hospital floor.
7. Carol ………… at the bus stop.

B Put the words in brackets into the present progressive.

Examples:
Mother (cook) a meal right now.
- Mother is cooking a meal right now.

At present Carol (work), she (not go) to school.
- At present Carol is working, she is not going to school.

1. Hi Carol, ….you (get on) well?
2. Look, Carol (sleep) because she is so tired.
3. Where are Carol's parents? They (visit) their neighbours.
4. Jason (not listen) to Carol.
5. Why ….. Carol (not go) to school at the moment?
6. Carol (not watch) TV, she (lie) in bed.
7. Carol always wears jeans, but in the kitchen she (wear) work clothing.
8. Why ….. you (run), Jason? Are you late again?
9. I am not hungry because I (work) in the kitchen at present.
10. Do you know what you (do)? You are going to cut your fingers with that knife.

1.2 Working in a Canteen Kitchen

What do people who work in the canteen kitchen of a hospital have to do? Some people have to prepare breakfast. They make tea and coffee. Some people put bread on the trays while others add cheese, butter, jam or other things for the patients. There is always a dietician who checks that the patients only get what they are allowed to eat. One person puts the tray onto a trolley and others deliver the food to the wards.

A Find these words in the text and add them to your vocabulary list.

Frühstück – Tablett – Patient – kontrollieren – hinzufügen – Diätassistent/-in
liefern – erlauben – Station (in einem Krankenhaus) – Stationswagen – Essen

B After breakfast, all the people who work in the kitchen have to do many different things. Who does what? Match the profession with the job description. (! Do not forget to add an 's' to the verb.)

Example:
A baker bakes bread and cakes.

I did not know…

… that jam and marmalade are not the same. Marmalade is made from citrus fruits like oranges.

Profession	Job Description
chef	check the delivered food
dietician	sweep the floor
baker	help chef to prepare the meal
dishwasher (person)	cook the meal
housekeeper	bake bread and cakes
housecleaner	prepare special diets
trainee	put plates, pots etc. into the dishwasher

C Translate these sentences into English. Use the present progressive.

1. Ich mache gerade ein Praktikum (to do a practical training)
2. Im Moment arbeite ich in einer Krankenhausküche.
3. Ich lerne gerade, einen Speiseplan zu schreiben.
4. Die Diätassistentinnen kontrollieren gerade das Essen.
5. Momentan gehe ich nicht zur Schule.

1.3 Working in a Hospital Ward

What about Jason? How is he doing? Let us have a look on the ward where Jason is working at present. It is the third day of his practical training.

Ward Nurse: Hi, Jason, why are you just standing around? Why are you staring into space? Is there nothing for you to do?

Jason: Well, it is only my third day here and nobody is really telling me what to do.

Ward Nurse: It is only your third day? It is already your third day! Time flies. Make sure that you learn something. I am sorry that we are so busy at the moment. Who is responsible for you?

Jason: Nurse Sadler, but she is off sick.

Ward Nurse: Yes, that is right, I forgot about that. I am going to ask Nurse Cooper if she has got time for you. Maybe you can shadow her and give her a hand. Just wait a minute.

(after a short time)

Ward Nurse: Jason, this is Nurse Cooper. She will be in charge of you as long as Nurse Sadler is off sick.

Nurse Cooper: Hi, Jason, don't be shy. Don't just stand around. We all need a helping hand. Just come and ask us what you can do.

Jason: But I am so afraid that I'll make a mistake, that I do something wrong.

Nurse Cooper: You don't have to. We were all beginners once, you see? I am just serving breakfast. You can help me. I'll keep an eye on you, I promise.

Jason: That's great. Thank you, Nurse Cooper.

Tips for your training

Do not try to be another person – just be yourself. Don't be afraid to ask if you are not sure whether you understood everything right the first time. Do not wait to be told – have a look for yourself to see if there is work for you to do.

A Questions on the text. Answer in whole sentences. RECEPTION

Example:
Why is Jason standing around?
Jason is standing around because he does not know what to do.
(! Do not just say: Because he does not know what to do.)

1. What does Jason not like? Jason does not like …
2. Who wants Jason to learn something?
3. Why is Nurse Sadler not taking responsibility for Jason?
4. Why is Jason afraid?
5. What is nurse Cooper doing at the moment?
6. What does she promise to Jason?

Tip

Whenever you have to answer questions on a text, do not just give the answer. It is always better to repeat a part of the question. Always answer in whole sentences.

B You have probably done a practical training, too. How was your first day? Tell your classmates about your experience.

Personal Pronouns

(→ See also page 170, „Grammatikalischer Anhang" in German)

Subject form: A noun is a naming word. You can say: Lisa reads a book. → *Lisa* is a noun. Instead of *Lisa* you can say: **She** reads a book. → *She* is a personal pronoun. When the pronoun is a subject, you use these pronouns: I, you, he, she, it, we, you, they

Object form: There are also object forms. You can say: Lisa likes Peter. Instead of *Peter* you can say: Lisa likes **him**. → *Him* is the object form.
When the pronoun is an object you use: me, you, him, her, it, us, you, them

She likes him.
She ⇩ Subject
him ⇩ Object

A Subject forms. Use the personal pronouns in the box and complete the sentences.

I – they – you – he – it
she – you – you – I

1. My name is Carol. … am at home.
2. This is Peter. … is my boyfriend.
3. There are mum and dad. … are my parents.
4. This is Lindsey. … is my sister.
5. Mum says to Lindsey: "Can … walk the dog? … am too busy."
6. What a lovely child. … is so quiet.
7. Peter says to Carol: " … look wonderful."
8. Teacher to the pupils: "… are too noisy."

Personal Pronouns Object Forms

me	mir, mich
you	dir, dich
him	ihm, ihn
her	ihr
it	es
us	uns
you	euch, Ihnen
them	ihnen, sie

B Object forms. Use the personal pronouns in the box and complete the sentences.

him – us – them – me – you
them – him – them – you

1. I do not know how to do my homework. Can you help … , please?
2. Where are you, Peter? I cannot hear …
3. I have a date with John. I meet … at the station. I work with …
4. Sue has got trouble with her parents because she told … not to go into her room.
5. Here are the children. Give … something to eat.
6. They should eat some apples, too. Put … on the table.
7. Please, tell … about your practical training, said her parents.
8. Not right now. I will tell … about it tomorrow.

1.4 Working Days

A Do you remember?

1. Jason does not go to school. What is he doing at present?
2. Jason lives in England. In which town does he go to school?
3. Why is Carol upset when Jason goes back to work?
4. What is Jason's problem on his third day?

It is Jason's second week now in his practical training in the hospital. He already knows a lot. Let us have a look at a normal working day. What is Jason doing right now?

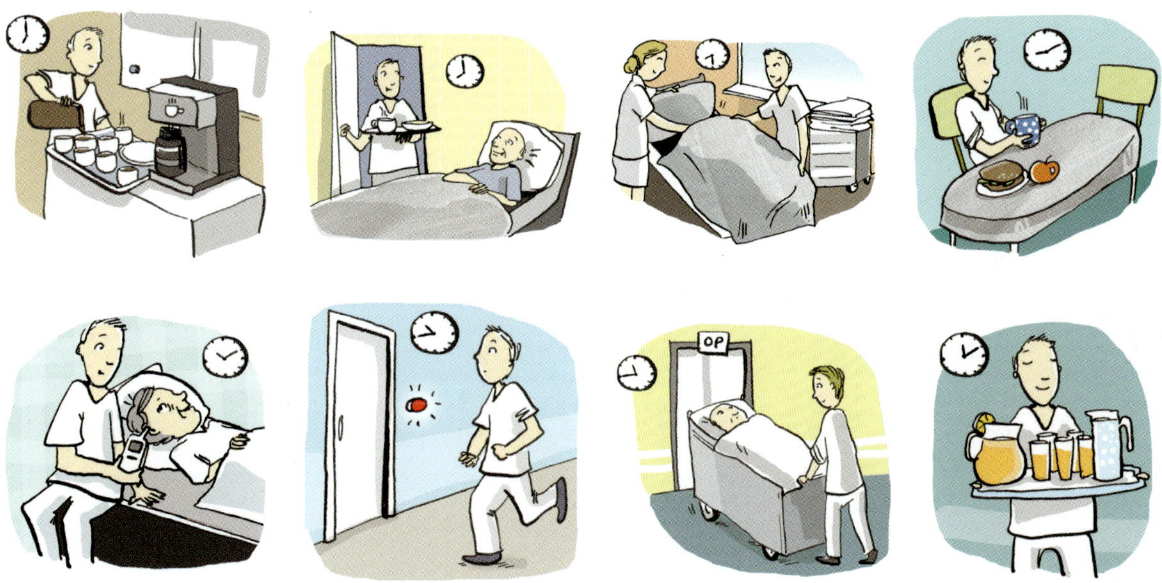

B Copy these sentences and fill in the gaps. Use the present progressive.

PRODUCTION

Example:
At seven o'clock Jason … (cook) coffee.
- At seven o'clock Jason is cooking coffee.

1. At eight o'clock he … (serve) breakfast.
2. At eight thirty he … (make) beds.
3. At ten minutes past nine he … (have) a break.
4. At … he … (check) the temperature.
5. At a quarter to eleven he … (answer) the bell.
6. At … he … (take) a patient to the theatre.
7. At … he … (serve) mineral water and orange juice.

Vocabulary

1.1 Our Practical Training		
(to) attend [ə'tend]	to go	etwas besuchen, an etwas teilnehmen
vocational school [vəʊ'keɪʃənəl sku:l]	a school for learning a job	Berufsbildende Schulen
housekeeper ['haʊsˌki:pər]	someone who does domestic tasks in a household	Hauswirtschafter/in
male nurse [meɪl nɜ:s]	someone who takes care of ill people	Krankenpfleger
geriatric nurse [ˌdʒer.i'æt.rɪk nɜ:s] (old people's nurse)	someone who takes care of old people	Altenpfleger/in
old people's home [əʊld 'pi:pl s həʊm]	a place where old people live	Altersheim/Altenwohnheim
surgical ward ['sɜ:dʒɪkəl wɔ:d]	block forming a division of a hospital shared by patients who need a similar kind of care after an operation	chirurgische Station eines Krankenhauses
(to) last [lɑ:st]	to take	dauern
(to) feel insecure [ˌɪnsɪ'kjʊər]	not to know if you do things right	sich unsicher fühlen
(to) be confused [kən'fju:zd]	unable to think with clarity	verwirrt sein
(to) scream [skri:m]	to cry loudly	schreien
(to) be proud [praʊd]	feeling self-respect	stolz sein
menu ['menju:]	a list of food which you can choose	Speiseplan
practical training ['præktɪkəl 'treɪnɪŋ]	a place where you can go to learn about jobs	Praktikumsplatz
(to) sigh [saɪ]	breathe deeply	seufzen
(to) look tired [lʊk taɪəd]	to look exhausted	müde aussehen
1.2 Working in a Canteen Kitchen		
tray [treɪ]	a box on which you can carry something, e.g. glasses, food	Tablett
dietician [ˌdaɪə'tɪʃən]	a specialist in the study of nutrition	Diätassistent/in
(to) deliver [dɪ'lɪvər]	bring something to a destiny	liefern
food [fu:d]	things you can eat	Nahrung / das Essen
plate [pleɪt]	a dish on which food is served	Teller
1.3 Working in a Hospital Ward		
(to) stare into space [steər 'ɪntu: speɪs]		Löcher in die Luft starren
(to) take care of s.o. [teɪk keər]	to watch what somebody is doing	sich um jemanden kümmern
(to) be off sick [ɒf sɪk]	to be unable to go to work because of an illness	krankgeschrieben sein
(to) give s.o. a hand [hænd]	to help somebody	helfen
(to) be in charge of s.o. [ɪn tʃɑ:dʒ]	to be responsible for somebody	verantwortlich sein für jemanden
(to) shadow ['ʃæd.əʊ]	to follow s.o. around	hier: der Anleiterin folgen
shy [ʃaɪ]	lacking of self-confidence	schüchtern sein
(to) promise ['prɒmɪs]	to tell that you will do something	versprechen
(to) be sad [sæd]	to feel unhappy	traurig sein
theatre ['θɪətər]	a place where people have an operation	Operationssaal

1

2

3

4

I have nine wishes

5

6

7

8

9

A Here is a list of things Peter would like to do or have. Which wish is which number? The wishes are not in the correct order.

a) a ski course
b) my own telephone
c) a TV set
d) holiday
e) a racing bicycle
f) go to pop concerts
g) go to parties
h) a new computer
i) a computer course

B Make a list of your own wishes. Then tell the others in your class what you would like to have or do.

Start like this:
I would like to have/go on/attend/ …

2.1 Money Problems

Sue, Liz and Peter go to a College of Further Education. They study full time. It is a school for domestic science, and they want to become housekeepers. Right now they are sitting at a table in their school cafeteria. They are talking about money, because they are always short of it. What do they think about their money problems?

Sue: "My parents give me some pocket money every week. I get £10, but I must buy the bus ticket and pay for my writing paper with it. If I want a new piece of clothing, they say: 'You must save your pocket money.' If I want an ice cream, then I cannot buy a new pullover. This is really hard."

Liz: "I think you are quite lucky! My parents pay everything for me, but I must ask them whenever I want to have money for an ice cream or a new T-shirt. They often say 'No'. My Mum works in a supermarket, but she does not earn a lot of money there. And my father is unemployed. So I always have a bad conscience when I ask them for money. And look, I am wearing really old clothes."

Peter: "My mum is divorced. We are five children in the family, and so my mum cannot go working. We live on social allowance. Money is a really big problem for us. My dad lives abroad and he does not send very much money. I must try to earn some extra money, that is why I help an old couple and do some odd jobs for them. For example I go shopping for them and clean their home and do the garden."

Do you like to fill in puzzles? Find out what the writing below means. Each symbol stands for a letter, the same symbols are the same letters. You will find the correct words in the text above.

1. A large shop where you can buy everything ⬧◆◻♏❒❍♋❒🙵♏⧫
2. Someone who works in a household ♒□◆⬧♏🙵♏♏◻♏❒
3. The pay which you get for an odd job ♏⌧⧫❒♋ ❍□■♏⍓
4. It is a cold, sweet food, tastes of chocolate, vanilla, etc. ♓♍♏ ♍❒♏♋❍
5. A school on which you train for a job 👍□●●♏♑♏ □♐ 👉◆❒⧫♒♏❒ 👈♎◆♍♋⧫♓□■
6. T-shirt, pullover, trousers, socks, shoes are ♍●□⧫♒♓■♑
7. He has no job, he is ◆■♏❍◻●□⍓♏♎
8. No longer married ♎♓❖□❒♍♏♎
9. If you only work for a few hours, you do an □♎♎ 🙰□♌

It is helpful when you draw a chart like this:

letter	1	2	3	etc.
1.	s			
2.				

hint: ⬧ = s

Solution: 👍♋■ ⍓□◆ ⧫♒♓■🙵 □♐ ♋■ □♎♎ 🙰□♌ ♋■♎ ♏♋❒■ ⬧□❍♏ ♏⌧⧫❒♋ ❍□■♏⍓?

B Look at Sue, Liz and Peter. Answer these questions on the text.

1. Find out what the young people have in common.
2. Why is Sue not happy with her pocket money?
3. Why must she be careful with her money?
4. Can Liz save her money better than Sue? Why or why not?
5. Why do Liz' parents often say "No" when she asks for money?
6. Why does Liz get a bad conscience when she asks her parents?
7. Do you believe that Peter asks for money, too?
8. Which of the three students can solve his or her money problems best? Why do you think so?

2.2 Looking for an Odd Job

In the United Kingdom a lot of young people are looking for odd jobs before or after school to make some extra money. Sue, Liz and Peter are discussing how they can find a good job with a fair pay.

Peter: "Before we make a big mistake and work like dogs for just a few pence, let's interview some fellow students who have odd jobs."

Liz: "That's a good idea. Let's start with you, Peter. You often help an old couple. What do you normally do for them?"

Peter: "Well, I go shopping for them. Then I clean their home and sometimes I even cook. But I do not earn much money. They both do not have a lot of money, you know."

Sue: "Well, then you are a nice boy, but it doesn't help you much! I don't want a job like that. My friend Peggy works on a farm every weekend. That is better."

Liz: "And what does she do there? Does she milk cows or does she plant potatoes?"

Peter: "Or does she breed kangaroos?"

Sue: "You two are making jokes. No, Peggy usually does household chores. The farmer's wife is lying in hospital for a couple of weeks."

Liz: "Well, that job sounds good. What exactly does she do?"

Sue: "Oh, she cooks meals and she washes the clothes. She also looks after the two children."

Peter: "Not bad. This is exactly what we are learning in school at the moment. So she is making her own experience and she is getting a fair pay, too."

Liz: "It is really good, but in this case it is no job for a longer period of time. Look, there is my friend Sara. – Nice clothes she is wearing. Hey Sara, do you own a clothes factory? You are wearing the latest fashion."

Sara: "No, but I work in a restaurant. I normally serve food from 9 p.m. to 12 p.m. The manager is really nice and he is looking for young waiters and waitresses. Why don't you ask him?"

A Read the dialogue and answer the questions.

1. Is Peter's job a good one? Why do you or why don't you think so?
2. What do you think of Peggy's odd job? Is it better than Peter's?
3. Why can Peggy's job be good for her training at school?
4. What problem might Peter, Sue and Liz get if they take an odd job like Sara's?

B Get into groups and answer the following questions in English. Present your results to the class on a flipchart. PRODUCTION

1. Why do many young people try to get an odd job?
2. What makes an odd job good for you? Name things which are important for you.
3. How can you find out if an odd job is good for you *before* you take it?

The Simple Present

Peter, Sue and Liz are interviewing Sally. She is lucky as she has got a job in an old people's home. As all of them are interested in the job, they visit the home and interview Sally about what she usually does. They do not want to know what Sue is doing right now (➜ for present progressive see Unit 1), but they want to know what Sally does **every day**. To ask such questions they use the simple present. ➜ See page 166 for rules

A Fill in the gaps, using the simple present.

> **Tip**
>
> Use do
> - for questions (Does she work?)
> - for negations (She doesn't work.)

> **Tip**
>
> Do not use do
> - with must, can, may (Can you help me?)
> - with forms of the verb to be (Is she ill?)
> - with have/has got (Have you got a minute?)

Peter: When **do you start** (you, start) work in the morning?

Sally: Well, when I **am** (be) on day shift, my working day starts (start) at 6 a.m.

Liz: **Do you have** (you, have) more shifts than the day shift?

Sally: Yes, of course. We **have** (have) the late shift and the night shift, too.

Sue: **1.** From when to when _____ (be) the shifts?

Sally: **2.** Well, the day shift _____ (be) from 6 a.m. to 3 p.m.

3. The late shift _____ (start) at 2 p.m. and _____ (end) at 11 p.m.

4. Finally, the night shift ______ (last) from 10 p.m. to 6 a.m.

Liz: **5.** Why _____ (the working hours overlap)?

Sally: **6.** Well, if an old person ______ (have) health problems, my colleague _____ (tell) me about those.

7. And he or she _______ (inform) me about the medicine I ______ (have) to give that person.

Peter: **8.** What ________ (you like) most about your job?

Sally: **9.** Well, I ______ (love) playing games with the old people.

10. And I _________ (sometimes, go) for a walk with them and __________ (push) their wheel chair.

Liz: **11.** And _____ (be) there anything you _______ (not like)?

Sally: **12.** Yes, I ______ (hate) when an old person ______ (die).

13. All of us ______ (be) very sad then.

14. But we _______ (not forget) that none of us _______ (live) forever.

Becoming a cook might be another good idea. So Peter, Sue and Liz go to "The Crown", a restaurant where Jake Smith works in the kitchen. They have a list of the questions they would like to ask Jake and they write down his answers in brief, so that they can remember them later when they discuss a cook's job routine.

B **Form questions and answers in simple present. Do it like this:**

Peter: Do you work at Christmas, too?

Jake: Yes, I often work at Christmas, but I don't do that every year.

Peter's, Sue's and Liz's Questions	Jake's Answers in Brief
1. wash the dishes, too?	yes, always wash dishes right after use
2. buy the food yourselves?	yes, mostly buy food ourselves
3. can eat free meals?	yes, sometimes eat what we cannot sell
4. use a cook book?	yes, sometimes use one, when try new dishes
5. work alone?	no, not alone; work in a team
6. can smoke?	no, never smoke during my work
7. get a day off per week?	yes, one day during the week
8. job stressful?	yes, sometimes, when too much work

So far Peter, Sue and Liz have only asked questions which Jake could answer with 'yes' or 'no'. They want to get some more precise answers and so they use the following question words, which are not in the correct order.

[how many, how much, how often, when, why, what, where, who]

Tip

Use 'to do' not with who!

→ Who helps you with the cooking?

C **Ask the questions and give Jake's answers. Use the right question word from the box.**

Peter's, Sue's and Liz's Questions	Jake's Answers
1. dishes cook per day? **Example:** How many dishes do you cook per day?	cook one hundred and fifty on an average day We cook one hundred and fifty dishes on an average day.
2. wear a hygienic hat?	because not want hairs in the food
3. peel the potatoes?	nobody, kitchen have a peeling machine
4. clean the kitchen (at what time)?	always clean right after a dish is ready
5. kind of food buy on the market?	buy vegetables, salads and fruit
6. cooks work in your kitchen?	on working days three, on Sundays five cooks
7. money you earn?	£300 per week, plus £15 per hour for working overtime
8. you buy the meat	buy at a local butcher's shop

Questions in Simple Present

How **do** the English form questions?
Do you know that?
Does your teacher tell you?
Look at this table.

If you leave the *question word* (wh-word) out, you will get an answer with ‚Yes, …' or ‚No, …'. We call those questions "Yes-/No-questions".
If you use a *question word*, you will get a longer answer. We call those questions "Wh-questions".

Question word				
Why	do	I	smoke	cigars?
When		you	work	there?
What	does	she	eat	… ?
Why		he	drink	milk?
How		it	help	you?
Where	do	we	do	that?
How much		you	earn	a week?
When		they	clean	the grill?

E Now form Yes-/No-questions in the simple present and give matching answers.
→ For rules see pages 166

Example:
you/smoke? – Do you smoke? – Yes, I do or No, I don't.

! CAUTION: Do not make a mistake – Look up the rules for "To do" on page 167.

1. you/work/in a kitchen? – No, …
2. she/do/the garden? – Yes, …
3. they/help old people? – Yes, …
4. Sara/serve food? – Yes, …
5. they/want/a job? – Yes, …
6. the old people/go/shopping? – No, …
7. the microwave oven/work/automatically? – Yes, …
8. Peter/is/at school? – No, …
9. Sue/can/cook well? Yes, …
10. They/are/in the cafeteria? – Yes, …

F Now form Wh-questions and give the matching answers. For your answers look in unit 2.2 "Looking for an Odd Job".

Example:
Why do you work in a restaurant?
– Because I need the money.

1. What/Peter/do/for the old couple?
2. Why/Peggy/work/on a farm?
3. When/Sara/serve/meals?
4. What/Liz, Peter and Sue/want?
5. How much/the three/know/about household chores?
6. What/Sara/can/do/with her money?
7. What training/you/get at school?

2.3 Hi Jean – No Idea of Hygiene?

Liz is happy. She has got a job in *The Old Crown*, an old restaurant in the city. She works there as a waitress. Her working hours are from 7 p.m. to 10 p.m. from Monday to Friday. On Saturdays she works from 11 a.m. to 6 p.m., for seven hours. On Sundays she works from 10 a.m. to 2 p.m. So she works more than 20 hours every week. She gets £3 an hour. That means she is able to buy nice clothes and she can go to the cinema or to the pub every now and then. She does not spend all her money – she wants to save £15 every week because she wants to get a driving licence and buy a small car, a Mini.

It's Monday evening, her first day in *The Old Crown*. She is serving the guests and is carrying trays with food and drink. Another girl named Jean is working in the kitchen. Jean is preparing the meals. The waitress must tell Jean what the guests have ordered.

Look at the picture above. Right now Liz is not serving the guests. She is waiting for the meals inside the kitchen. The kitchen is really looking dirty. Liz knows: Jean doesn't work very well. Liz remembers what her domestic science teacher has told her. She is getting angrier and angrier.

Liz: "Hey Jean, what are you doing there? Why are you wearing rings on your fingers?"
Jean: "Why – I always wear these rings. They are really hip, aren't they?"
Liz: "But your kitchen is not. You must never wear rings when you work with food. And this kitchen doesn't look very clean. It's a rubbish tip!"
Jean: "Well, I never clean the kitchen when I have to cook. I can do that later."
Liz: "After your guests have eaten the dirt? Hell, no! And why don't you wear a hygienic hat? Do you wear that later, too?"
Jean: "Yes, much later. I never wear a hygienic hat, because I am not an old lady."
Liz: "Look, some of your nice long hairs are swimming in the soup. I am not serving hairy soup. Believe me: old or young, a hairy cook is never nice."

A Are the following statements on the text true or false? Say why!

Example:
*The Old Crown is a country pub. – No, that's **false** because it's a restaurant in the city.*

1. She gives people something to eat and something to drink.
2. Liz works as a cook.
3. Liz needs all her money for living.
4. Jean is a good cook.
6. You must clean things right after you used them.

B

Answer the following questions on the text on page 21.

1. What does Liz want to do with her money?
2. How much money does Liz get every week?
3. Why does Liz want to save some money?
4. Why must Liz enter the kitchen?
5. What does Liz know about hygiene?

C

Do you want to have a clean workplace? Then you can draw posters for your kitchen and illustrate them with icons like this one on the right.
Form sentences with words from the two boxes. Be careful, the words are not in the correct order.

For example, the icon on the right can mean:
Do not wear rings on your fingers!

Now it's your turn to do the others:
Wash …
Do not …

not wear	the kitchen clean
wash	dirty utensils for cooking
wear	in a dirty kitchen
not taste	head scarf
keep	rings on your fingers
not work	food with a dirty spoon
not use	your hands after toilet

D

"Waitress, the bill, please!"
Liz must add up the prices very quickly. Look at the price list below. Read what the guest had and tell the guest what he or she must pay.

beer, 1 pint	£ 1.85
orange juice	£ 1.60
lemonade	£ 0.60
coke	£ 0.55

steak	£ 3.90
chicken	£ 1.90
fish'n'chips	£ 3.90
hamburger	£ 0,75

Example:
"Two pints of beer: three pounds seventy pence, three cokes: one pound sixty-five, two fish and chips: seven pounds eighty. That's thirteen pounds fifteen, madam/sir."

1. 2 glasses of orange juice, 3 hamburgers, 1 chicken
2. 2 pints of beer, 2 cokes, 1 steak, 1 chicken
3. 2 cokes, 5 beer, 12 hamburgers

E

Design a better menu for *The Old Crown*. You can even convert the pounds into euro prices.

F

Look at the pronouns. Copy the table „Pronouns", write down the German meaning of the words and learn them.

Pronouns

Subject Case	Object Case	Possessive
I	me	my
you	you	your
he	him	his
she	her	her
it	it	its
we	us	our
you	you	your
they	them	their

G

The landlord of The Old Crown is a nice man. He tells Liz what she must do, so Liz can learn her job quickly.
Replace the underlined noun by the right pronoun. Choose them from the table on the bottom of page 22.

Example:
*"Liz, I am thirsty. Bring **the landlord** a cup of coffee, please."*
*- "Bring **me** a cup of coffee, please."*

Landlord: "Liz, I am hungry. Bring the landlord a hamburger, please."
Liz: "Yes, sir. And shall I bring the landlord a coke, too?"
Landlord: "Yes, please. There are my friends. Make five pints of beer for my friends."
Liz: "Yes, sir. Who will pay your friends' bill?"
Landlord: "They are the landlord's guests. Give the landlord the bill."
Liz: "That man is drunken, sir. Shall I give that man another beer?"
Landlord: "No, call the man a taxi. The man cannot drive the man's car."
Liz: "The telephone. The telephone is ringing. - It's the man's wife."
Landlord: "Tell the man's wife that the wife's husband has just left. Then the landlord and Liz will have no trouble."

H

Do you love puzzles?
Find out the right word for these descriptions.

1. A school restaurant
2. A girl or a woman who serves food in a restaurant
3. It gives dirt no chance
4. The day before Sunday
5. The place where you cook meals
6. A sweet non-alcoholic drink
7. If you combine the fields with the question marks (= ?) in the right order, you get what girls look for when they go shopping.

1.	?	✌	☞	☜	❄	☜	☼	🖐	✌
2.	⌖	✌	🖐	?	☼	☜	💧	💧	
3.	?	✡	☝	🖐	☜	☠	☜		
4.	?	✌	❄	✞	☼	👎	✌	✡	
5.	😐	🖐	❄	👍	👇	?	☠		
6.	?	☜	💣	?	☠	✌	👎	☜	
7.	?	?	?	?	?	?	?		

I

Internet research

INTERACTION

Are the prices really up-to-date? Surf the Internet and find out.
A helpful internet link may be: http://www.whatprice.co.uk/food-drink/beer-prices.html
Then tell the class what you found out. Compare your prices with the prices your classmates found.

Example:
Today, a pint of lager costs ______ in ______.

Vocabulary

2.1 Money Problems		
vocational school [vəʊ'keɪʃənl skuːl]	College of Further Education (in UK)	berufsbildende Schule
domestic science [dəʊ'mestɪk 'saɪəns]	housekeeping	Hauswirtschaft
housekeeper [haʊs'kiːpə]	someone with a housekeeping job	Hauswirtschafter/-in
(to) be short of money [bɪ ʃɔːt əv 'mʌnɪ]	You have not enough money.	mit dem Geld knapp sein
(to) save money [seɪv 'mʌnɪ]	not to spend so much money	Geld sparen
piece of clothing [piːs əv 'kləʊðɪŋ]	something you can wear	ein Stück Kleidung
(to) be lucky [bɪ 'lʌkɪ]	Lottery winners were lucky.	Glück haben
(to) be unemployed [bɪ ʌnɪm'plɔɪd]	to have no job	arbeitslos sein
(to) have a bad conscience [hæv ə bæd 'kɒnʃəns]	You feel bad because of this.	ein schlechtes Gewissen haben
(to) be divorced [bɪ dɪ'vɔːsd]	no longer married	geschieden sein
social allowance ['səʊʃl ə'laʊəns]	The money that poor people get from the government	Sozialfürsorge
old couple [əʊld 'kʌpl]	an old man and woman	ein altes Paar
an odd job [ɒd dʒɒb]	a job you do for some hours, usually not regularly	Gelegenheitsarbeit
(to) do the garden [duː ðə 'gɑːdn]	to work in the garden	den Garten machen
in common [ɪn 'kɒmən]	We have something in common!	gemeinsam
2.2 Looking for an Odd Job		
(to) discuss [dɪ'skʌs]	to talk and share opinions with someone	diskutieren
fellow students ['felaʊ 'stjuːdntz]	your classmates	Mitschüler
(to) mow the lawn [maʊ ðə lɔːn]	to cut the grass	Rasen mähen
boring ['bɔːrɪŋ]	dull, not interesting	langweilig
(to) breed kangaroos [briːd ˌkæŋgə'ruː]	to raise kangaroos	Känguruhs züchten
household chores ['haʊshaʊld tʃɔːs]	the work you do in a home	Hausarbeiten
(to) sound good [saʊnd gʊd]	Something seems to be good.	gut klingen
experience [ɪk'spɪərɪəns]	You get it automatically when you do something.	Erfahrung
fair pay [fea peɪ]	enough money for your work	angemessene Bezahlung
clothes factory [kləʊðz 'fæktərɪ]	a place where shirts and other pieces of clothing are made	Textilfabrik
(to) overlap [ˌəʊ.və'læp]		ineinandergreifen, überlappen
hygienic hat [haɪ'dʒiːnɪk hæt]	a cloth to cover your hair	Kopftuch
2.3 Hi Jean - No Idea of Hygiene?		
(to) serve food [sɜːv fuːd]	to take the food to the guests	Essen servieren
waiter, waitress [weɪtə] ['weɪtrɪs]	people who work in a restaurant	Kellner, Kellnerin
team [tiːm]	a group of people working together	Mannschaft
(to) tidy up ['taɪdɪ ʌp]	to clean everything and put things back where they belong	aufräumen
somewhere else ['sʌmweə els]	in another place	woanders
rubbish tip ['rʌbɪʃ tɪp]	place where all the dirt goes	Müllhalde
every now and then ['evrɪ naʊ ænd ðen]	from time to time	ab und zu
tray [treɪ]	a board on which you put the food	Tablett
Hell, no! [hel nəʊ]		Zur Hölle, nein!
hairy ['heərɪ]	full of hairs (auch: unpleasant)	haarig (auch: unangenehm)

Unit 3 Clothes for Work

A Why are these people wearing their specific clothing?

3.1 Starting at a Vocational School

Jane works in a vocational school where young people are trained for many jobs. She is responsible for supplying the trainees with work clothes. The first term has just begun and the pupils are getting their uniforms.

Jane: Well, Barry, what do you want to be?
Barry: I want to become a baker.
Jane: Good. You are rather tall. What size do you take?
Barry: I do not know.
Jane: It doesn't matter. Just put on this jacket. Let's see if it fits you. However, you must take off your pullover first.
Barry: Well, the jacket is a bit tight.
Jane: Yes. This jacket here is a bigger size. It will fit you. And you get a baker's hat, too.
So, Jill, you're next. What do you want to be?

Jill: I want to become a geriatric nurse. But I don't want to wear any uniform.
Jane: Hm, why not?

Jill: I don't want to wear a uniform. I have my own style of dress. I love fashion. It's the way I express my feelings. I like to wear what I want and nobody should take away my identity.

Jane: But a nurse's tunic is not a uniform. It must be worn for hygienic reasons. And moreover, it is quite practical as work clothes are regularly washed and ironed by the training college.
Jill: I don't know ...
Jane: I think you will look quite dressy in your work clothes. Try them and see. Okay?

Jill hesitantly takes the clothes.

Jane: And now to you, Patrick. What do you want to become?
Patrick: A butcher.

Jane: Okay. You then get a blue-white striped shirt, a white plastic apron and white safety shoes with steel toe caps. An apron must be worn in the butchery.
Patrick: Thank you.

Jane: And now it's your turn, Shirley - what training course are you going to do?
Shirley: I want to become a cook.
Jane: Right. For you I have a beautiful white chef's hat and a white chef's tunic. You have to make sure that you always wear clean clothes in the kitchen. And now over to you, Harry. Which profession would you like to take up?

Harry: I'm going to be a waiter.
Jane: I see. Then you will be trained in our guest house. Here are a white shirt, a black bow tie, a black waistcoat, black trousers and black shoes. Make sure that these clothes are always well ironed, as you need to look smart in your job.
Harry: No problem. Thanks.

A Do you know the names of these clothes? Look at the pictures and match the numbers of the items with the words in the box.

baker's jacket – apron – chef's hat – waiter's shirt – boots – waistcoat – baker's hat – chef's tunic – butcher's shirt – nurse's tunic – bow tie

3.2 Laura and Mark Are Buying a Pullover

"I'm Laura. I'm nineteen. I attend a vocational school for domestic science and I live with my mother. My parents are separated. At the moment I'm on holiday, and I'm shopping at C&A. I'm looking for some bargains, because the sales are on. Mark is with me. He is my boyfriend, and we're getting married next month. Mark is twenty-two. He is a social worker, that means he usually works in the evening. Mark helps students with their personal problems. At the moment he is in the men's wear department, because Mark is looking for a new pullover."
This large department store has got almost everything you need. Here you can buy sweaters, cardigans, blouses, skirts, coats, suits and many other things. Let's watch Mark and Laura:

Shop assistant: "Good morning, madam. Good morning, sir. Can I help you?"
Mark: "Good morning. That pullover you have in the window – it is pure wool, isn't it?"
Shop assistant: "No, it isn't. But it is very good quality, and the price is only fifty-five pounds."
Mark: "Well, it is size XXL – a little big, I think. The pullover I'm wearing now is only size XL. Have you got a smaller size?"
Shop assistant: "Yes, sir. Here you are – size XL. You can try it on, of course, if you like."
Mark: "Yes, thank you."
Laura: "May I see the care label, please? You know, Mark, your old pullover is too small now, because you probably washed it too hot."

XL
50 % Acrylic • Acrylique • Polyacryl • Acryl • Acrilico • Acrilica • Acrico
50 % Wool • Laine • Wolle • Wol • Lana • La

Laura looks at the label.

Laura: "Oh, dear! I don't understand all the signs on this label."
Shop assistant: "Well, may I explain it to you? On top of this label you see the size of the pullover – XL. Then you have the information for example what kind of material the pullover is made of. At the bottom there are five signs. The left sign tells you how to wash the pullover. The other signs give you information about the ironing, the bleaching, the dry-cleaning and the drying."
Mark: "Laura, do you think that I can wash this pullover properly in our washing machine?"
Laura: "Yes, I think so."
Mark: "Alright. I will buy this pullover."
Shop assistant: "Fine. Anything else?"
Mark: "No, thank you, that is all."

Mark goes to the pay desk. He inserts his bank card into the card reader, checks the displayed amount, enters his PIN and confirms.

Shop assistant: "Shall I wrap the pullover up for you?"
Mark: "No, thanks. I'll put it into this bag with the other clothes I have bought."

A Read the text and the dialogue and answer these questions.

1. When are Mark and Laura getting married?
2. What is Mark's profession?
3. Why are Mark and Laura in the department store?
4. How does Mark pay for the new pullover?

B Mark and Laura are leaving the department store. At the exit they meet Mr Kelly. He is working for a market research institute.
Read the following survey and complete the sentences. Use the words in the box. **PRODUCTION**

symbols on the labels – a pullover – twenty-two – nineteen – social worker blouses – skirts – coats – suits – in the evenings – of domestic science

Mr Kelly: "Excuse me, please. I'm interviewing the customers to get more information for the management of this department store. May I ask you a few questions?"

Mark and Laura agree.

Mr Kelly: "What did you buy?"
Mark: "I bought … ."
Mr Kelly: "How old are you?"
Mark: "I'm … ."
Laura: "I'm … ."
Mr Kelly: "Do you remember what items you can buy in this store?"
Mark: "You can buy … and … ."
Mr Kelly: "What do you think about the information you get in this department store?"
Laura: "The shop assistant in the men's wear department knows a lot about the …."
Mr Kelly "Good. It's three o'clock in the afternoon - you are not working. May I ask for the reason?"
Laura: "I'm on holiday. I'm a student of …"
Mark: "I'm a … . I work … ."
Mr Kelly: "Now I understand that you are relaxing at this time of the day. Thank you very much for the interview!"

How about a role play? Form groups. One of you could be the interviewer and the others are the customers. You can ask each other different questions on textiles and shopping. On page 147 there is more information about role plays.

Present Progressive or Simple Present?

When do you use present progressive and when do you use simple present?
The progressive form of the present tense is used to express an activity which is happening *at the time of speaking*.

- **Signal words:** at the moment - now - today - just - these days - Look!

The simple form of the present tense is used to express what always occurs or to express what happens again and again.

- **Signal words:** always - never - normally - regularly - sometimes
usually - every day - every month - every year
on Saturdays/on Sundays/on ...

A **Put the verb in brackets in the present progressive or the simple present.**
→ For rules see page 166

Examples:
At the moment I (look) for some bargains.
*- At the moment **I'm looking** for some bargains.*

Mark usually (work) in the evening.
*- Mark usually **works** in the evening.*

1. At the moment I (shop) in a department store.
2. Mark (help) students with their personal problems.
3. The pullover I (wear) now is only size L.
4. The signs on the label (give) you some information about the cleaning and the drying of the pullover.
5. Look! Mark and Laura (leave) the department store.
6. Mr Kelly, what are you doing this afternoon?
- I (interview) the customers.
7. Laura (have) a shower every morning.
8. Mark: "I (work) every day from 4 o'clock in the afternoon to 10:30 p.m."

3.3 Care Labels

Mr Brown has found a new job. He works in the washhouse of a vocational school. Look at Mr Brown in this picture. Why is he unhappy?

It may be that Mr Brown doesn't know enough about washing. Washing is a very complicated business because of many improvements in fabrics, washing machines and washing powders.

To give more information about the necessary care of clothes most textile articles have a care label. It contains instructions about the right care of a textile. It is very useful, but only when you are able to understand the instructions. Otherwise you may be as unhappy as Mr Brown.

"I am going to learn more about washing."

Mark and Laura are studying a care label (see page 28):

Mark: "Laura, I'm going to wash the pullover that I bought at C & A. But I don't understand every symbol on the care label. Can you help me, please?"

Laura: "Of course. Which symbols do you mean?"

Mark: "Well, I understand the first – it gives the size of the pullover. The XL means EXTRA LARGE. The next information is quite clear as well – the pullover is made of acrylic and wool. But I don't understand the tub with the broken bar underneath it."

Laura: "Oh, you always leave the difficult questions for me to answer! I know that the number inside the wash tub stands for the temperature of the washing water. And the bar underneath the tub means, … let me think, oh yes: The machine action should be reduced when you wash this pullover."

Mark: "I think I understand the next symbol. It has something to do with ironing."

Laura: "That's right. An iron with two dots means 'warm' and an iron with three dots means 'hot'. But I don't know the next symbol. I'll look it up in my book about domestic science. Wait a minute. … There it is: 'Do not use chlorine bleach'."

Mark: "The next symbol looks funny. Let me look in your book, please: The 'P' means that the pullover may be dry-cleaned. The 'P' stands for the solvent, perclorethylene, which is used by the dry-cleaner."

Laura: "I know the last symbol: 'The pullover may not be tumble dried.'"

Mark: "That's not a problem for me, because I don't have a tumble dryer."

A Look at the symbols on the right – something is wrong with the descriptions.
In two cases the meaning of the care label does not match the symbol. Can you find them?

1	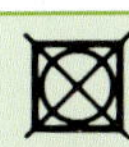	**a** Do not tumble dry
2		**b** May be dry-cleaned
3		**c** Use a warm iron
4		**d** Do not use chlorine bleach
5		**e** Maximum temperature of the washing water 95 °C

B Laura and Mark do the housework in their apartment.
Here is what they usually do, but right now they are doing something else. Put the words in brackets into the simple present or the present progressive.

Example:
Mark usually (hang) up the laundry, but at the moment he (iron) a shirt.
- Mark usually hangs up the laundry, but at the moment he is ironing a shirt.

1. Laura mostly (wash) the clothes, but at the moment she (tidy) up the wardrobe.
2. Mark normally (hoover) the carpets, but now he (empty) the dustbin.
3. Laura (unload) the dishwasher every day, but today she (water) the flowers.
4. Mark usually (clean) the bathroom, but just now he (sweep) the kitchen.

C Which part of the housework do members of your family regularly do? Tell the class what the other members and you yourself usually do.
Form sentences like these:

INTERACTION

Examples:
My mother normally prepares the meals.
On Sundays my father makes the beds.

3.4 Mr Brown – The Washing Expert

Laura: "Mr Brown, everybody knows that clean, well-cared for clothes look better and last longer. You know a lot about the care of clothes. May I ask you for some guidelines about washing?"

Mr Brown: "Stained or dirty clothes should be cleaned as soon as possible. Most clothes can be washed in automatic washing machines.
Before you wash the clothes you should check whether there are stains on them. Sometimes it is advisable to soak the clothes in soapy water before you wash them.
If you want to wash silk which needs a gentle handling, a handwash may be the right method.
The washing powder normally contains perfume and sometimes bleach. In case you want the clothes very soft, you may finish the washing by using a fabric conditioner."

"Now I know how to wash my clothes."

The Present Progressive is used for the Future

The present progressive is also used for the *future* and for expressing *plans*.

Examples:

Laura: *Mark and I* ***are getting*** *married next month.*
→ They have agreed to marry next month. It is going to happen in the future.

Mr Brown: *I'****m going*** *to learn more about washing.*
→ It is Mr Brown's plan.

A **The following sentences tell you something about the future or about certain plans. Put the words in brackets into the present progressive tense or use *going to*.**

Examples:

Laura asks Mark: "What you (do) on Monday evening?"
Mark: "I (work). I'm on duty."
- "What ***are*** *you* ***doing*** *on Monday evening?"*
*"****I'm working****. I'm on duty."*

Jim: "There's a football match tomorrow, but I (not go). I (meet) Laura and Mark."
- "There's a football match tomorrow but ***I'm not going****.* ***I'm meeting*** *Laura and Mark."*

1. Mark: "My parents (go) on holiday next week. They have already booked the flight."
2. Laura: "Oh, that's nice. Where they (go)? What are their plans?"
3. Gina asks Fiona: "I (go) out with some friends tonight. Why don't you come, too? We (meet) at Mark's house at 8 o'clock. That's what Mark suggested."
4. Mark asks Laura: "How you (get) home after the party tomorrow? By taxi?"
5. Laura: "No, I can go by bus."
6. Gina and Jim (have) supper with Ken and Fiona on Friday. They have invited them.
7. Mr Brown (buy) a new washing machine. It is his plan.

B **What are you doing in the next few days? Form questions and answers. Don't forget to use the present progressive.**

Example:

Question: "What are you doing tonight"?
Answer: "I/stay/at home."
If you plan to stay at home, you may say:
*"****I'm staying*** *at home tonight."*

Question: What are you doing on …
(Monday, Tuesday, etc.)?

Answers:
1. I/visit/my aunt
2. I/play/football
3. …

A Test your knowledge about washing. What are the right answers to the following questions? You may use the underlined words in Mr Brown's guidelines on page 32.
In case you don't know the answer, the number in the brackets may be of some help.

Example:
What kind of washing machines can most clothes be washed in? (9)
- Most clothes can be washed in ***automatic*** *washing machines.*
(The word "automatic" has nine letters.)

1. What is added to washing powder to make it smell nice? (7)
2. What do you call dirty marks on clothes? (6)
3. What is a wash without using a machine? (8)
4. What is added to washing powder to make clothes whiter? (6)
5. What kind of textile needs a gentle wash? (4)
6. What do you do when you leave clothes in soapy water? (4)
7. What do you use when you want clothes to be very soft? (11)

3.5 Protect the Environment

Here are five rules how to save money and protect the environment:

1. Read the amount of washing powder needed for washing which is printed on the packing. In order to decide the correct quantity, you have to know two things:
   - the degree of hardness of the water and
   - how dirty your laundry is.

   You can get information about the degree of hardness of the water from your local waterworks. Soft water may need less washing powder. If the clothes are not very dirty, you may use less water.

2. Always make full use of your washing machine. Otherwise it means waste of water, waste of energy, and waste of washing powder. This is true even for an economy programme.

3. Wash without prewash. You can clean normal dirty laundry without prewash. The main wash course then needs only 75 to 80 percent of the washing powder which is necessary for both washing programmes!

4. Wash without fabric conditioner! The fabric conditioner lowers the absorbency of textiles and can eventually cause skin problems.

5. Wash your boiling laundry with the 60 °C wash programme. By doing so you save 40 percent energy in comparison to the 95 °C wash programme! A hygienic clean washing is still ensured. Only in special cases (for example with clothes of sick people or baby laundry) a 95 °C wash programme is necessary.

One way to check all the things you learned about textiles is to prepare a quiz with your classmates. On page 154 you will find information about "Preparing a Quiz". Ask your teacher.

3.6 Mark and Laura and the Five 'Green Guidelines'

A Fill in the gaps in the dialogue with the correct vocabulary. Use the guidelines and rules on the pages 33 and 34 for help.

Mark: "Mr Brown told me that it is important to know the degree of … of the water and how dirty the laundry is."
Laura: "Well, it's easy to see how dirty the laundry is. But what about the degree of hardness of the water?"
Mark: "That is easy to find out. You can ring the … and they will tell you."
Laura: "I think we use quite a lot of water for washing. Is it possible to reduce the amount of water?"
Mark: "Mr Brown told me that we should always make … of our washing machine."
Laura: "Well, that is a silly 'guideline'. Everybody knows that!"
Mark: "That's right. But he advised as well to clean normal dirty … without prewash."
Laura: "That's a good idea, if the clothes become really clean. How much washing powder can you save?"
Mark: "About … to … %. By the way, if you wash without … you save money and you protect your health because –"
Laura: "I know, Mark, because fabric conditioners eventually cause … . Well, I see that most things Mr Brown told you are known by everybody. I guess he also told you something about saving … by using the 60 °C washing programme."
Mark: "Well, if you know everything anyway, I won't talk to you about this anymore."
Laura: "You don't have to. Let me put it like this: When you save your money, you protect the … at the same time."

Look at the packet label in the picture on the right.

B This packet contains 1.05 kg washing powder and it costs £ 4.20. Calculate: How much money does a kilo of this washing powder cost in euros?

C Compare the price of this washing powder with the price of other washing powders. What do you find out?

D Try to find a washing powder which is less harmful for the environment. Are you successful?

Vocabulary

3.1 Starting at a Vocational School		
geriatric nurse [ˌdʒer.i'æt.rɪk nɜːs]	a person whose job is to care for old people	Altenpfleger/-in
identity [aɪ'den.tɪ.ti]	something which makes a person different from others	Individualität
tunic ['tjuː.nɪk]	a piece of clothing which fits loosely over a person's body	Kittel
dressy ['dres.i]	describes clothes which are very suitable	schick
hesitantly ['hez.ɪ.tənt.li]	doing something not immediately or quickly	zögernd
steel toe cap [stiːl toʊ kæp]	strong metal, any of the five separate parts at the end of the foot, a kind of hat	Stahlkappe (in einem Schuh)
bow tie [baʊ taɪ]	a strip of cloth put around a collar in the shape of a bow	Fliege
waistcoat ['weɪst .kəʊt]	a piece of clothing that covers the upper body but not the arms	Weste
3.2 Laura and Mark Are Buying a Pullover		
(to) separate ['sepəreɪt]	when married people stop living together	sich trennen, scheiden
bargain ['bɑːgɪn]	something that costs much less than usual	Gelegenheitskauf
sales [seɪlz]	when things are sold at low prices	Schlussverkauf
sweater ['swetə]	a woollen piece of clothing worn on the top half of the body	Pullover
cardigan ['kɑːdɪgən]	a woollen piece of clothing worn on the top half of the body with buttons	Strickjacke
suit [suːt]	a jacket and trousers worn together	Anzug
(to) care [keə] for	to look after	pflegen
(to) iron ['aɪən]	to press clothes flat	bügeln
(to) bleach [bliːtʃ]	to make something white	bleichen
change [tʃeɪndʒ]	any money you get back after you pay for something	Wechselgeld
(to) wrap [ræp]	to put package around something	einpacken
survey ['sɜː.veɪ]	a study of something	Untersuchung, Umfrage
customer ['kʌstəmə]	someone who buys something in a shop	Kunde
(to) agree [ə'griː]	to think the same as someone else	(jemandem) zustimmen
an item ['aɪtəm]	any one thing on a list	Sache, Gegenstand
reason ['riːzn]	anything that explains why something has happened	Grund, Ursache
rule [ruːl]	something that everyone must do; rules have to be followed	Regel
3.3 Care Labels		
an improvement [ɪm'pruːvmənt]	much better than it was	Verbesserung
fabric ['fæbrɪk]	material or cloth	Gewebe
(to) contain [kən'teɪn]	to have something inside	enthalten, aufweisen
tub [tʌb]	a container, for example for water	Wanne
bar [bɑː]	a thick short line	Strich, Balken
(to) reduce [rɪ'djuːs]	to lower or to make small or less	reduzieren
chlorine ['klɔːriːn]	a certain gas	Chlor, auch: chlorhaltig
(to) dry-clean [draɪ kliːn]	to clean clothes with solvent	chemisch reinigen
solvent [sɒlvənt]	a liquid that dissolves	Lösungsmittel
tumble dryer (also: tumble drier) ['tʌmbl 'draɪə]	a machine that dries clothes	Wäschetrockner
laundry ['lɔːndrɪ]	dirty clothes that need to be washed	(Schmutz-) Wäsche
wardrobe ['wɔːdrəʊb]	a tall cupboard in which you keep your clothes	Kleiderschrank
3.4 Mr Brown – The Washing Expert		
guideline [gaɪd laɪn]	information to help you do something	Richtlinie
stain [steɪn]	a dirty mark	Fleck
(to) soak [səʊk]	to leave something in water	einweichen
gentle ['dʒentl]	mild, soft	sanft
(to) handle something ['hændl]	to treat something	behandeln
fabric conditioner ['fæbrɪk kən'dɪʃnə]	liquid used to make clothes soft	Weichspülmittel
3.5 Protect the Environment		
(to) protect [prə'tekt]	to look after	schützen
environment [ɪn'vaɪərənmənt]	everything around you	Umwelt
degree [dɪ'griː]	the amount of something	Grad
waste [weɪst]	to use more of something than is needed	Verschwendung
prewash [priːwɑʃ]	a wash done before the main wash	Vorwäsche
(to) lower ['laʊə]	here: to make something smaller	hier: herabsetzen, verringern
absorbency [əb'sɔːbənsɪ]	how much liquid something can hold	Aufnahmefähigkeit
3.6 Mark and Laura and the Five 'Green Guidelines'		
(to) cause [kɔːz]	to make something happen	verursachen
(to) ensure [ɪn'ʃʊə]	to make certain	sichern
harmful [hɑːmfʊl]	not good for you	schädlich

Listening Comprehension

Tom Barnes from a British Youth Radio Station interviews some teenagers who have an odd job. He wants to find an answer to a controversial question: Do students who have an odd job sacrifice their future in order to enjoy the present?

Hi, my name is Tom Barnes and I am reporting from a fast food restaurant where 17-year-old Jessica works after school.

RECEPTION

A **Read these questions before you listen to the audio-track. Decide who in your class has to answer which of the following questions. Later compare your answers.**

1. What is Tom Barnes' job?
2. Why does he interview Jessica?
3. Where does Jessica work?
4. Why does she work there?
5. Why can her parents not give her more pocket money?
6. What does she spend the money she earns on? List a few examples.
7. Does she save any money? If so, what is she saving the money for?
8. What job would she like to do after she has finished school?
9. What are her chances of gettig such a dream job?
10. Why does Jessica not work harder for her exams?

B Listen to the audio-track "**Sacrifices for an Odd Job?**" (available on audio-CD for teachers*).

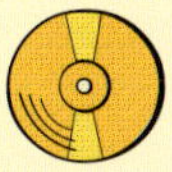

PRODUCTION

C **Listen to the dialogue again and complete the following sentences in your own words.**

1. The problem students with an odd job often have is …
2. If students who have an odd job want to work less so that they can do their homework properly, …
3. You cannot get a good job if …
4. If you want to earn more money later on, you should …
5. Tom Barnes interviews young people with an odd job because …

[*Transcript available in HT 1622 Lösungsheft Living Together]

Mediation

Mediation

A Situation: You heard the interview "Sacrifices for an Odd Job?" on the radio.
Now report about the interview in German for your German school magazine and comment the interview.
(If that is too difficult, have your teacher copy the audio transcript* for you.)

Tip

Look for question words on page 20.

INTERACTION

B Here are the answers another student gave to questions he was asked.
Work out the questions.

1. I work at a garage.
2. Oh, I wash cars or I work on the till.
3. I only work on Saturdays and Sundays when I have no lessons.
4. No, I don't need to work every weekend. When we have exams, I can stay at home and revise.
5. I get £3.50 per hour.
6. No, of course that's not enough money, but it's better than nothing.
7. I need the money for my hobbies. I love cooking and need to buy cooking equipment.
8. The garage is only a ten-minutes' walk from my home.
9. I always do my homework right after school.
10. Because I need good grades to get the job as a cook in the Sheraton Hotel.

[*Transcript available in HT 1622 Lösungsheft Living Together]

A Choose three of these competences which you think are important for you personally. Tell your classmates why they are important for the work you do or would like to do.

4.1 Professional Experiences

A Before listening to or reading the following text: What should a young trainee who works in a hospital do when a patient dies? What advice would you give him or her? Talk to your classmate next to you about it and present at least two ideas.

INTERACTION

Mary has had a very hard day today. She has been working as a trainee in a hospital for three weeks and today an old patient has passed away. After work she goes to her favourite ice-cream parlour and talks to her boyfriend John and some other friends about her working day.

Mary: Hi, thank God I'm here now. Nice to see you all. I've got to tell you something straightaway. Today a patient died on the ward where I am doing my practical training at the moment. I really feel terrible.
John: Oh, dear, I 'm sorry about that.
Eileen: Poor Mary, tell us about it.
Marvin: Yes, tell us everything. Maybe that will help you a bit.
Jill: Oh no, you're talking about problems? About death? Not with me, I'll have to go. Sorry ...
Jane: Tell us about your patient, Mary. Was it a man or a woman? How old?
Mary: It was an old lady, she died of old age, I think.
Jane: But why was she in hospital then?
Mary: I do not really know, but I heard someone say that she had problems with her heart or something. I did not really get what they said.
John: How do you feel, Mary?
Mary: It was so awful, I just came into the room and there she was just lying there, not moving a muscle. I have never seen a dead body before.
Ben: How do you feel, Mary? How did you cope with all that?
Mary: I left the room and yelled for help. I felt so helpless and now I feel sad, really, really sad.
Marvin: Do not be too sad, Mary, you said she was an old lady. She had a long life. We all have to die one day.
John: I can understand your feelings. I lost my grandfather one year ago. But there is a difference between you and me.
Mary: What difference, what do you mean?
John: You are doing an internship in a hospital, aren't you? You said you want to work with people, didn't you?
Mary: So, what?
John: I think you've just got to learn to cope with situations like this. You should learn to be a bit more professional, try to accept that old people might die on the ward where you work.
Marvin: It's good that you told us about it. It's always better to talk than to bottle up your emotions. Why don't you talk with the ward nurse? Maybe she can comfort you better than we can. Maybe she can give you some professional advice.

RECEPTION

B What did Mary do to handle her problems? What advice did she get? Make a list. Compare this list with your ideas. Did you have the same ideas or were your ideas different?

C
1. Do you think Mary felt better after she had talked to her friends? Give reasons for your opinion.
2. What do you think about Jill's reaction?

D

PRODUCTION

Activity - Instead of saying someone 'died', you can also say someone 'has passed away'. Have a look at the obituaries in your local newspaper. Cut out five of them which you consider are interesting and bring them into class. Find out

a) how the word 'death' is paraphrased in your obituaries,

b) what might have been the reason for the person's death,

c) the English expressions for your German findings. Use the Internet or a dictionary for help.

E

Match the expressions from the text (1-6) to the German translations (A-F).

1	trainee	A	schrecklich
2	to cope	B	professionell
3	awful	C	fertig werden mit
4	advice	D	Gefühle
5	emotions	E	Ratschlag
6	professional	F	Praktikant/in, Auszubildende/r

F

One of the social competences you will have to learn is the prevention of burn-out and stress. Here are some ideas about what people can do when they have a lot of stress.

go for a walk - sleep on it - talk to friends - talk to parents/colleagues
autogenic training - dance it off - go to a pub - cry - eat a lot
go out with friends - play computer games - watch TV

INTERACTION

Make a ranking list of all these 12 ideas and say which one you consider the best in order to cope with stress. What you would rather not do? Compare your list with a classmate. Do you have other ideas? Add them to your list.

G

Another social competence is motivation. What is your motivation to learn the profession you want to do later? What is good about this job? Are there disadvantages? Make a list and find at least six positive and three negative aspects about your future job.

4.2 A Night at the Disco

A Combine the pictures with the texts. Start like this:
Picture A belongs to text number four.

PRODUCTION

1. Mary is in love with John. They have known each other for three months now.
2. John is an attractive, tall guy with brown eyes and blond hair. Mary has got blue eyes and is a bit overweight.
3. They usually meet each other at the ice-cream parlour in the city once or twice a week.
4. Mary goes to a vocational school and John has got a job as a carpenter.
5. They always go to a disco together at the weekends.
6. The last time they went to the disco, Mary brought her classmate Cathy with her.
7. Cathy looked good and she danced perfectly.
8. John only had eyes for Cathy and he danced with her all night long. He didn't care about Mary anymore.
9. Mary was very disappointed. When she arrived at her mother's house that night, she cried.

B Look at the pictures and repeat the story of Mary, John and Cathy.

C Has anything like that ever happened to you or to a friend of yours?

4.3 The Night after the Disco

Mary was still very upset. She hated John and Cathy for what had happened. She simply hated everybody.
She and John had such a good time with each other. They had so much fun. She loved him so much and he meant everything to her. All the kisses he had given her and all the promises he had made!

She could not wait to see him last night but then he only had eyes for Cathy. Nobody seemed to love her. John didn't, Cathy didn't, and her Mum was always working. Mary hadn't seen her Dad for ages. Her parents got divorced when she was eight years old.

She finally got up and went to school with hanging shoulders and full of sorrow. Her eyes were still red from all the crying in the night. She didn't know what to do. Life seemed to be so senseless without John. "John", she sighed, "oh, John."

A Read the two texts. Which of these answers is correct – A, B or C? RECEPTION

1. Mary and John went to the disco
   A once a month. B at the weekends. C on Wednesdays and Saturdays.
2. They used to meet each other
   A in the park. B at the bus station. C in an ice-cream parlour.
3. Mary
   A has got normal weight. B is underweight. C is a bit overweight.
4. John
   A goes to school. B works as a carpenter. C has got no job.
5. Mary has got
   A brown eyes. B blue eyes. C green eyes.
6. Mary's parents
   A got divorced. B married eight years ago. C were never married.
7. Mary lives
   A in her father's house. B on her own. C together with her mother.
8. Cathy
   A works in a restaurant. B doesn't go to school. C is in the same class as Mary.

B Find the right word in the texts.
If you need help - the numbers in brackets tell you how many letters the word has.

1. A place where many young people go to on Friday or Saturday night is a ... (5)
2. People who are not married any longer are ... (8)
3. When somebody hurts your feelings you are very ... (12)
4. The opposite of hatred is ... (4)
5. A person who makes wooden objects is a ... (9)
6. A good-looking person is very ... (10)

C Start a discussion in class and talk about these aspects: INTERACTION

1. Which disco do you like to go to and why? Give reasons.
2. What do you think Mary should do - should she forget John or should she fight for her love?
3. What is the opinion of your classmates?

D Activity - Probably not all of you are allowed to go to a disco at night. INTERACTION
Imagine that you desperately want to go to a disco next Saturday and your parents are against it.
Form two teams. One team has to find arguments you might have and the other team has to find arguments *your parents* might use.
Start with arguments from the list below.

In Favour of (Pro)	Against (Contra)
- all friends go	- too expensive
- help in the household	- too young
- late night bus	- no transport

You can find more information about discussions on page 151.

If you want to, you could play this situation in a role play. Do you want to know how to do that? Look on page 147 for details.

4.3 What Happened to Mary?

Let us have a look at Mary's situation again. She is still sad but she also knows that life goes on. In the first days she always compared herself to Cathy. Was Cathy better than she was? Was Cathy prettier?

Yes, Cathy was prettier. But was Cathy also better? Last year Cathy was as good at school as she was, but this year Mary seems to be better. Cathy's marks in maths and religion were worse than hers, but Cathy was the best of her class in sports.

Mary decided to forget John - he just didn't deserve her. He was the worst guy she had ever looked at.

In the meantime she has found a new friend, who is as nice as Cathy was when they were friends. The new girl is fairer to Mary. What about the boys? Well, at the moment Mary is not interested in a new relationship.

Simple Past

Statement Clause (Aussagesatz)			
I You He She It We You They	walk**ed**	to the disco	last night.

Negative Clause (Verneinung)			
I You He She It We You They	**didn't walk (did not walk)**	to the disco	last night.

Questions (Fragesatz)				
Why **When** **How**	**did**	I You He She It We You They	**walk** to the disco	last night.

How do you form the simple past?

- When you have *regular verbs* you add either -***d*** or -***ed*** to the verb.
  love → love**d**
  walk → walk**ed**
- When you have *irregular verbs* you use ***the second form*** of the verb.
  go → **went**
  see → **saw**

→ There is a list of the irregular verbs on page 164

- You form negative sentences with ***didn't (or did not) + the infinitive***

  didn't go
  didn't see
- You form questions with ***did or didn't + the infinitive***

  Did you **go** there?
  Didn't you **see** me?
- You can also form questions with a ***question word + did*** or ***didn't + infinitive***

  Why did you **go** there?

When do you use the simple past?
You use the simple past when something is *definitely over*.
Signal words: Last month - last year - yesterday - two weeks ago - in 2010 - …

A You already know some signal words which tell you that you have to use the simple past. Can you think of some more signal words? Try to find ten others for this tense.

B Combine the words from the box and form sentences.
Start like this: *She played in the garden an hour ago.*
How many sentences can you find?

→ For rules see page 167

I	**played**	the train	yesterday.
You	ran	home	last month.
He/**She**/It	missed	**in the garden**	**an hour ago.**
We	went	to the bus	last night.
You	came	here	in May 2008.
They	came	home at 4 o'clock	two days ago.

C Put the verbs from the box below into the simple past. Then look at the statement clauses and find the correct place for the verb in the sentences.
Do the same with the negative clauses.

love - like - dance get divorced - find - look think - meet - be	not look - not believe - not like not care - not want - not want not sleep - not love

Statement Clauses

1. Mary ... John and ... Cathy very much.
2. They ... each other once a week when they were friends.
3. During the night at the disco John ... with Cathy all the time.
4. He only ... at Cathy, and Mary stood aside.
5. She ... very disappointed.
6. Her parents ... some time ago.
7. Mary ... a lot about her problems.
8. She ... another girlfriend.

Negative Clauses

9. Mary ... John, and ... Cathy anymore.
10. John ... at her during the whole night.
11. She ... in love anymore.
12. Her father ... for Mary either.
13. The night after the disco she ... well.
14. She ... to go to school the next day.
15. She promised herself that she .... to give up hope.

D Mary's new friend Sheila had a date with a nice young guy last weekend. When the girls met at school on Monday morning, Mary was very curious and asked Sheila a lot of questions.
Form questions which Mary might have asked. Use the *simple past*.

Comparison

Sentences with Comparison

- When we compare things which are the same we can use ***as*** … ***as*** …. with an adjective.

Example: *I'm **as** tall **as** my mother.*

- In negative sentences we can use not as … as … with an adjective.

Example:
*I'm **not as** good at school **as** my brother.*

A Now it's your turn. Choose eight words from the box below and form sentences like this one:
I'm as tall as Georg, but I'm not as tall as Phillip.

> tall - loud - quiet - nice - old - good - happy - rich - young - thirsty
> brave - bad

→ For rules see pages 171 f.

The Comparison of Adjectives

- You compare adjectives with one syllable and adjectives with two syllables and -***y***,-***er***, -***le***, -ure or -***ow*** at the end like this:

clean hot	clean**er** hott**er**	(the) clean**est** (the) hott**est**	One syllable
lucky	luck**ier**	(the) luck**iest**	Two syllables and -y at the end

B Write down the comparison of the following adjectives.

Be careful! There is always an exception to every rule:
Good and *bad* have also got only one syllable. However, here you say:

good	better	(the) best
bad	worse	(the) worst

There are some more exceptions:

much, many	much, many	(the) most
little	little	(the) least
far	far	(the) furthest

C Make a list of all the adjectives you find in the text "What Happened to Mary?" and compare them.
Example:
***sad** (in the text)* *sadder* *(the) saddest*
good ***better** (in the text)* *(the) best*

D Do the same with the adjectives in the box of exercise A - compare them.

Vocabulary

responsibility [rɪˌspɒnt .sɪ'bɪl.ɪ.ti]	to be in charge of something	Verantwortung
knowledge ['nɒl.ɪdʒ]	when you know much you have a good knowledge	Wissen
self-awareness [ˌself.ə'weə.nəs]	a person's sense of his/her own qualities, skills, behaviour	Selbstwahrnehmung
self-esteem [ˌself.ɪ'stiːm]	the respect you have for yourself	Selbstwertgefühl, Selbstachtung
ability [ə'bɪl.ɪ.ti]	to be able to do something	Fähigkeit
prevention [prɪ'vent .ʃən]	to take care that something does not happen	Verhütung, Vermeidung
(to) solve a problem [sɒlv ə 'prɒb.ləm]	to know what to do with a problem	ein Problem lösen
confidence ['kɒn.fɪ.dənt s]	belief in yourself and your abilities	Selbstvertrauen
4.1 Professional Experiences		
advice [əd'vaɪs]	to tell someone what to do	Rat, Ratschlag
(to) pass away [pɑːs ə'weɪ]	to die	sterben, dahinscheiden
(to) paraphrase ['pær.ə.freɪz]	to say it in other words	umschreiben
straightaway [streɪt.ə'weɪ]	right now	sofort
awful ['ɔː.fəl]	something that is really bad	furchtbar, entsetzlich
(to) cope with sth. [kəʊp]	to be able to handle a problem	mit etwas fertig werden
(to) yell [jel]	to cry out	schreien
(to) feel helpless ['hel.pləs]	not to know what to do	sich hilflos fühlen
difference ['dɪf.ər.ənt s]	the quality of being unlike	Unterschied
(to) bottle up emotions (ugs.) ['bɒt.l ʌp]	not to tell anybody how you feel	Gefühle in sich hineinfressen
(to) comfort ['kʌm.fət]	a child that cries wants to be comforted	trösten
(to) handle a problem ['hæn.dl ə 'prɒb.ləm]	to be able to live with a problem	mit einem Problem umgehen
instead of [ɪn'sted]		anstelle von
obituary [əʊ'bɪtʃ.ʊə.ri]	to announce that someone has died, e.g. in a newspaper	Todesanzeige
(to) consider [kən'sɪd.ər]	to think, to believe	betrachten, ansehen als
rather ['rɑː.ðər]	preferably	eher, lieber
disadvantage [ˌdɪs.əd'vɑːn.tɪdʒ]	the opposite of advantage	Nachteil
4.2 A Night at the Disco		
(to) be overweight [bɪ 'əʊvəweɪt]	to weigh more than normal	übergewichtig sein
once [wʌns]	one time	einmal
twice [twaɪs]	two times	zweimal
carpenter ['kɑːpəntə]	someone who works with wood	Zimmermann
classmate [klɑːs meɪt]	a pupil who goes in the same class as you	Klassenkamerad
not to care about [nɒt tʊ keə ə'baʊt]	to ignore	sich nicht kümmern um
(to) be disappointed [bɪ dɪsə'pɔɪntɪd]	not be able to fulfill hopes	enttäuscht sein
4.3 The Night after the Disco		
(to) be upset [bɪ ʌpset]	to be angry and disappointed	bestürzt sein
(to) make a promise [meɪk ə 'prɒmɪs]	to say that something will be done	ein Versprechen machen
for ages [fɔː eɪdʒɪz]	since a long time	seit Ewigkeiten
(to) get a divorce [get ə dɪ'vɔːs]	to end a marriage	sich scheiden lassen
finally ['faɪnəlɪ]	at last	schließlich, endlich
sorrow ['sɒrəʊ]	unhappiness, sadness	Traurigkeit
senseless [senslɪs]	without sense, without meaning	sinnlos
probably ['prɒbəblɪ]	almost sure	wahrscheinlich
definitely ['defɪnɪtlɪ]	without doubt, clearly	ganz bestimmt
gap [gæp]	an empty space	Lücke
(to) be curious [bɪ 'kjʊərɪəs]	to want to know everything	neugierig sein
4.4 What happened to Mary?		
maths [mæθs]	a subject in school	Mathematik
(to) deserve something/someone [dɪ'zɜːv]		jemand oder etwas verdienen
brave [breɪv]	a brave soldier	tapfer (nicht: brav)
narrow ['nærəʊ]	a small street is very narrow	eng
secure [sɪ'kjʊə]	safe	sicher

The Majestic Hotel

is looking for an
ambitious young man
to help in our hotel kitchen.
Send applications to

The Majestic Hotel
7 Ipswich Road
Bristol

Dear Sirs,

My ... is Ryan Shanks, and I am 17 years .... At present, I go to a College of Further Education and I will ... my exams in housekeeping this summer.
I would very much like to ... for the job you offered in today's ... I have always wanted to be a .., and my teacher says that I am quite good ...
I am ... and hard-working and I promise I will do my best if you give me a ....
You can find my last ... and my curriculum vitae in the ....

Yours ...,

Ryan Shanks

A Complete Ryan's letter with the words from the list below.
Be careful - they are not in the correct order.

to apply - certificate - cook - old - sincerely - chance - local newspaper - envelope - at cooking - name - to pass - reliable

B You want a job, don't you? Try to answer these questions.

1. How and where can you get information? Make a list.
2. What must you do to get a job? Form sentences and write them down.
   Here are some words to help you:

write/application - ask for/interview - phone/manager - go to/firm and speak to ... - employment office - Internet

3. If you write an application, what do you have to write?
4. What must you enclose in your envelope?

5.1 Ryan's Dreams

Ryan Shanks was very happy when school was over. He sat down, wrote some applications and sent them to hotels, factory canteens and hospital kitchens. He wanted a good training, because his Mum and Dad always said that "a good training is really important, Ryan". They often said so, until Ryan really believed it. He had learned domestic science at school, but his marks were not very good. He had spent too much time doing odd jobs. "Money is more important than school", he used to say. He was very optimistic when he started writing applications, but he often got answers which said that they did not need someone like him. Some employers did not even send an answer.

After sixty applications he was ready to take any training place. Ryan was listening to his Heavy Metal records when his mother came in and showed him a letter from *The Majestic Hotel*, that was what it said on the envelope. "Another refusal", he moaned and opened the letter with indifference. He felt frustrated by the many negative answers, but then he could hardly believe his eyes. They wrote that they were hoping to get "an ambitious young man" for their hotel kitchen. That was exactly what Ryan wanted! While he was making dinner he was dreaming: Ryan – the cook, the chef, designer of culinary art.

A There are some key words in the text which you must know to understand the text. Here they are in German. Can you find the English words in the text?
Copy the words into your vocabulary notebook and complete them with the English words.

English	German
	Noten, Zensuren
	maulen
	Bewerbung
	Gleichgültigkeit
	Berufsausbildung
	ehrgeizig
	Kochkunst
	Briefumschlag
	Chefkoch, -köchin
	schicken
	wichtiger als
	bereit sein
	Arbeitgeber/in

B Answer the following questions on the text.

1. How did Ryan feel when school was over?
2. What did he do to get a job?
3. Where did Ryan want to work?
4. What job was he dreaming of?
5. Why did Ryan want a training?
6. What is the reason that Ryan's marks were not very good?
7. What job does *The Majestic Hotel* offer Ryan?
8. Do you think *The Majestic Hotel* wants to make Ryan a chef?

C Read the headline of text 5.2. What does it mean? These two explanations can help you:
a rookie – someone who is new and has no experience of an activity
a booby – a stupid, foolish person; an idiot

D How did everybody treat Ryan? What do you think?

5.2 Rookie Ryan – Everybody's Booby?

Ryan was sitting in the hotel lounge. He was wearing a blue pair of jeans and a white T-shirt. He wanted to be punctual. In the letter they had told him to be there by 6 o'clock. And now he was waiting for someone to come out of the kitchen and tell him what to do. It was ten to six already. But nobody came. So he tried to go through the kitchen door which said "OUT". He was slowly trying to open it, when there was a loud bang and a terrible clatter of plates with porridge flying through the air. The porridge felt pretty hot on Ryan's new trousers and T-shirt and the plates soon turned into bits and pieces on the tiled floor. The pretty waitress who had carried the tray was full of porridge on her blue costume. She screamed and ran away. Ryan could not – he was standing there and thought he was in a nightmare.

"Who the hell are you?", a huge man with a chef's hat thundered.
"I ... am ... Ryan Shanks, the new man," Ryan stuttered.
"And what does an idiot like you want here?", the man questioned.
"I want to be a cook. My teacher at school said I can cook quite well", Ryan hurried to say.
"Booby", the cook started. He was looking like the devil himself.
"The first thing you want is new clean clothes. Then you want to sweep up the bits and pieces, and wipe and polish the floor until it is as shining as a mirror!"
It was horrible. From the very beginning on, Ryan had his nickname: "Hey Booby", everybody shouted, and after that they always had something to do for him. He had to peel mountains of onions till there was no water left in his eyes, or he had to scrub pots and pans until they shone like mirrors. Whenever he was looking out of the window and dreaming of better times, someone always came and had a job for him.
"Hey Booby, you are not paid for dreaming. Move it!", everybody used to say. When he had to get potatoes from the cellar to peel them, someone else said: "Why do you walk around with empty hands? Here is a brush. Scrub the chopping block. And you hurry, Booby!"
While he was cleaning the chopping block, there was a scream: "Where the hell are my potatoes? I did not tell you to grow them but to get them from the cellar!"
Ryan was already thinking of quitting the job when Dora Mae, a friendly woman of around forty, said, "Ryan, why don't you have a talk with the chef? You want to learn something. You have to change, but the others must, too."

A

Write down all the words in the text 5.2 which you don't know. Then form groups and share the job to look the words up in a dictionary. Ask the others for words you don't know, complete your list and help the others with the words you looked up.

There is more information about working with a dictionary on page 152.
You could use Ryan's story for a role-play. Interested? Look on page 147.

Example:
You can ask like this: *"What is the meaning of …"*
or *"Can you tell me what … means?"*

B

Are the following statements right or wrong? Say why.

1. Ryan was unpunctual on his first day.
2. Ryan did not find the entrance for the hotel staff.
3. The accident which happened at the kitchen door was Ryan's fault.
4. Ryan was very busy in the kitchen.
5. The colleagues were happy to have Ryan around.

C

What did Ryan do wrong? What did his colleagues do wrong? Try to complete the following sentences. Use the simple past. → For rules see page 167

1. Not tell the receptionist he had arrived
2. Not ask for the staff entrance
3. Not read the writing on the kitchen door
4. Not ask what job Ryan was doing at the moment
5. Call him "Booby"
6. Not teach Ryan anything
7. Only shout at him

INTERACTION

D

A reporter interviews Ryan. Read texts 5.1 and 5.2 again and answer the reporter's questions in Ryan's place.

1. Ryan, how did you feel when school was over?
2. Ryan, why were you frustrated after some time?
3. Why was it not exactly easy for you to find a job?
4. How did you feel when The Majestic Hotel offered you a job as a cook?
5. Ryan, on your first day you had a funny accident in The Majestic Hotel. Can you explain to us what happened?
6. How did everybody treat you at the beginning?
7. Did you have any mistakes for which the others could attack you?
8. In how far did Dora Mae help you to solve your problem?

Tip
Answer in the simple past:
Well, I felt quite happy because …

Past Progressive

➜ For rules how to form the past progressive, see page 168, "Grammatikalischer Anhang"

What the hell were they all doing?

In *The Majestic Hotel*, most of the hotel staff are football supporters - some are for Arsenal, others are for United. But today there is an important conference at the hotel, with one hundred hungry guests. So the chef told his team to prepare today's food yesterday evening (he was not there himself). Some people, however, preferred watching the football match. Now the food is not ready and the chef is foaming with rage. He asks Ryan to describe what **was** go**ing** on in the kitchen yesterday.

A Help Ryan and use the past progressive.

Example:
I (Ryan) / peel / mountains of onions when Arsenal scored the first goal.
➜ I **was** peel**ing** mountains of onions when Arsenal scored the first goal.

1. Two girls / peel / potatoes.
2. They / chat / about their friends.
3. John cut his finger when / he / watch / TV.
4. Sally broke an egg when she saw / Arsenal /win.
5. Two waiters / lay the table while they / watch TV.
6. Tom / smoke / while he /watch / the football match.

- When the kitchen staff were working, something happened.
- While Ryan was doing his job, the girls were doing their job.

After the boss had asked Ryan, he also asked others what they were doing.
Look how the boss asks questions and how the staff answered.
➜ What were you doing yesterday evening? Were you chatting about your friends again?
➜ No, we were not (weren't) chatting about our friends, we were peeling potatoes.

B Form questions and answer them.

1. You / dream again, Booby? No, I / not dream - I / peel / potatoes.
2. The waiters / lay / the tables? - No, they / not lay / the tables - They / support / Arsenal.
3. Dora Mae / make / the soup? - No, she / not make / the soup - She / pray / for United.
4. The girls / watch / the football match, too? - No, they / not watch / the football match - They / chat / about their friends.
5. Most of the staff / work / in the kitchen? - No, they / not work / in the kitchen - They / help / either Arsenal or United to win the match.

Tip

Ask your teacher to write the rules of how to form questions and how to negate sentences in the past progressive on the blackboard. Or can you write them on the blackboard?

C Fill in the right preposition or conjunction.

- Prepositions are words that are used with a noun, pronoun or an -ing-form: *in, on, at*.
- Conjunctions are words that connect parts of sentences: *and, but, or, while, when*. Choose them from the box below.

while - when (2x) - for - from - of - where - but

1. Ryan got a letter … *The Majestic Hotel*.
2. He was very happy … he read that they wanted him.
3. He wanted to be a cook, … his marks at school were not very good.
4. He was waiting … the chef.
5. … he was preparing dinner, he was dreaming … being the chef.
6. … he was cleaning the chopping block, somebody shouted, "… are my potatoes?"

Simple Past or Past Progressive?

Remember:
You take *simple past* for events,
past progressive for a period of time.
Look at the following sentence:

When Ryan **was dreaming**, someone **shouted** at him. The dreaming took a *period of time* and in this time *the event* happened, that someone shouted at him.

Some verbs do not usually take the *progressive*. For further information look at page 166.

There can also be ***two parallel actions***, which occurred *at the same time*:
While Ryan **was peeling** onions, the girls **were peeling** potatoes.
Both actions were periods of time - so you take the *past progressive* for both.

D Now do the following exercise and use the *past progressive* and the *simple past*.

1. When Dora Mae (make) salad, the telephone (ring).
2. When Ryan (chop) carrots, he suddenly (cut) his finger.
3. While the waiters (lay) the table, the cooks (prepare) the porridge.
4. When Ryan (scrub) pots and pans, a girl (drop) a plate.
5. When she (sweep) the bits and pieces away, Ryan (go) to her and (ask) if he could help her.

5.3 A Man-to-Man Talk

Ryan was pretty nervous. It was five to nine. He was waiting in front of the chef's office. Today he wanted to talk with his boss. When the long hand of the hotel clock had reached the twelve, he knocked on the wooden door.

"What can I do for you, Booby?"

Chef: "Come in! Ah, it's you Booby. What can I do for you?"

Ryan: "Oh, quite a lot, sir. First, please don't call me 'Booby'. My name is Ryan. Did you know that? It hurts me if everybody calls me 'Booby', and it makes me angry."

Chef: "Okay, Ryan, sorry. And when you are angry, you start dreaming?"

Ryan: "Yes, I know, I was dreaming several times. But it is not easy when everybody treats you like a fool. And then I escape in dreams."

Chef: "But your dreams make things even worse. The staff think a dreamer must be a booby."

Ryan: "I am not a booby and I am not a dreamer. I really want to learn something, but I can't if everybody sends me around and never shows me anything."

Chef: "So you want to change yourself?"

Ryan: "Yes, and I want to change the situation here. I cannot stand it much longer."

Chef: "And how can I help you?"

Ryan: "Well, sir, why don't you give me more responsibility? I really know when the chopping block needs cleaning, and I know what we need for the breakfast buffet."

Chef: "Okay, young man - more responsibility. And let me give you a hint: Do not look so furious when people try to send you around. Tell them with a smile that you are busy at the moment. And another bit of advice: When the others notice that you *see* work and *do* it, they will see that they can rely on you, and you will no longer be 'Booby'."

A Answer the following questions in full sentences. Use the words in brackets for your answers.

1. Why did Ryan wait for five minutes before he knocked on the door? (he/want to be/punctual)
2. How did Ryan feel about his nickname? (he/get angry; it/hurt/him; he/not like it)
3. What did Ryan want the chef to do for him? (should not call/Booby; more responsibility)
4. What bit of advice did the chef give Ryan? Name three points (see text 5.3).
5. What does it mean that someone "sees" work? Explain in your own words.

B Ryan meets his girlfriend after the talk with the chef. Write down her questions to Ryan's answers. **PRODUCTION**

Example:
Ryan, how did you feel before you entered the chef's office?/
Oh, I was pretty nervous before I entered the chef's office.

1. _____ / I told him not to call me 'Booby' again because it hurts me.
2. _____ / He told me I was often daydreaming.
3. _____ / I told him that was because everybody treated me like a fool.
4. _____ / He asked me how he could help me.
5. _____ / I told him to give me more responsibility.
6. _____ / He told me not to look so furious when others want to send me around.
7. _____ / I think the talk was quite helpful for me and it will help me to do my job better than before.

Vocabulary

5.1 Ryan's Dreams		
(to) be over [bɪ 'əʊvə]	to have ended	vorbei sein
an application ['æplɪ'keɪʃn]	a letter to ask for a job	Bewerbungsschreiben
training ['treɪnɪŋ]	education on the job	Ausbildung
housekeeping [haʊs 'kiːpɪŋ]	working in a household	Hauswirtschaft
(to) spend; spent; spent (time) [spend· spent· spent]	to do something for some time	(Zeit) verbringen
employer [ɒm'plɔɪə]	someone who gives you a job	Arbeitgeber/-in
(to) be ready for something [bɪ 'redɪ fɔː]	to accept something	bereit sein
(to) force one's way [fɔːs wʌnz weɪ]	to try to get through	seinen Weg bahnen
noise [nɔɪz]	something very loud	Lärm
envelope ['envələʊp]	You put a letter in it.	Briefumschlag
refusal [rɪ'fjuːzl]	act of saying "No"	Ablehnung
(to) moan [məʊn]	to complain	maulen
indifference [ɪn'dɪfrəns]	no interest	Gleichgültigkeit
(to) be ambitious [bɪ æm'bɪʃəs]	to be ready to work well	ehrgeizig sein
culinary art ['kʌlɪnərɪ ɑːt]	skill of cooking	Kochkunst
key word [kiː wɜːd]	very important word	Schlüsselwort
5.2 Rookie Ryan – Everybody's Booby?		
hotel lounge [həʊ'tel laʊndʒ]	place where hotel guests can sit	Hotelsalon
by six o'clock [baɪ sɪks ə'klɒk]	not later than six o'clock	bis spätestens sechs Uhr
clatter ['klætə]	A noise that breaking plates make	Geklirr
porridge ['pɒrɪdʒ]	a soup with milk and oatmeal	Haferflockensuppe
bits and pieces [bɪts ænd pɪːsɪz]	broken parts of plates	Scherben
nightmare ['naɪtmeə]	a very bad dream	Alptraum
(to) thunder ['θʌndə]	to speak very loud and harsh	donnern
(to) sweep [swiːp]	to clean a floor by using a brush	fegen
(to) polish ['pɒlɪʃ]	make something shine	polieren
(to) scrub [skrʌb]	to clean something by using a brush	schrubben
chopping block [tʃɒpɪŋ blɒk]	a table where you cut meat	Hackklotz
(to) quit [kwɪt]	to stop working	kündigen
receptionist [rɪ'sepʃənɪst]	someone who welcomes guests	Empfangsdame, Portier
staff entrance [stɑːf 'entrəns]	a door through which people go who work in the hotel	Personaleingang
furious ['fjʊərɪəs]	very angry	wütend
(to) lay the table [leɪ ðe 'teɪbl]	to put things on the table	den Tisch decken
the hell [hel]		zur Hölle, zum Teufel, verflucht noch mal
staff [stɑːf]	people who work at a hotel	das Hotelpersonal
football supporters [sə'pɔː.tərs]	people who favour a special football club	Fußballfans
(to) foam with rage (ugs.) [fəʊm wɪð reɪdʒ]	to be very furious	vor Wut schäumen
(to) prefer [prɪ'fɜːr]	to like better	vorziehen, lieber tun
5.3 A Man-to-Man Talk		
hand of a clock [hænd əv ə klɒk]	a clock has two of them	Zeiger einer Uhr
wooden ['wʊdn]	made of wood	hölzern
(to) hurt someone [hɜːt]	to make someone feel pain	jemanden verletzen
(to) treat [triːt]	to behave towards someone	(jemanden) behandeln
hint [hɪnt]	a small suggestion	ein Tipp
in brackets [ɪn 'brækɪts]	These are brackets: (...)	in Klammern
an advice [əd'vaɪz]	a hint	Rat

A

Why do so many young people leave their parents' home?

Many young people <u>want to</u> leave home because …		Many young people <u>have to</u> leave home because …	
avoid	more freedom	be	in another town
dream of	conflicts with parents this way	have to work	when learning
want to live	more privacy, no control in their …	must concentrate	trouble with their parents
enjoy	with a friend	have	not enough place in their

Do it like this: *Many young people want to leave home because they want to avoid conflicts with their parents this way.*

6.1 Home or Hell?

A Out of the saucepan into the fire?
Some kids begin to see what a good time they had when they still lived in "Hotel Mama". They feel that their life has become worse than it was at their parents' home. But what are the reasons for that? Living on your own can be a **dream** – but it can also be a **NIGHTMARE**.
Look at what the four young people say. Living on their own is a nightmare for them, but why?

Match the following facts to the young people in the picture:

1. … lives in the middle of nowhere.
2. … has a flat above a rave disco.
3. … is always short of money.
4. … has a home with a poor insulation.

B Chas' Mum could be a little (diplomatic) **more diplomatic** with her son. It is often (easy) **easier** to tell someone indirectly what he has to do …
Use the comparative form of the adjectives in brackets.

> How do you do use comparison? Look at the grammar box Comparison in Unit 4 (page 47) and in the appendix.

Now, what does Chas' Mum want? Are you a good psychologist?
Look at the text "Home Or Hell?".

Do it like this: *The air in your room could be (good).*
You say: *The air in your room could be* ***better****.*
What does Chas' Mum want? You say:
She wants ***him to*** *open the window. (= that* ***he*** *opens the window.)*

1. "It is (dangerous) for your girlfriend to go home after 10 p.m."
2. "It would be (hygienic) if there was not so much dust on the floor."
3. "Chas, your washing gets (dirty) when it is lying on the floor."
4. "Chas, wouldn't it be (intelligent) to learn vocabulary than to read that youth magazine?"
5. "Sorry, Chas, could you speak a little (loud)?"
6. "Chas, couldn't you be a little (understanding)?"

6.2 Flat-Hunting in Bristol

Chas Banks was very optimistic. He had got a job in a factory where they produce fish fingers. There was only one problem – he was from Ipswich. That is on the east coast. Bristol – where the fish finger factory is – lies on the west coast of England. So he needed a flat somewhere in Bristol. He earned £850 a month and he soon found out that this was not enough for renting a good flat. In the factory he met Holger, a young German who wanted to stay in England for one year on the "Leonardo da Vinci programme", a European programme that helps you to finance your practical training abroad. Holger was a nice guy and he also needed a flat. Therefore Holger had the idea of sharing a flat with Chas and George, another colleague.
They are sitting together in the canteen and discussing what they can do.

Holger: Why don't we surf the Internet to find a suitable flat for the three of us?
Chas: Ah, you mean 'property hunting' via the Internet. That's really a good idea because we'll save money on bus tickets and phoning around.
George: Yes, that's right! We can weed out the bad offers more cheaply. You know, flats which are too far away from our workplace, noisy flats above a disco or flats in the middle of nowhere which are cheap at first sight – but where you'd end up spending the money you saved on the flat buying bus or train tickets.
Holger: And wouldn't it be horrible if girls weren't allowed in our flat ...?
Chas: And if we could not take a shower after 9 o'clock ...?
George: And if some old dragon of a landlady checked up on whatever we did?
Holger: Okay, we have to be very careful with our choice, but we can save a lot of money if we share the kitchen, living room and bathroom.
Chas: True. And it's better than staying on your own in a bedsitter.
Holger: Bedsitter? I do not understand all the English words for flats. What exactly is a bedsitter?

INTERACTION

A **Read text 6.2 again and complete the following sentences in your own words.**

1. In Bristol Chas had the problem of ...
2. Chas met Holger who ...
3. Holger suggested to ...
4. On the Internet you can ...
5. George thinks that some older landladies ...
6. The three young men do not want a flat which ...
7. The three think sharing a flat will have the advantage that ...
8. George tells Holger that a bedsitter is ...

Leonardo da Vinci Programme

→ see page 99 for more information

6.3 Property Hunting via the Internet

After they had had their tea, the three young men decided to go to an Internet café. They found this homepage. It was a little difficult for Holger to understand all the English terms, so he made a list of them. Here is his list:

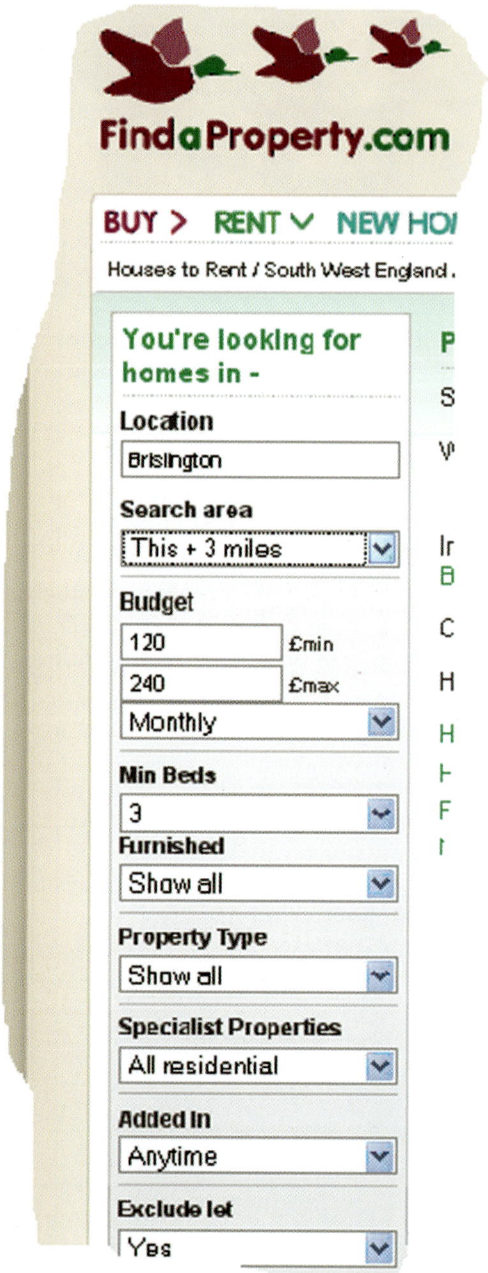

location - search area - budget - monthly - weekly - min beds - furnished - unfurnished - part furnished - exclude let - flat - terraced house - semi-detached house - detached house - shared house

His friends wanted to help Holger to improve his English. So they gave Holger a list of explanations and told him to put the fifteen terms in the right place. "And, why don't you give us the German terms, too, Holger?" they asked. "Perhaps we can do a practical training in Germany one day, who knows?"

RECEPTION

A **Here is the list. Match the terms to the explanations and write down the German term as well. Enter the words into your vocabulary notebook.**

1. a house in which three young people live
2. the place where you want to live
3. one of a row of houses
4. a house for two families
5. a house for one family only
6. how far your home can be away from your workplace
7. no cupboards, tables, chairs etc.
8. just a few cupboards
9. all you need to move in is your suitcase
10. you do not want to buy but rent it - so tick 'no'!
11. if we want to share the flat, we need three of them
12. accomodation in a larger house with kitchen, bathroom, bedrooms, living room
13. how much money you can pay for rent
14. paid twelve times a year
15. paid every Monday

Tuesday 8 March

FISHPONDS: Smart Double and Single Rooms - Manor Rd area From £60pw inc bills — FEATURED AD — £60pw
Fishponds Date available: 28 Feb

2 Double bed flat — FEATURED AD — £150pw
Bedminster Date available: 1 Mar

4 Bed Furnished House on Shaldon Road, Horfield, Great Sharers & Students. — FEATURED AD — £242pw
Horfield Agency Date available: 8 Aug

Lovely 3 Bedroom house with a massive south facing garden — FEATURED AD — £168pw
Horfield Date available: 4 Mar

B

When they surfed the Internet, the three young men spotted these entries. Which one do you think is the best one for them? Form sentences like this:

1. The rooms in Fishponds are the *cheapest* (cheap), but they are also much *smaller* (small) than the 4-bed furnished house.
2. The 3-bedroom house is _____ (cheap) than the 4-bed furnished house, but it is ____ (expensive) than the 2-double-bed flat.

C

Which property is better and which one is the best? **PRODUCTION**

"Stop!" Holger shouted. "There are too many entries and if we do it like this, we will not make the best decision."
"So what do you suggest?" George wanted to know.
"Let's make a checklist to compare the best three properties," Holger said. And so the three sat together and made the list which you find on page 62. Before you look at it, think of what you have to bear in mind when choosing the right flat.

D

Look at the picture. Would you like to live in this semi-detached house? Explain why or why not. Some factors to consider: garden, fence, rooms, space, loft (room under the roof)

E

Form sentences in order to compare the three properties. Use the comparative (page 47). The adjectives in brackets in the table can help you to form the sentences.

→ see page 47 for comparison

Example:

There are **more** rooms in ... than in ..., but ... has **the most** rooms of the three.

Holger's list of the best three properties - a comparison

	Horfield 3-Bedroom	Brislington terraced	Knowle flat
1. rooms (many)	3 bedrooms, combined kitchen/living room, utility room, bathroom with WC, shower, balcony	2 bedrooms, kitchen, living room, bathroom, patio	large living room, 1 large + 1 small bedroom, kitchenette, bathroom
2. living space (large)	100 square metres	75 square metres	68 square metres
3. noise (noisy)	100 metres near the railroad line	near a park	bus stop in front of the house
4. insulation (good)	walls 36 cm thick, porous concrete, facing brick	walls 28 cm thick, concrete, brickwork	wooden walls, 5 cm thick, 8 cm mineral rock wool
5. shops (close)	15-minutes' walk to a shopping mall	next shopping centre 15 minutes by bike	larger shopping centre 5 miles away
6. extra costs (high)	£60 per month	£20 per week	£50 per month
7. rent (expensive)	£168 per week	£400 per month	£80 per week
8. age (old)	built in 2001	built in 1992	built in 1968
9. home (comfortable)	laminate floor, tiled kitchen + bathroom, gas central heating	stripped floor, linoleum in kitchen and bathroom, underfloor heating	carpets or tiles, coal central heating
10. distance from work (far)	5 miles	10 miles	17 miles

If you don't understand an English word and it is not in the vocabulary list, then you can look it up in an English-English dictionary. See page 152.

F

State your opinion - Do you think the three young men will take one of those properties above? Say why or why not. You can start like this:

1. I think all three flats are too ... for the three because ...
2. In my opinion, the flat in Knowle is too ... as it has ...
3. The flat in ... is the cheapest but ...
4. If the three take the terraced house in Brislington, they ...
5. If I had my way, I wouldn't rent the flat in Horfield because ...

G Another Try

Holger, Chas and George do not give up that easily. They study the advertisements in the Evening Post. It is difficult for the German native Holger to understand all the English abbreviations and technical terms the advertisers use in their newspaper adverts and so his friends Chas and George give Holger another riddle.

"Holger," George grinned. "If you manage to match all the terms and abbreviations to the right explanations, you will find what we are at the moment and we will buy you a pint of lager tonight as a prize." So, here you are. Holger is thirsty and needs your help.

1. Match them to the explanations. The terms are not in the correct order.

Terms and Abbreviations	Explanation	
1 a match	a home you can rent	R
2 on bus route	there is no furniture there	T
3 Gas central heating	the bus stop is quite near	R
4 £40 per week	this is the rent you have to pay per month	H
5 plus bills	a sum of money paid into an account as a guarantee if repairs are necessary	R
6 deposit required	these are additional costs, for example for heating, gas, water, electricity, sewage	E
7 employed only	a house in which several tenants live	Y
8 shared house	this is only for people who have a job	T
9 £115 pcm	the rent you have to pay per week	P
10 4/5 house	this matches what you are looking for	P
11 furnished	central heating which is run by gas	O
12 unfurnished	it means that there are already tables, cupboards, bed etc. in the home	N
13 nicely dec.	four other tenants are wanted, one is already there	U
14 room to let	a flat which looks good	E

2. If you match the letters to the right numbers, you will find a helpful Internet homepage which you can use to find a home quickly.

1	2	3	4	5
P (10)				

INTERACTION

H

In the end, Holger, Chas and George found the advert of a "lovely 3 Bedroom house" you can see in the picture below. Discuss whether the three made the right decision or not by completing the following sentences.

Example:
I think it is quieter in a cul de sac than in a through road.

1. In my opinion a large garden is ... because ...
2. It's good that there is a ... in the kitchen. So we don't need to ...
3. If they installed a brand new boiler for the gas central heating, ...
4. They completely repainted the house. But I hope they will like ...
5. I think a separate toilet is ...
6. One double bedroom? I would toss a coin to decide who gets ...
7. Go on and discuss the other items, too! Is really everything positive?

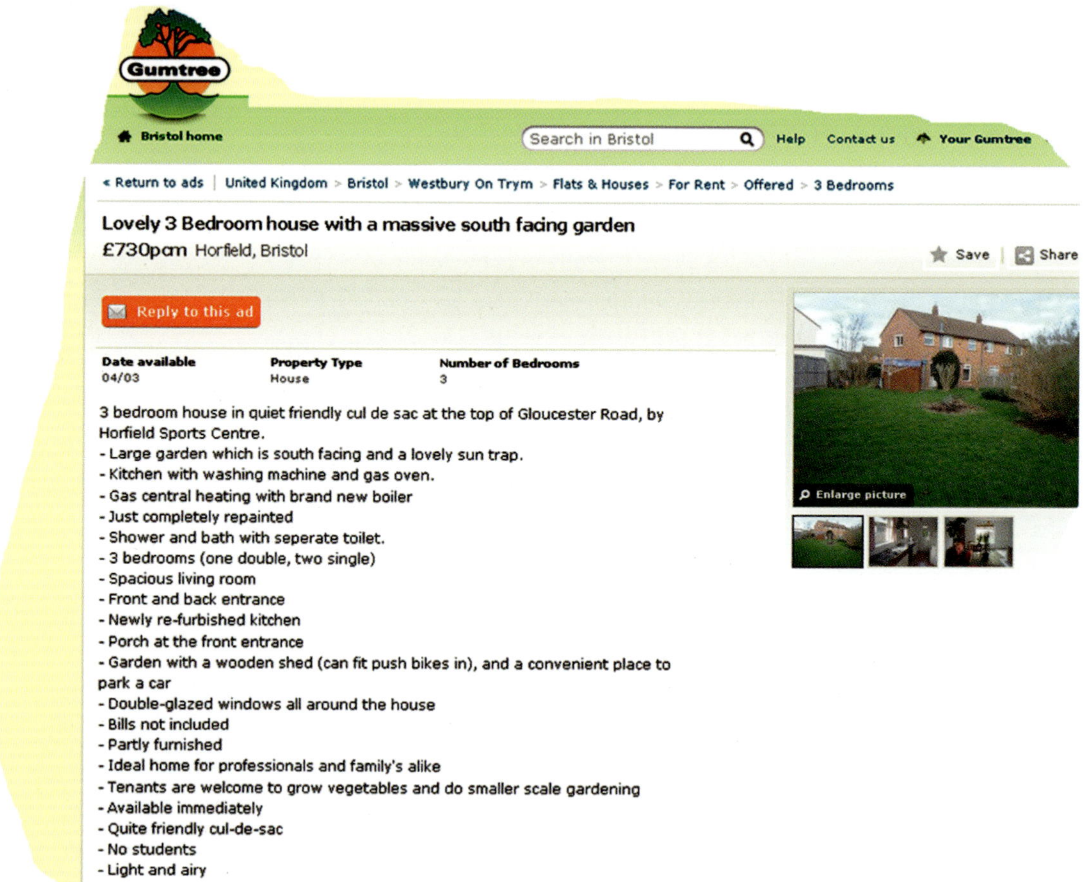
Gumtree

Bristol home | Search in Bristol | Help | Contact us | Your Gumtree

« Return to ads | United Kingdom > Bristol > Westbury On Trym > Flats & Houses > For Rent > Offered > 3 Bedrooms

Lovely 3 Bedroom house with a massive south facing garden
£730pcm Horfield, Bristol

Save | Share

Reply to this ad

Enlarge picture

Date available	Property Type	Number of Bedrooms
04/03	House	3

3 bedroom house in quiet friendly cul de sac at the top of Gloucester Road, by Horfield Sports Centre.
- Large garden which is south facing and a lovely sun trap.
- Kitchen with washing machine and gas oven.
- Gas central heating with brand new boiler
- Just completely repainted
- Shower and bath with seperate toilet.
- 3 bedrooms (one double, two single)
- Spacious living room
- Front and back entrance
- Newly re-furbished kitchen
- Porch at the front entrance
- Garden with a wooden shed (can fit push bikes in), and a convenient place to park a car
- Double-glazed windows all around the house
- Bills not included
- Partly furnished
- Ideal home for professionals and family's alike
- Tenants are welcome to grow vegetables and do smaller scale gardening
- Available immediately
- Quite friendly cul-de-sac
- No students
- Light and airy

For planning a discussion, look at page 151.

6.4 A Nice Elderly Landlady

Chas, George and Holger were sitting in a café. They were discussing the flat in Horfield which they liked best. They could even grow their own vegetables and fruit there. If only this lovely house in Horfield was not so expensive! It was such a nice property, much quieter than many other.
Finally they returned to the advertisement in the Evening Post:

> **Semi in Garden Street to let.**
> £600 pcm. 1 living room, 3 bedrooms, kitchen, bathroom, patio, utility room, garage, large garden.
>
> Contact Mrs Underwood, 4 Garden Street, Bristol BS 9 JJ

They had seen the semi-detached house before. Mrs Underwood owned the semi-detached house. She lived in the house on the left and the right-hand side was to let. Actually the house was quite good, but it needed some repairing, and the garden needed to be looked after a little more.
"Isn't the semi a good compromise?" Chas asked.
"Well, £200 from each of us is still quite a lot of money," George remarked.
"Why don't we go and see Mrs Underwood again?" Holger suggested. "Perhaps we can beat down the price a little. If everybody only had to pay £180, wouldn't that be okay?"
The other two agreed. "We could try at least," Chas replied.

The old lady was working in the front garden when the young men arrived there.
"Hello, Mrs Underwood, here we are again," Holger started the conversation.

The landlady got up and tried to straighten her back.
"Ouch," she said.
"I am getting old, the garden is too much for me. So, do you three want to rent the semi?"
"Well, Mrs Underwood, we would really love to take it, but to be honest, it's a little too expensive for use because we do not earn very much," said George. "Is there any chance to talk the rent over?"
Mrs Underwood gave George a sad look. "I am a widow," she replied. "My husband died two years ago. I decided to let the place because I need the money. With my back full of pain I will need a gardener, too. Someone offered to do my garden for £40 a month. And, as you see, the fence needs painting and the guttering has to be repaired as well. How am I to pay the tradesmen from the little old-age pension I get? I need the money and so I cannot reduce the rent."

"Can I make a suggestion?" Holger asked politely.
"Yes, go on," Mrs Underwood replied.
"If we could rent the semi for £180 each, we would love to do the garden for you and do all the repairing and painting. We are DIY enthusiasts. In the end, that would be good for all of us," Chas went on.

Mrs Underwood did not hesitate long: "Really? I would be happy if you three could look after the house and the garden. Then let's sign the rent contract! Young and old sitting in one boat," she laughed.

A

Read the text again. Look up the words you do not understand and write them down. Then answer the following questions in full sentences.

RECEPTION

1. Why did the three young men not take the flat in Horfield which they liked best? Find three reasons.
2. Why was the semi in Garden Street not their top favourite in the beginning?
3. Why could the three not afford to pay £ 200 each?
4. What were Mrs Underwood's problems?
5. How could the three young men help Mrs Underwood to solve her problems?
6. Is the suggestion Holger made a fair offer? What do you think?
7. What does Mrs Underwood mean with her statement "Young and old sitting in one boat"?

PRODUCTION

B

Holger wants to write a letter to his English teacher in Germany to say that he has now found a home at last. Of course, he writes in English to show that his English has improved.
Take Holger's part.

C

Getting ready for a housewarming party ...

Chas had asked Mrs Underwood if she would allow him to arrange a housewarming party. She suggested a garden party. Now Chas is sitting down and is making a list of who to invite. Why should or shouldn't he invite the following people?
Use the words in brackets to give reasons.

1. Mrs Underwood (the landlady, her garden, noise)
2. some of his new colleagues (to make friends)
3. his old friends from Ipswich (enough accomodation?)
4. his new neighbours (to make friends, music, noise)

D

Writing an invitation

Chas wants to write an invitation on his computer, but he doesn't know how to put the words.

1. Would you like to go to the computer room and design a nice invitation card with cliparts and texts? Ask your teacher.
2. You can write the invitation on simple paper as well. Your invitation card should give answers to the following questions:

   - What do you want to do?
   - Why do you want to celebrate?
   - For whom is the invitation?
   - When is the party?
   - Where is it?
   - Shall the guests bring anything?
   - Till when do you need an answer?

E Helping hands

Everybody was delighted when they got Holger's invitation. His colleagues, his friends and the neighbours knew how much work a garden party would mean for a young man and many people offered to help him. In the afternoon they were working hard to have a nice party.
Form sentences and use either *past progressive* or *simple past*. It's quite easy if you remember the rules.

Here is a small revision:

While Chas (suspend) Chinese lanterns from the trees/two girls (prepare) the potato salad.	
While Chas was suspend***ing*** Chinese lanterns from the trees, two girls ***were*** prepar***ing*** the potato salad.	These are two actions happening at the same time (2x past progressive).
When Chas (come) into his kitchen, George (fry) meatballs.	
George ***was*** fry***ing*** meatballs, when Chas ***came*** into the kitchen.	Entering a room is an event (simple past), frying meatballs takes a period of time (past progressive).

1. When Chas and two friends (put up) a large tent, Mr Miller (bring) two crates of beer.
2. While Lucy and Sara (lay) the garden tables, Sue Ellen (clean) the garden chairs.
3. Jack (make) sandwiches when a Chinese lantern (fall) on his head.
4. Mrs Smith (squeeze out) some oranges while the Millers (wash up) beer glasses.
5. Mrs Underwood (make) a party soup while Mary (cut) cheese cubes for a cheese platter.
6. When Chas (play) on his guitar, the guests suddenly (applaud).

In this unit there are a lot of words and vocabulary that you don't know. If you can't find the words in the following vocabulary, you can look them up in an English-English dictionary. Do you know how to use a dictionary like that? You will find all the information you need on page 152 - "How to Work with an English-English Dictionary".

Vocabulary

6.1 Home or Hell?		
laundry basket ['lɔːndrɪ 'bɑːskɪt]	you collect dirty washing in it	Wäschekorb
(to) hoover ['huːvə]	British word for (to) vacuumclean	staubsaugen
(to) dust [dʌst]	to wipe away dust with a cloth	staubwischen
by 10 p.m. [baɪ ten pɪem]	10 p.m. is the latest point of time	bis (spätestens) 22 Uhr
(to) turn down [tɜːn daʊn]	to reduce the noise	leiser drehen
freedom ['friːdəm]	the state of being free	Freiheit
privacy ['prɪvəsɪ]	the state that you can do something without being watched by others	Ungestörtheit
(to) concentrate ['kɒnsəntreɪt]	to direct one's attention to something	sich konzentrieren
"out of the saucepan into the fire"	to get into something that is worse than before	„vom Regen in die Traufe kommen"
fridge [frɪdʒ]	refrigderator, for keeping something cool	Kühlschrank
insulation [ˌɪnsjʊ'leɪʃn]	it prevents the heat from escaping	Isolation
fish fingers [fɪʃ 'fɪŋgəz]	fish pressed in a rectangular form	Fischstäbchen
bedsitter or bedsit ['bed 'sɪtə] ['bedsɪt]	a room for both living and sleeping in	Wohnschlafzimmer, Einzimmer-apartment
6.2 Flat-Hunting in Bristol		
flat-hunting [flæt hʌntɪŋ]	trying to find a good flat	Wohnungssuche
landlord ['lænlɔːd]/ landlady ['lænleɪdɪ]	man who offers a flat/ woman who offers a flat	Vermieter/ Vermieterin
maisonette [ˌmeɪzə'net]		Einliegerwohnung
hole [həʊl]	small platform between two flights of stairs	Bruchbude
lavatory ['lævətərɪ]		Toilette, Waschraum
landing ['lændɪŋ]	a certain gas	Trepppenabsatz
6.3 Property Hunting via the Internet		
minimum criteria ['mɪnɪməm kraɪ'tɪərɪə]		Mindestkriterien, -eingabedaten
location [ləʊ'keɪʃn]	place where to live	Wohnort
rental period ['rentl 'pɪərɪəd]	the time for which you pay rent	Mietzeitraum
furnished ['fɜːnɪʃt]	with furniture	möbliert
distance ['dɪstəns]	how far it is from A to B	Entfernung
window pane ['wɪndəʊ]	the glassy part of the window	Fensterscheibe
property ['prɒpətɪ]	something you own	Eigentum, Besitz
detached house [dɪ'tætʃt haʊs]	a single house	Einzelhaus
semi-detached house [semɪdɪ'tætʃt haʊs]	one of two houses that are linked to each other	Doppelhaushälfte
cottage ['kɒtɪdʒ]	a small house, often in the country	kleines Landhaus
(to) be confused [bɪ kən'fjuːzt]	no longer able to think clearly	verwirrt sein
terraced houses ['terəst haʊs]	several houses in a row	Reihenhäuser
mews [mjuːz]	a flat in a former shed	zur Wohnung umgebauter Stall
apartment (AmE); flat (BrE)	a set of rooms in a house	Wohnung
(to) include [ɪn'kluːd]	to have as a part, to contain	einschließen
porous concrete ['pɔː.rəs 'kɒŋ.kriːt]		Schaumbeton
facing brick ['feɪ.sɪŋ brɪk]	you can see the bricks	Verblender
brickwork ['brɪk.wɜːk]	a wall built up with bricks	Mauerwerk
concrete ['kɒŋ.kriːt]	a liquid building material that hardens	Beton
mineral rock wool ['mɪn.ər.əl rɒk wʊl]	material for insulation	(Mineral-)Steinwolle
tiled [taɪld]	like the walls in a bathroom	gefliest
cul de sac ['kʌl.də.sæk]	dead-end street	Sackgasse
spacious ['speɪ.ʃəs]	large	geräumig
6.4 A Nice Elderly Landlady		
elderly ['eldəlɪ]	looking somewhat old	ältlich
(to) beat the price down [biːt ðe rent daʊn]	to get a lower price	die Miete herunterhandeln
at least [ət liːst]		wenigstens
ouch! [aʊtʃ]	that's what you say when you feel pain	Aua!
(to) talk over [tɔːk 'əʊvə]	to speak about it in order to solve a problem	darüber reden, durchsprechen
widow ['wɪdəʊ]	a wife whose husband has died	Witwe
tradesman [treɪdzmən]	someone who works with hands and tools	Handwerker
guttering ['gʌt.ər.ɪŋ]		Regenrinnen
enthusiastic [ɪn'θjuːzɪ'æstɪk]	very happy	begeistert
lodger [lɒdʒə]	someone who pays rent	Mieter
housewarming party [haʊs'wɔːmɪŋ 'pɑːtɪ]	a party you give after you moved in	Kistenparty, Einzugsparty
accommodation [əˌkɒmə'deɪʃn]	a place where you can stay and sleep	Unterkunft
meatballs [miːt bɔːl]	minced meat that is fried	Frikadellen
(to) squeeze out [skwiːz aʊt]	to get the juice out of it	auspressen
cheese platter [tʃiːz 'plætə]	a plate with various sorts of cheese	Käseplatte
DIY [ˌdiː.aɪ'waɪ]		do it yourself
DIY enthusiast [ˌdiː.aɪ'waɪ ɪn'θjuː.zi.æst]		Heimwerker

Listening Comprehension

A Listen to the audio-track "School Exchange: Six months on Vancouver Island" (available on audio-CD for teachers*).

B Which of the following sentences is true? RECEPTION

1. Vancouver Island lies
   a) off the west coast of Canada
   b) off the west coast of the USA
   c) off the east coast of Canada

2. Lily was part of a family with
   a) four children
   b) five children
   c) six children

3. Lily's host mother was a
   a) speech therapist
   b) cook
   c) food inspector

4. The British Columbian winter is
   a) cold without much snow
   b) cold with a lot of snow
   c) cold and wet

5. In Canada you get Christmas presents
   a) on Christmas Day
   b) on Christmas Eve
   c) on Christmas Night

6. In Canada young people can go to the disco when they are
   a) eighteen years
   b) sixteen years
   c) twenty years

C Listen to the audio-track again. Have a look at these pictures. What do they have to do with the text?

[*Transcript available in HT 1622 Lösungsheft Living Together]

Mediation

Mediation

Christmas in Great Britain

Christmas Day is on the 25th December, but preparations start long before that. The Christmas tree is put up from the 1st December. The decorating is a family occasion, with everyone helping. Christmas cards are written and sent to relatives and friends all over the world. On Christmas Eve, younger kids hang up their stockings on the ends of beds or by the chimney for Father Christmas. The kids prepare special gifts for Father Christmas and his reindeer and put everything in front of the chimney. On Christmas morning, presents are opened. At lunchtime the main Christmas meal is eaten. It starts usually with a toast and popping the crackers. At the traditional Christmas meal it is common to have turkey (or goose), roast potatoes, vegetables, sausages, bacon, and dessert is often Christmas pudding. In the afternoon people visit family and friends.

A **Make up a dialogue between Lily and Mary in German.**

Lily: Wie wird Weihnachten in Großbritannien gefeiert?
Mary: … (beschreibt das britische Weihnachtsfest)

Two days later they meet Brian, an exchange student from Seattle in the USA.
He asks them about German Christmas customs.

B **Make up a dialogue between Lily and Brian in English.**
Lily describes German Christmas customs.

Lily: …
Brian: …

Switzerland

The Netherlands

Austria

Ireland

Italy

A Which of the named countries would you like to go to?

7.1 Sarah and Michael Are Going Abroad

Sarah and Michael go to a vocational school in Papenburg, which is a small town near the Dutch border. They are in a class for domestic and social science. Sarah wants to become a nurse in a hospital and Michael wants to become a geriatric nurse. They've already had a lot of practical experience in their future job this year. They have both worked full time for eight weeks: Michael in an old people's home and Sarah in a hospital.

In many lessons, their class has worked on an international project about traditional home remedies. Another school in Groningen/ Netherlands and one in Ballymahon/Ireland are also taking part in this project.

Sarah and Michael are now on their way to their twinned school in Ireland. They are going to prepare a presentation of the project with students from their twinned schools.

Michael and Sarah went by train to an airport near Amsterdam. They are now waiting to be checked in. The plane to Dublin is delayed.

Training Abroad?
The Leonardo Mobility Programme might be useful for you.
Target group: Trainees in initial vocational training
Activity: Supporting trainees to go abroad for a certain period of time
More information: Your class teacher or the Internet (www.leonardo.org.uk)

A **Choose one of the alternatives (a–c) to complete the sentences.**

1. Sarah wants to become
   a) a doctor.
   b) a nurse.
   c) a pilot.
2. Michael got a lot of practical experience by
   a) reading a book about caring for people.
   b) working in an old people's home.
   c) taking pictures of old people with his camera.
3. Sarah and Michael travel to their partner school
   a) by car.
   b) by bicycle.
   c) by plane.
4. Sarah and Michael are travelling to Ballymahon because they
   a) want to prepare a presentation of a project.
   b) want to get married.
   c) want to spend their holidays in Ballymahon.
5. In which country has Michael been before?
   a) Ireland
   b) United States of America
   c) Great Britain

It can be fun to work on a project - you can learn and make your own experiences at the same time. Our friends Michael and Sarah are working on a project about traditional home remedies. You can work on other projects as well, for example you could plan an English breakfast for your class. Look on page 148 for more information and ask your teacher about it.

Present Perfect

When do you use the present perfect?

The present perfect expresses an action which began in the past and still continues. It also expresses the effect of past actions on the present. ➜ For rules see page 168

Examples:

- *The class* ***has worked*** *on an international project. (The results can be seen now.)*
- *Michael* ***has been*** *to the Netherlands and to Great Britain. (Michael has some knowledge about these countries now, it has an effect on him.)*

➜ *Sarah and Michael* ***have had*** *a lot of practical experience this year. (So they are better informed now.)*

How do you form the present perfect?

You form the present perfect with a present tense form of *have* + the third verb form (past participle).

Past participle:

- Most verbs have a regular past participle: *verb + -ed* (work***ed***)
- Some verbs have an irregular past participle: been, had, written, made, held etc.

➜ *There is a list of the irregular verbs and their verb forms on page 164.*

Statement Clause		
I We You They	**have**	work**ed**.
He She It	**has**	

Negative Clause			
I We You They	**have**	not	work**ed**.
He She It	**has**		

Questions		
Have	I we you they	work**ed?**
Has	he she it	

A Put the words in brackets into the ***present perfect*** tense.

Examples:

- *Michael … on an international project (work).*
  - Michael ***has worked*** *on an international project.*
- *It is Sarah's birthday tomorrow and Michael … her a present yet (not, buy).*
  - It is Sarah's birthday tomorrow and Michael ***has not bought*** *her a present yet.*
- *Ken: "Can I take this newspaper? … you … with it (finish)?"*
  - Ken: "Can I take this newspaper? ***Have*** *you* ***finished*** *with it?"*
- *Sarah: "Michael, this is Mary." Michael: "Yes, I know. We … already … (meet)."*
  - Sarah: "Michael, this is Mary." Michael: "Yes, I know. We ***have*** *already* ***met****."*

1. Ken and Gina … in the same house for six years (live).
2. Sarah … to Great Britain yet (not, be).
3. Ken: "Are Fiona and Jim here?" Gina: "Yes, they … just … (arrive)."
4. Mark asks Laura: "When does Mr Kelly start his new job?" Laura: "He … already … (start)".
5. Ken: "Where is the recipe for apple crumble?" Fiona: "I don't know. I … it (not, see)."
6. Mr Kelly … as an interviewer since January 2011 (work).
7. Jim: "Hmm, that's a lovely meal. Who … it (cook)?"
8. Gina: "I … plum pudding before (not try). It is very nice."

B Look at the pictures of the flags. Which flag goes with which text? Name the country.

1. This country has a population of 4.2 million. It is an island in the North Atlantic Ocean, west of Great Britain. The landscape is beautiful. The people are very fond of tea. Flag: three equal vertical bands of green, white, and orange.
2. This country has a population of 16.5 million. The people travel a lot, learn foreign languages and buy a lot of bicycles.
3. This country has a population of 60.5 million. It is an island off the North West coast of Europe. The people have small families and love their own national food. The people smoke and drink more than their European neighbours. The national colours are red, white and blue.
4. This country has a population of 82.2 million. As a country with many immigrants, it has adopted many international dishes into daily eating habits. Italian dishes like pizza and pasta, Turkish and Arab dishes like doner kebab and falafel are well established, especially in big cities. The people like to drink coffee.

Working Abroad?
The EURES Programme might be useful for you.
Target group: Workers who want to live and work temporarily or permanently in a European Union's Member State different to that of their country of origin
Activity: EURES Advisers help jobseekers to find suitable employers
More information: A job centre or the Internet (**http://ec.europa.eu/eures**)

C This is the flag of the European Union.

1. Which countries belong to the European Union?
2. What are the capitals of these countries?

7.2 The Meeting

When Sarah and Michael arrive in Ballymahon, they are heartily welcomed by those students from the Ballymahon Vocational School who take part in the project.

Juliana and Wim from the twinned school in Groningen/Netherlands have arrived as well.

Soon they are talking about the kind of work they have been doing for the project and are sharing their experiences. Look at their conversation:

Sarah: "This week we have learned how to put a compress on somebody."
Wim: …

A What else has been done for the project? Here are some words which give you ideas what has been done already. Use the *present perfect* of the verbs.
→ For rules see page 168

Examples:
Wim: we/already/produce/bath salts
Wim: "We ***have*** *already* ***produced*** *bath salts."*

William: our class/make/a herbal garden
William: "Our class ***has made*** *a herbal garden."*

1. Marian: a team in our class/collect/herbs for steam baths
2. John: this year/my mother/dry/herbs/for making tea
3. Patrick: I/buy/a guide book about home remedies
4. Juliana: our project team/make/a video for an exhibition in a pharmacy
5. Michael: we/write/an essay for the journal *Examples – Teaching in Lower Saxony*
6. Mary: Bernadette/design/a professional homepage about the project
7. Marian: Annie and I/recently/start/a survey about the use of natural cosmetics
8. Annie: I/press/plants for a herbarium …
9. Annie: … but/my three-year-old sister Ruth/tear/quite a lot of the pressed plants

7.3 In a Pub

It was a successful presentation and the students are all very happy. They have worked very well! Moreover, many of them have actually made friends with the students from another country.

Irish Pub

Juliana: "What are we going to do in the evening?"
Michael: "Well, we could just go to a pub!"
Geert: "I think that's a good idea. Does anybody know if there is live music in any pub?"
William: "On Thursdays there is usually music in *The Plough*."
Juliana: "Oh, that's nice. Shall we meet there at – let's say 9 o' clock?"

Later on the students meet in the pub. They are really disappointed because they don't see any musicians. They order their drinks. Most of them have a coke. Some of the older students have a pint of lager or a glass of stout.

Sarah: "I think it is very funny that the Irish still keep to their traditional measurements."
John: "It is not only the measurements. The traffic regulations are another example. Unfortunately if you don't drive on the left, you are likely to have an accident. "
Geert: "But I think that they have changed their distances from miles to kilometres, haven't they?"
Tom: "That's right. But only in Ireland. In Great Britain the traffic signs are still showing the distances in miles."
Michael: "I think it is nice when a country keeps to its traditions. As far as I know, the British have the oldest monarchy in the world. And the majority are still very fond of it. Is that right, Mary? You have worked in England for nearly a year, you must know."
Mary: "That is true. Many official events begin or end with the national anthem 'God Save The Queen'."
Juliana: "Oh, a few days ago I saw some students wearing a uniform. Is there a special reason for that?"
Mary: "Well, it is quite common here to wear uniforms at school. Most schools have their own special uniform."

School uniforms

In the meantime three musicians have arrived at the pub and have started to play. The Dutch and German students listen very carefully - they have never heard some of the instruments before, for example the harp. They all enjoy the music and the musicians play very well.

Mary: "There are many things here in Ireland that are different, compared to your country, for example Christmas. It is a great, big festival here: We decorate the houses colourfully, for that we often use balloons, holly and mistletoe. We have a traditional dinner with turkey and plum pudding."

Michael: "When I listen to you talking, I think it would be lovely to stay here."

Mary: "Well, dear Michael - why don't you? You know, I will really miss you when you leave."

When the pub closes at 1 a.m., Michael and Mary go home silently. The stay of the foreign students is almost over. Two days later Michael has to fly home.

A week later Mary gets a letter from Michael:

Mary Barrins
21 Parnell Street
Ballymahon
Co. Longford
Ireland

Dear Mary,
thank you so much for being so kind and hospitable to me last week. I really had a wonderful time and I especially enjoyed my stay with you. Thank you for the interesting tours and the entertaining evenings. And I will never forget the night in our pub "The Plough".
I will send you the tourist information about Germany that you asked for as soon as possible.
You are welcome to stay in our house anytime!
Best regards,

Michael

Plum pudding is a famous, traditional English dessert on Christmas Day.

RECEPTION

A

Read the text "In a Pub" again. Now look at these sentences. Each of the sentences has a mistake. Find it and correct it.

Examples:

In Great Britain the traffic signs show the distances in kilometres.
- In Great Britain the traffic signs show the distances in ***miles****.*

In Ireland the pubs can stay open all night.
- In Ireland the pubs ***close at 1 a.m****.*

1. The Irish have the oldest monarchy in the world.
2. On Sundays there is usually music in *The Plough*.
3. Many official events begin with the song 'What shall we do with the drunken sailor'.
4. About 10% of the people in Great Britain are fond of the monarchy.
5. At Christmas the Irish have a traditional dinner with turkey and plums.
6. The students want to go to a cinema.
7. When you buy a beer in a pub you order either half a litre or a litre.
8. The musicians started to play before 8:30 p. m.

Adjectives and Adverbs

When do you use adjectives and when do you use adverbs?

- Adjectives describe *nouns*.
  Example: *It was a* ***successful presentation****. (a presentation = noun)*

- Adverbs describe ***verbs.***
  Example: *The students* ***worked successfully****. (to work = verb)*

How do you form an adverb?

- You form regular adverbs with **adjective + *-ly***

→ For rules see pages 171/172

Spelling rule: Adjectives that end in ***-y*** change to ***-ily***.

Adjective	Adverb
quick	quickly
bad	badly
careful	carefully
easy	easily
successful	successfully

Be careful, because some adverbs are irregular:

Adjective	Adverb
good	well
hard	hard
early	early
fast	fast

A **Do you know? Are the underlined words adjectives or adverbs?**

1. Michael and Mary go home <u>silently</u>.
2. The Irish have a <u>traditional</u> dinner with turkey and plum pudding.
3. There is <u>live</u> music in *The Plough*.
4. Many <u>official</u> events begin or end with the national anthem.
5. Most schools have their own <u>special</u> uniform.
6. The Irish decorate the houses <u>colourfully</u>.
7. The Dutch and German students listen very <u>carefully</u> to the music.
8. That is a very <u>good</u> idea.
9. The musicians play very <u>well</u>.

B **Fill in the gaps by using the following words.**

quick – quickly – bad – badly – careful – carefully – easy – easily – good – well – hard

1. Lunch is a … meal for many people.
2. Many people eat their food in a fish and chip shop …
3. Manchester United played … and lost the match.
4. Smoking is a … habit.
5. Ken is a … driver.
6. The students work on their project …
7. Gina is very good at tennis. She won the game …
8. The homework is …
9. Gina and Ken know Jim …
10. Jim is a … cook.
11. Nurses work … and don't earn much money.

Vocabulary

7.1 Sarah and Michael Are Going Abroad		
old people's nurse [əʊld 'pi:plz nɜ:s]	someone who looks after old people	Altenpflegerin, Altenpfleger
old people's home [əʊld 'pi:plz həʊm]	a place where old people live	Altenheim
practical experience ['præktɪkl ɪk'spɪərɪəns]	learning by doing	praktische Erfahrung
home remedy [həʊm 'remɪdɪ]	medicine which is produced at home	Hausmittel
twin [twɪn], be twinned with	If a school in one country is twinned with a school in another country, they have a special relationship	durch eine Partnerschaft verbunden
presentation [ˌprezən'teɪʃn]	to show your work	Darbietung, Vorstellung
destination [ˌdestɪ'neɪʃn]	the place to go to	Zielort
flight [flaɪt]	the plane you will fly in	Flug
remark [rɪ'mɑ:k]	a short piece of information	Bemerkung
on time [ɒn taɪm]	not late	pünktlich
delay [dɪ'leɪ]	something is too late, not on time	Verspätung
to express [ɪk'spres]	to put an idea into words	ausdrücken
mobility [məʊ'bɪl.ɪ.ti]	the ability to move freely	Mobilität
target ['tɑ:.gɪt]	a subject at which activities are aimed	Ziel
trainee [ˌtreɪ'ni:]	a person who is learning the skills of a particular job	Auszubildende, Auszubildender
initial [ɪ'nɪʃ.əl]	at the beginning	am Anfang, hier: erste
7.2 The Meeting		
temporarily ['tem.pər.ər.ili]	not lasting or needed for very long	zeitlich begrenzt
permanently ['pɜ:.mə.nənt.li]	for ever	dauerhaft
jobseeker ['dʒɑ:bˌsi:.kɚ]	someone who is trying to find a job	Arbeitssuchende/r
compress [kəm'pres]	a cloth used to stop high temperature	Kompresse, Wickel
bath salts [bɑ:θ sɔ:lt]	herbal remedies used in bath water	Badezusatz, Badesalz
herb [hɜ:b]	a plant used for flavouring or for medicines	Kraut, Kräuter
herbal garden [hɜ:bl gɑ:dn]	a garden with many herbs	Kräutergarten
steam bath [sti:m bɑ:θ]	very hot bath	Dampfbad
an exhibition [ˌeksɪ'bɪʃn]	a show	Ausstellung
pharmacy ['fɑ:məsɪ]	a medicine shop	Apotheke
an essay ['eseɪ]	a small piece of written work	Aufsatz, Zeitschriftenartikel
7.3 In the Pub		
pub [pʌb]	a place where alcohol is served	Gaststätte
successful [sak'sesfʊl]	with success, a good result	erfolgreich
a pint [paɪnt]	a glass which contains 0,568 litre, a British measurement	0,568 Liter
lager ['lɑ:gə]	beer with a golden colour	helles Bier
a glass (of stout etc.) [ə glɑ:s (əv staʊt)]	the half of a pint	0,284 Liter
stout [staʊt]	strong dark beer	dunkles Starkbier
measurement ['meʒəmənt]	unit which is used to find the quantity of a thing	Maßeinheit
unfortunately [ʌn'fɔ:tʃnətlɪ]	to have bad luck	unglücklicherweise
likely [laɪklɪ]	it may happen	wahrscheinlich
monarchy ['mɒnəkɪ]	a country which is ruled by a king or queen	Monarchie
majority [mə'dʒɒrətɪ]	the most	Mehrheit
event [ɪ'vent]	an activity or an action	Ereignis
national anthem ['næʃənl 'ænθəm]	a piece of music belonging to a country and its people	Nationalhymne
holly ['hɒlɪ] 	an evergreen plant with prickly leaves and red berries	Stechpalme
mistletoe ['mɪsltəʊ] 	a plant with white berries	Mistel
turkey ['tɜ:kɪ]	a large bird which is eaten	Truthahn
plum pudding [plʌm 'pʊdɪŋ]	a kind of boiled cake with fruit	Plumpudding

Unit 8 People at Work

A Carol and Jason have not decided yet which profession they want to learn later on. Have you already made a decision?

8.1 Carol's Second Practical Training

Carol attends the vocational school in Manchester. In her first year she did some practical training in the kitchen of St. George's hospital. She is in her second year now and has to do a second training. This time she has the chance to work in a nursery school.
Carol is always well supported by the nursery nurse. This is what her typical day looks like.

A Describe her day in complete sentences. Use the expressions from the right. Use the *simple present* and start like this:
Carol gets up at 6:30 a.m.

1. (get) up at 6:30 a.m.
2. (arrive) at the nursery school at 7:30 a.m.
3. (prepare) breakfast
4. (help) the children to brush their teeth
5. (go) for a walk
6. (put) the children in a circle and (study) a new song
7. (help) them to draw pictures
8. the mothers (come) at 1 p.m. and (take) their children home
9. Carol (go) home. She (be) very tired and (take) a nap.

B In the evening her mother wants to know what Carol did during her working day. Give Carol's mother a full report. Use the *simple past* and start like this:
I got up at 6:30 a.m.

C Would you like to be in Carol's place? Give reasons why or why not. The words from the box below might help you. Discuss it with your classmates. **PRODUCTION**

interesting – boring – fascinating – like to work with children – useful job – monsters – good / bad working hours – work with people – colleagues – help children – hate children – low income – dangerous – mothers know everything better – responsible work – a lot of different activities – stay young myself – see world new

D Unfortunately a friend of Carol's nursery teacher has lost her job and is now unemployed. She has made a big mistake. What could she have done wrong? Here are some explanations. Use the *present perfect* for your sentences.

Example:
*steal something – She probably has lost her job because she **has stolen** something.*

steal something – not be at work sometimes – be late too often – have arguments with colleagues – be ill too often – not inform a mother that her child walk home – drink alcohol at work – be too lazy – not see problems of children – not be hygienic enough

→ For rules, see page 168 ff.

E What tense do you have to use in these sentences? ***Present perfect*** or ***simple past***?

1. I (read) this magazine last month.
2. There (be) an accident. You have to drive another way.
3. We (live) in London from 1997 to 2010.
4. Sorry, can you say that again? When … (you live) there?
5. I (never be) there, but my father (go) there last Christmas.
6. We (see) each other every day when we (be) small kids.
7. When Mary was young, she (be) a little overweight.
8. During the last three months she (lose) five kilos and looks pretty good.
9. … you … (go) to the party last night? No, I (do). I (go) to Melanie instead.
10. What … you … (wear)? My green shirt and my black trousers.

8.2 What about Jason's Second Practical Training?

Jason did his first practical training on a surgical ward in St. George's Hospital in Manchester. Just like Carol, he also has to do a second placement. He applied to do it in an old people's home where he had the opportunity to have a closer look at what it is like to work with old people.

The teacher at school has told him to write a report about his working routine, the residents and the skills needed when working with old people. This is what he wrote in his report:

My Work Routine

I had to work shifts. In my first week I was on the morning shift and had to start at 8 a.m. I had to work for seven hours. In the following two weeks I was on the late shift. I liked the late shift better, because there is not so much work to do as in the morning and I could sleep longer. The late shift started at 1 p.m. Once I also had to work at the weekend.

Residents
In the old people's home there were 38 residents. Most of them were in their eighties or nineties. One resident was only 45 years old. She had tried to commit suicide but she survived. The woman was now paralysed and therefore unable to care for herself. Most of the residents were female. We only had three male residents. Some of the old people were confused and so we had to explain things over and over again, because they couldn't remember. The ones who were not confused liked to talk about their lives - and I listened very carefully, because it was really interesting. They also wanted to do something useful. Some of them liked to help the cook, so they peeled potatoes or cleaned the dishes.

Qualifications
During the three weeks of my practical training I learned quite a lot. You need a lot of skills when working with the elderly. I learned to be very patient and sensitive. I tried to put myself into their situation to understand them better. I also asked them about their professions and what they liked to do when they were younger. There was a patient who always got up at 2 a.m. - almost in the middle of the night. I could not really understand that. So I asked him what his profession was and - believe it or not - he was a baker!

You also need a lot of physical strength. It is not so easy to turn those residents over in bed who are unable to move. I was told to be very careful with my back. Nobody was allowed to turn them over without the help of a second person. Those residents were turned over every two hours, even at night, to prevent bedsores.

A RECEPTION

1. What does Jason say about the working routine?
2. What do you know about the residents?
3. Which skills do you need in this job?

8.3 Evaluation of the Practical Training

After the three weeks of training, all the pupils had to go back to their vocational school in Manchester. On their first day they took the time to evaluate and to talk about the experiences they had had. All of them were very excited and it was really noisy in the classroom, because they had so much to talk about. They started with a breakfast which the teachers had made for them. Then they received their task for the first day.

A **Use the words in the box and describe what the pupils had to do. Choose the right order and form complete sentences. Start like this:** *At first we had to find a partner. Secondly …*

got pencils - had to lie on the ground - secondly - then
had to find a partner - at first - then
drew lines around our bodies - after that -
fixed the paper onto the walls in our classroom -
had to complete the sentences - finally

Tip
There is no simple past for 'must'.
Use 'had to'+ infinitive instead.

This is an example of a body outline.

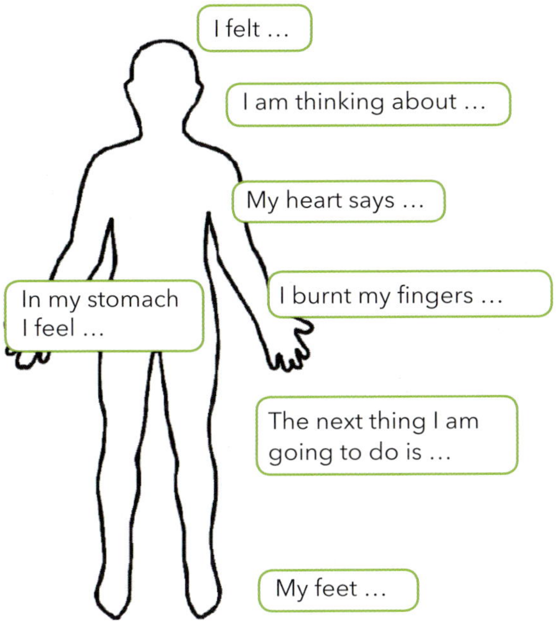

B **Now it is your turn. Copy this body outline and complete the sentences with your own experiences in your practical training. You can just as well create your own body outline and go on as described above.**

8.4 A Day in Ann's Life

Ann works in the kitchen of a hospital. Today she is on the morning shift. They are very busy and the chef gave her a lot of work to do. He wanted everything to be ready by 10 o'clock.

A **Look at the pictures. Form complete sentences – what did the chef tell Ann to do?**

Start like this:
He told her to wash the cabbage.
He told her to …

At 10 a.m. he wanted to know what Ann had already done. Ann said:
I ***have*** *already* ***washed*** *the cabbage.*
I have …
I haven't … yet.

B **Complete the sentences. Use the *present perfect* this time to show that there is a visible result of what you have done.**

➜ For rules see page 168

8.5 The Future Is Yours

What do you want to do when you leave school? Here are some ideas:

Professional Life

nurse - baker - cook - social worker - hang about - gardener - odd jobs - further education - social assistant - doctor's assistant - teacher - domestic science - nursery nurse - no idea - help disabled people ...

Private Life

sports (basketball/football/gym ...) - have a lot of friends - go to pubs - discos - computer - stay at home a lot - have children - get married - build a house - go abroad - travel a lot - go to the church more often ...

A Choose two professions and two private activities which come close to your wishes for the future and form sentences like this:

When I leave this class, I am going to qualify as a baker or a cook. In my private life I plan to get married and I also want to have some children.

B What is your classmate sitting next to you going to do in his professional and private future? Interview him or her.
Tell the class what you have found out about the other person's plans.

INTERACTION

The Future

Going-To-Future

Statements and Negative Clauses			
I	**am**	(not) **going to**	**play** football.
You	**are**		
He She It	**is**		
We You They	**are**		

Statements and Negative Clauses			
what	**am**	I	**going to do?**
	are	you	
	is	he she it	
	are	we you they	

How do you form the going-to-future?
You form the going-to-future with
am/is/are + going to + infinitive.

When do you use it?
- You use going to when you talk about *concrete future plans and intentions*.
- You use going to *when you can see* what is going to happen in the future.

Examples:
- *What **are** you **going to do** after school? Have you got any plans?*
- *I **am going to be** a nurse when I leave school. I have already applied at the hospital.*
- *It's **going to rain**, just look at the clouds!*
- *John **is going to be** quite fat. This is his fifth hamburger.*

➜ For rules see page 169

Will-Future

Statements and Negative Clauses		
I You He She It We You They	**will** **will not** **(won't)**	**hely** you.

How do you form the will-future?
You form the will-future with
will or will not (won't) + infinitive.

When do you use it?
- You use the will-future instead of the going-to-future when you do something *spontaneously*.
- You use the will-future *when you have no influence* on what is going to happen.

Examples:
- *Oh, dear! These bags are too heavy for you. I will carry one of them.*
- *What will the town look like in ten years?*
- *I think there will be many high-rise buildings.*

If you are not sure which tense you have to use – take the will-future.

Vocabulary

8.1 Carol's Second Practical Training		
nursery nurse ['nɜːsrɪ nɜːs]	a woman who works with small children	Kinderpflegerin, Erzieherin
nursery school ['nɜːsrɪ skuːl]	a place for children aged 0 – 6	Kindergarten
tooth (singular), teeth (plural) [tuːθ] [tiːθ]	You show them when you smile.	Zahn, Zähne
exactly [ɪg'zæktlɪ]	very precise	genau
low income [ləʊ 'ɪŋkʌm]	not enough money for your work	geringes Einkommen
responsible [rɪ'spɒnsəbl]	When you do baby-sitting your are responsible for the baby.	verantwortlich, verantwortungsvoll
(to) have arguments [həv 'ɑːgjʊməntz]	to quarrel	Streit haben
(to) be hygienic [bɪ haɪ'dʒiːnɪk]	to be washed and dressed properly	hygienisch sein
8.2 What about Jason's Second Practical Training?		
(to) be unable [bɪ ʌn'eɪbl]	not to be able	unfähig sein
(to) work on shifts [wɜːk ən ʃɪftz]	You work either the morning shift, the late shift or the night shift.	im Schichtdienst arbeiten
resident ['rezɪdənt]	a person who lives in an old people's home	Bewohner, Heiminsasse
(to) commit suicide [kə'mɪt sjʊɪsaɪd]		Selbstmord begehen
(to) succeed [sak'siːd]	to have success	Erfolg haben, gewinnen
(to) be paralysed [bɪ 'pærəlaɪzd]	to be unable to move your body	gelähmt sein
(to) be patient [bɪ 'peɪʃnt]	to be able to wait	geduldig sein
(to) be sensitive [bɪ 'sənsɪtɪv]	to understand the feelings of others	sensibel sein
physical strength ['fɪzɪkl streŋθ]	the strength of your body	körperliche Stärke
(to) prevent [prɪ'vent]	to avoid	verhindern
bedsore [bedsɔː]		Druckgeschwür; Dekubitus
8.3 Evaluation of the Practical Training		
evaluation [ɪˌvæl.ju'eɪ.ʃən]	review	Auswertung / Bewertung
(to) be excited [ɪk'saɪ.tɪd]	to feel happy	aufgeregt sein
noisy ['nɔɪ.zi]	with a lot of noise	laut
(to) lie on the ground [ləɪ on ðə graʊnd]		auf dem Boden liegen
8.5 The Future Is Yours		
(to) hang about [hæŋ ə'baʊt]	not to know what to do	herumlümmeln
(to) be disabled [bɪ dɪs'eɪbld]	to be handicapped	behindert sein
(to) go abroad [gəʊ ə'brɔːd]	to go into another country	ins Ausland gehen
intention [ɪn'tenʃn]		Absicht

Unit 9 Living with Special Needs

The NOVOTOWN Hotel in Birmingham belongs to the ACCOR Hotel Group with 150.525 employees in 4065 Hotels in almost 100 countries. "For many years, the Group has been committed to facilitating the professional integration of disabled workers." (Website of Accor Group)

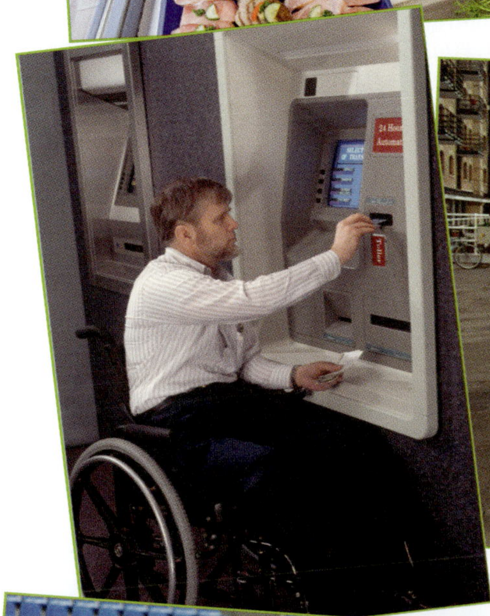

Did you know?
All London BLACK CABS are wheel-chair accessible and include additional aids.

A What is Integration?
An example (look at picture 1): Integration is, when disabled and other employees work together in the kitchen of a hotel. Now it is your turn. Give more examples for 'integration'. "Integration is, when all taxis in a town …"

9.1 Harry Lives in a Hotel

Joan and Thomas Baker are on the way to visit their son Harry. They meet their friend Mary Miller at the bus stop.

Joan: Good morning, Mary.

Mary: Good morning to you, Joan. How are you?

Thomas: Thanks, very well. We are just on the way to visit Harry.

Mary: Harry? Why? Doesn't he live with you anymore?

Joan: Oh, my goodness. I haven't told you, I'm sorry. Yes, Harry has moved out about six weeks ago. He's now 19 years of age, you know, and he wants to lead an independent life. He feels that my husband and I are patronising him too much. We usually visit him once a week.

Mary: Hm, I'm really astonished. Can Harry cope properly with his disability on his own? Where does he live now?

Joan: He lives at the NOVOTOWN Hotel.

Mary: Isn't that quite expensive for you?

Joan: Fortunately not. Harry isn't a guest in the hotel. He works there as an employee. Have you ever heard anything about the NOVOTOWN Hotel in New Street?

Mary: Isn't that a hotel for disabled people?

Thomas: That's right. It is a hotel for disabled guests. Non-disabled guests can stay there of course as well. The hotel belongs to a well-known Hotel Group. It is mainly run by people with disabilities. The employees there have their own room in the hotel. Harry receives a salary from which he can pay for his board and lodging and the other cost of living as well.

Mary: Very interesting. I've heard that there's a similar hotel in Germany – in Hamburg, I think.

Thomas: I think you mean the "Stadthaushotel". It is the most famous integration hotel in Europe. Ah, there's the bus. We're going to see the new film "The King's Speech". Goodbye.

Mary: Give Harry my best regards. Have a nice day.

A Which of the following statements are true, which are false?

RECEPTION

1. Harry moved out of his parents' home about six weeks ago.
2. Harry is 21 years old.
3. Harry felt being patronised by his parents.
4. The NOVOTOWN Hotel is especially suitable for customers with disabilities.
5. People without disabilities can stay at the NOVOTOWN Hotel.
6. Since Harry has lived at the NOVOTOWN Hotel his parents have had to pay a lot of money for his cost of living.
7. Harry gets paid for his work.
8. Joan and Harry would like to see the movie "My Left Foot".

True	False
✓	

B Find out information about the "Stadthaushotel" and the movie "The King's Speech" by using the Internet. Which answers to the following questions are correct? You will find the answers e.g. at Wikipedia.

1. Who founded the "Stadthaushotel"?
   a) The NOVOTOWN Hotel Group
   b) Some parents of disabled children
   c) The city council of Hamburg

2. The main character of the film "The King's Speech" is a man who is ...
   a) a stutterer.
   b) blind.
   c) deaf.

C Talking about people with special needs
In many towns there are sheltered workshops for people with disabilities.

PRODUCTION

1. Find out and report where the nearest sheltered workshop is.
2. What kind of disabilities do the people have who work there?
3. What kind of work is carried out in this sheltered workshop?

The following words may be a help:

hearing impairment – visual impairment
learning difficulty (mild, moderate, severe) – autism – speech disorder
multiple disabilities – behavioural disorder – hyperactivity disorder

producing: bags – toys – decoration
repairing: bicycles – houses
gardening: growing and preparing vegetables for sale
working in hotels: serving – cooking – cleaning

9.2 Checking In

Mr Harrow and his son Robert enter the NOVOTOWN Hotel in Birmingham. Robert sits in a wheelchair. He is partly paralysed.

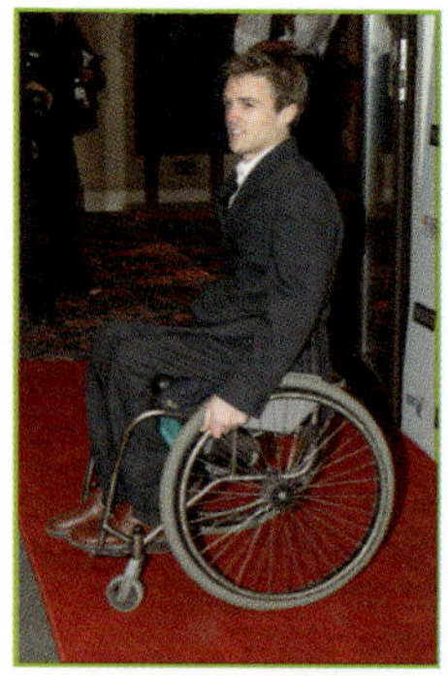

Mr Harrow: Good evening, my name is Harrow. I have booked two single rooms.
Receptionist: Good evening. Ah, there we are: a room for Mr Jack Harrow and a room for Mr Robert Harrow. You have reserved two single rooms, one of which should be fully adapted for disabled people. Well, your adjoining rooms are located on the first floor. They have wheelchair access and connecting doors.

Robert: What are the facilities in my room?
Receptionist: There is a disability-adapted WC and a roll-in shower. The lights can be operated by remote control. The doors open and close automatically. The windows and the curtains can easily be opened and closed by an electrical device. There is an emergency assistance system at the press of a button in your room as well.
Robert: All right.

Mr Harrow: Can we have dinner?
Receptionist: Yes, it's being served now. The dining-room is over there on the right. Can you see it? Okay. I will arrange for your luggage to be brought in.
Robert: Can we be called at seven o'clock tomorrow morning?
Receptionist: Certainly, sir. There are your keycards. Your room numbers are 108 and 109.
Robert: Thank you very much.
Receptionist: Would you please sign the register?
Mr Harrow: Oh yes. I'll fill it in.
Receptionist: Have a nice stay.
Mr Harrow and Robert: Thank you.

A Fill in the spaces by using some of the following words. One word will not be necessary.

single rooms	disabled	emergency	wheelchair	buttons
dining-room	luggage	seven o'clock	register	key card

1. Mr Harrow has booked two …
2. Robert sits in a …
3. One of the booked rooms is fully adapted for … people.
4. There are … in some rooms, which are part of an emergency assistance system.
5. In many hotels you don't have to bring your … to your room yourself.
6. Many hotels serve evening meals in a …
7. Robert wants to be called at …
8. You need a … to open the door of your room in a hotel.
9. When you are checking in at a hotel, you have to fill in a …

9.3 Famous Persons with Disabilities

Helen Keller	Helen Keller (1880 -1968) was the first deaf and blind person to get a degree at a university. She was an American author, political activist and lecturer. Helen Keller wrote twelve books. Many schools in Germany have been named after Helen Keller. In 1962 the story of her life was made into a film, "The miracle worker" (http://en.wikipedia.org/wiki/The_Miracle_Worker).	 Helen Keller
Stephen Hawking	Stephen Hawking was born in 1942. He is a professor of mathematics and physics at the Universities of Cambridge (Great Britain) and Pasadena (USA). He is possibly the world's most famous living scientist. When Hawking was 21, he gradually lost the use of his arms, legs and voice. Since 2009 he has been almost completely paralysed. He uses a device that enables him to write with the help of a computer with small movements of his body. A voice synthesizer speaks what he has typed. Hawking has been honoured many times for his scientific work and the way he has coped with his disabilities.	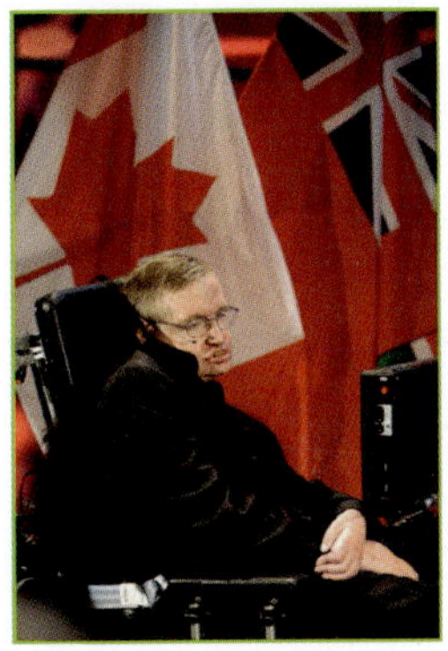 Stephen Hawking
Andrea Bocelli	Andrea Bocelli was born in Italy in 1958. He had difficulties with his eyesight from birth. In 1970, at the age of 12, he completely lost his sight following an accident during a football game. The single "Time to Say Goodbye" topped music charts all over Europe, breaking the all-time sales record, with over 12 million copies sold worldwide. The song "Time to Say Goodbye" is the most popular secular song at funerals in Protestant communities. Listen to Andrea Bocelli's song "Time to Say Goodbye" e.g. on YouTube.	 Andrea Bocelli at a live concert

A **Search for more information about these three persons. You may use the Internet, for example http://en.wikipedia.org.**

PRODUCTION

1. How did Helen Keller learn to write?
2. Find out more about Hawking's illness.
   You may use the German version of Wikipedia as well.
3. Who was Andrea Bocelli's partner when he sang "Time to Say Goodbye"?

Prepositions of Place

Ken asks: "What are the proper usages of the words 'in', 'at' and 'on' in a sentence? Often I cannot decide which preposition I must use." He asks his teacher: "Why do you say: 'Thomas lives in a bungalow, but Harry lives at the NOVOTOWN Hotel'?"
His teacher, Mrs Webster, explains: "The use of prepositions in English is quite difficult. General guidelines exist, but be prepared to learn individual expressions in which the preposition does not adhere to (= sich richten nach) the guidelines. Here are a few rules for using the prepositions which might help."

We use **in** (= inside) with	
a) something big enough to be all around a person	Robert is **in** the hotel room.
b) a road or a street	Jane and Thomas live **in** Liverpool Street.
c) a building or a large space	It was very warm **in** the cinema (= inside the cinema).
d) a village, town or country	The Bakers live **in** Birmingham.

We use **at** with	
a) a position	Mary is **at** the bus stop.
b) a house or address	Harry lives **at** the NOVOTOWN Hotel.
c) a place for doing things	Harry is **at** the cinema (= watching a film).
d) a village or town on a journey	Mr Kinley stopped **at** a village near Birmingham.

A **Now it's your turn. Use the words in the box to fill the gaps.**

in - in - in - in - in - in - in - in - in - in

at - at - at - at - at - at - at

1. Jenny works ... a home for disabled people.
2. Mary lives ... Oxford Road.
3. It was cold ... the swimming pool.
4. Andrea Bocelli was born ... Italy.
5. Mr Kinley is working ... his desk.
6. Adriana works as a receptionist ... the NOVOTOWN Hotel.
7. Many students work part-time ... fast food restaurants.
8. When we visited Ireland, we stopped ... Ballymahon, a village near Longford.
9. Sarah and Michael arrive ... England.
10. Harry likes to live ... a town and not ... the country.

11. I was in England last summer and I visited a school ... Birmingham. ... that school they wore school uniforms.
12. Here is a photo with Harry taken in his classroom. Can you recognise him ... it?
13. Harry is ... the kitchen.
14. When the lecturer is very boring, many students fall asleep ... their desks.
15. If you want to know more about disabilities, you will find plenty of information ... Wikipedia.

We use **on** to indicate proximity (= Nähe) and position above.	
a) proximity	There are several emergency service buttons **on** the walls.
b) above	Don't sit **on** the table. It's not very hygienic.

B **Now it's your turn again. Use the words in the box to fill the gaps.**

on - on - on - on - on - on - on - on - on

at - at - at - at - at - at

1. The dining-room is over there ... the right.
2. Mary, please don't sit ... the grass. It's wet.
3. Joan and Thomas are waiting ... the bus stop.
4. Daren writes his address ... the top of the page.
5. There are some books ... the shelf.
6. The NOVOTOWN Hotel is ... the end of the street.
7. There are some fine pictures ... the wall.
8. Many students work part-time ... fast food restaurants.
9. Teacher: "Open your textbook ... page 53."
10. I did some research for more information ... the Internet.
11. Announcement: "Don't leave any belongings unattended ... the station."
12. There are a lot of apples ... those trees.
13. Who is that girl ... the bicycle?
14. The movie "The Kings Speech" can be seen ... TV.
15. There is a stamp ... the envelope.

9.4 An Application

THE NOVOTOWN HOTEL

THE NOVOTOWN HOTEL is a fully adapted hotel for people with special needs. Part of our staff has a disability.

We are offering a full-time job for a well-trained

Cook

Applicants must be at least 27 years of age and have a minimum of three years' previous work experience.
Applicants must also be able to work with people with special needs.
More information upon request. Starting salary will be in the range £15-20,000 per year depending on experience and qualification.

Please send your letter of application and enclose a full CV with copies of your reference papers by E-mail to our personnel officer Mr Patrick Kinley (p.kinley@novotown.com).

The Interview

Daren Miller has been invited for a job interview at the NOVOTOWN Hotel. On the way to the interview he unfortunately gets caught in a traffic jam. With a red face and sweaty palms he arrives ten minutes late.

As he enters the personnel officer's room, he mentions the traffic jam and the problem of finding a parking space. The personnel officer, Mr Kinley, seems to be a bit reserved. He interrupts Daren and asks him to sit down.

Mr Kinley: Well, Mr Miller, in your CV there are two jobs mentioned for which you haven't enclosed any certificates.

Daren: Hm, oh dear, I have forgotten them because of the rush I was in. They are still in the car. Would you like me to get them?

Mr Kinley: No, thanks. Could you tell me, please, why are you applying for the post of a cook in our hotel?

Daren: Well, you're offering a good salary. And I think I might be given the opportunity to become a chef quite soon.

During the conversation Daren has crossed his legs. Now he starts to play with the phone cable.

Mr. Kinley: Why do you want to leave the job you are doing now?
Daren: The people I have to work with are very strange, especially the boss.

Mr Kinley (looking at his watch and getting up): Thank you very much.
Daren (getting up as well): But I have a lot of professional experience.

Mr Kinley: Yes, I can see that. Goodbye.
Daren: Goodbye.

Daren leaves the room with a feeling that he will not get the job.

"**AER RIANTA** encourages employment of people with disabilities in all its departments. This private Irish airline has 1200 employees, 2.6 % have a disability.

AER RIANTA organises different kinds of training including a special programme for people with learning difficulties that has helped to establish an extremely good working atmosphere." Ann Dinnigarn, Aer Rianta, Dublin Airport

----

"In 2007, 37 % of the ACCOR HOTELS employed 6 % of disabled people among their staff and 65 % of these disabled workers were working in the group for more than 5 years." Françoise Darmond, Human Ressources Manager, ACCOR Hotel Group

----

"The hotel '**IN OUT**' in the town of Vallvidriera (near Barcelona) is the first establishment in Spain and Europe almost totally managed by disabled workers – 90 % of the staff."

www.tourismforall.org.uk/10-good-reasons.html

"The absenteeism rate is not higher for disabled than for other employees." Wolfgang Neumann, president for the HILTON hotel chain

A Do you think Daren will get the job?
Explain to a partner what you would have done differently. The following hints may help you.

Your partner says …	What would you have done?	
	In German	In English
Daren was ten minutes late.	*Ich wäre so früh losgefahren, dass ich auf jeden Fall pünktlich da gewesen wäre.*	*I would have started out so early, that I definitely would have been there in time.*
Daren was speaking when he entered the room.	*Ich hätte erst mal Herrn Kinley begrüßt und mich ihm vorgestellt.*	
The submitted application papers were incomplete.	*Ich hätte*	
Two certificates were left in the car.		
What about Daren's reasons for applying?		
What is your opinion of a candidate crossing his legs and playing with the phone cable in an interview?		
What about criticising current colleagues in an interview?		
Daren talks about his "professional experience" when he leaves the room.		

Would you like to know whether Daren has got the job? Here is the answer.
A few days after the interview Daren got this written reply from Mr Kinley:

THE NOVOTOWN HOTEL

Mr Daren Miller
46 Portland Street South
App. 112
Dublin 1
Ireland

Ref: Your application for a position as a cook

Dear Mr Miller,

We thank you very much for your application.
Unfortunately, we cannot give you a positive reply.

Yours sincerely

P. Kinley
Personnel Officer
NOVOTOWN HOTEL
7 New street
B1 2HT BIRMINGHAM
UNITED KINGDOM

Word Order

In statements (=Aussagesätzen) the word order is subject - verb - object.
This word order must not be changed.

Subject	Verb	Object
Joan	visits	Harry.

The subject (Joan) tells who or what is doing something.
The verb (visits) tells what is being done.
The object (Harry) tells to whom the activity refers.

Adverbs of Place and Time
The verb and the object are usually together. An adverb of time can come either at the beginning or at the end of a statement.

Subject	Verb	Object	Time
Joan	visits	Harry	once a week.

or

Time	Subject	Verb	Object
Once a week	Joan	visits	Harry.

When there are two adverbs of place and time in a sentence, the adverb of place is usually before the adverb of time.

Subject	Verb	Object	Place	Time
Joan	visits	Harry	in the hotel	once a week.

A Right or wrong? Copy the table and correct the sentences that are wrong.

Statement	Right, Wrong	If wrong: Correction
1. Harry reads a newspaper every day.	Right	--
2. Joan watched all evening television.	Wrong	Joan watched television all evening.
3. Harry started last week his new job.		
4. Mary drinks three cups of coffee every day.		
5. Mr Harrow wrote this morning a letter.		
6. The hotel manager did a lot of work at home yesterday.		
7. Mr Harrow met yesterday at the airport a friend.		
8. Every day the receptionist walks to work.		
9. Joan and her husband have lived since 1990 in Birmingham.		
10. Harry was born in Birmingham in 1993.		

Vocabulary

9.1 Harry Lives in a Hotel		
people with special needs ['pi:pl wɪð 'speʃəl ni:dz]	special needs is a term to describe individuals who require assistance for disabilities	Menschen mit Behinderungen
independent [ˌɪn.dɪ'pen.dənt]	no help from anybody necessary	eigenständiges Leben
(to) patronise ['pæt.rən.aɪz]	to behave towards someone as if they are unable to look after themselves	beschützen
(to) cope [kəʊp]	to deal successfully with a difficult situation	zurechtkommen
disability [ˌdɪs.ə'bɪl.ɪ.ti]	a condition that makes it difficult for someone to do the things that other people do	Behinderung
disabled [dɪ'seɪ.bl ˌd]	not having all abilities that most people have	behindert
mainly ['meɪn.li]	to a large degree	überwiegend
salary ['sæl.ər.i]	a fixed amount of money as pay for an employee	Einkommen
board and lodging [bɔ:d ə nd 'lɒdʒ.ɪŋ]	the meals and room when someone pays to stay somewhere	Verpflegung und Unterkunft
costs of living [kɒst əv 'lɪ.vɪŋ]	the amount of money that a person needs to live on	Lebensunterhalt
integration [ˌɪn.tɪ'greɪ.ʃən]	mixing with and joining a group of people	Integration
(to) found [ˌfaʊn.d]	to set up	gründen
city council ['sɪt.i 'kaʊnt.səl]	group of people in a town chosen to make decisions	Stadtverwaltung
stutterer ['stʌt.ər]	a person who speaks or says something with difficulty	Stotterer
deaf [def]	unable to hear	gehörlos
impairment [ɪm'peə.mənt]	abnormality of physiological, psychological, or anatomical structure	Beeinträchtigung
autism ['ɔ:tɪ.zəm]	impaired social interaction and communication	Autismus
disorder [dɪ'sɔ:.dər]	a state of untidiness or lack of organization	Fehlsteuerung
behavioural [bɪ'heɪ vjə rəl]	way of acting	auf das Verhalten bezogen
9.2 Checking In		
(to) paralyse ['pær.əl.aɪz]	to cause a person/part of the body to lose the ability to move or feel	lähmen
(to) adapt [ə'dæpt]	to change something to different conditions	anpassen
adjoining [ə'dʒɔɪ.nɪŋ]	next to	angrenzend
wheelchair ['wi:l.tʃeər]	a chair on wheels which people who are unable to walk use for moving around	Rollstuhl
connecting door [kə'nek.tɪŋ dɔ:r]	being joined by a door	Verbindungstür
facility [fə'sɪl.ɪ.ti]	equipment provided for a particular purpose	Ausstattung
roll-in shower [rəʊl ɪn ʃaʊər]	shower usable with a wheelchair	mit Rollstuhl benutzbare Dusche
remote control [rɪ'məʊt kən'trəʊl]	to operate equipment from a distance	Fernbedienung
device [ˌdɪ'vaɪs]	a useful machine	Gerät
emergency [ɪ'mɜ:.dʒənt.si]	something dangerous or serious which happens suddenly	Notfall
assistance [ə'sɪs.tənts]	help	Hilfe
button ['bʌt.ən]	a small, usually circular object used for various reasons to operate equipment or other items.	Knopf
(to) arrange [ə'reɪndʒ]	to organise	für etwas sorgen
keycard ['ki:.kɑ:d]	a small plastic electronic card which is used to open a door.	Kartenschlüssel
register ['redʒ.ɪ.stər]	an official list or record	Verzeichnis
9.3 Famous Persons with Disabilities		
political activist [pə'lɪtɪkəl 'æk.tɪ.vɪst]	a person who works hard for political or social change	politischer aktiver Mensch
lecturer ['lekt.ʃər.ər]	someone who teaches at a university	Hochschullehrer
synthesizer ['sɪn.θə.saɪ.zər]	a machine that transforms a written text into spoken words.	Umwandler
(to) honour ['ɒn.ər]	to show great respect for someone	ehren
scientific [ˌsaɪən'tɪf.ɪk]	using an objective method to get new findings	wissenschaftlich
secular ['sek.jʊ.lər]	not having any connection with religion	weltlich
funeral ['fju:nər.əl]	a ceremony for burying the body of a dead person	Begräbnisfeier

Listening Comprehension

The Leonardo da Vinci Programme

Education and Culture DG
Lifelong Learning Programme

Sitting in a classroom for only two hours per week is not really the best way of learning English. So then, where can you learn English more quickly and more efficiently?

Silly question, isn't it? Of course, it would be a good idea to go to England or another Englishspeaking country like Ireland for some time. And doing practical training enables you to learn a really useful job-related English in the workplace. By seeing what others want you to do, you will understand things much more quickly than in a classroom.
Of course, this costs money. But don't you worry: The Leonardo da Vinci Programme helps young Europeans like you financially, so that you can do practical projects in the field of vocational education and training. You can go abroad on your own or you can take part in larger projects. If you want to inform yourself about what you can do, surf the web: Just "google" Leonardo da Vinci Program(me) to get some German (or English) information.

RECEPTION

A **Listen to the personal stories of Anja, Jessica and Petra (audio-track "The Leonardo da Vinci Programme"*) and answer the questions below.**

1. The pictures are not in the correct order. Who is who? Say why you think so.
2. Whose English was good in the beginning, and whose English was not so good?
3. Why was Anja Kaiser quite a good help for those where she worked?
4. What were Anja Kaiser's impressions of the people living in her guest country?
5. How do the young people in Anja's host country differ from those in Germany?
6. What could German young people learn from their Irish counterparts?
7. Why did Jessica Sachs go to her host country?
8. What did Jessica learn in the hotel kitchen besides cooking?
9. What did Jessica learn about British pub life?
10. Petra said that children are quite good teachers if you want to learn a foreign language. Explain this.
11. Why did Petra's colleague not speak German with her, although she could speak German quite well?
12. What could we Germans learn from the Irish?
13. Why is a stay abroad good for you, if you follow Petra's words?
14. Which of the stories did you like best? Say why.

[*available on Audio-CD, transcript in HT 1622 Lösungsheft]

Mediation

A Listen to the three girls on the audio-track again. Get into groups and develop an interview with a dialogue (questions and answers) for one of the girls. You should use the following words from the vocabulary list.

for Anja Kaiser

to select	auswählen	opportunity	günstige Gelegenheit, Chance
handicapped	behindert	to entertain	unterhalten
games	Spiele	to get washed and dressed	gewaschen und angezogen werden
to be surprised	überrascht sein	to be impressed	beeindruckt sein
to have the courage	den Mut haben	hospitality	Gastfreundschaft
to offer help	Hilfe anbieten	button acordion	Knopfharmonika

for Jessica Sachs

trainee cook	Kochlehrling	aim	Zweck, Ziel
to broaden one's mind	seinen Geist erweitern, sich weiterbilden	to gain new experiences	neue Erfahrungen gewinnen, sammeln
to calculate calories	Kalorien berechnen	to develop a diet plan	einen Diätplan entwickeln
team	Mannschaft	member	Mitglied
never a dull moment	überhaupt keine Langeweile	to join someone	jemanden begleiten
		it will be your turn	du bist an der Reihe

for Petra Roter

my first goal	mein erstes Ziel	to improve	verbessern
different way of life	andere Lebensart	adventure	Abenteuer
orphanage	Waisenhaus	innovative ideas	innovative Ideen
no specific mission	keinen besonderen Auftrag	children's books	Kinderbücher
quite soon	ziemlich schnell	to take one's time	sich Zeit lassen
to share a cup	eine Tasse gemeinsam trinken	stout beer	dunkles Bier (Guinness)
small talk	ein Schwätzchen	a strong accent	ein starker Akzent
to develop one's personality	seine Persönlichkeit entwickeln	to become more patient and tolerant	geduldiger und toleranter werden

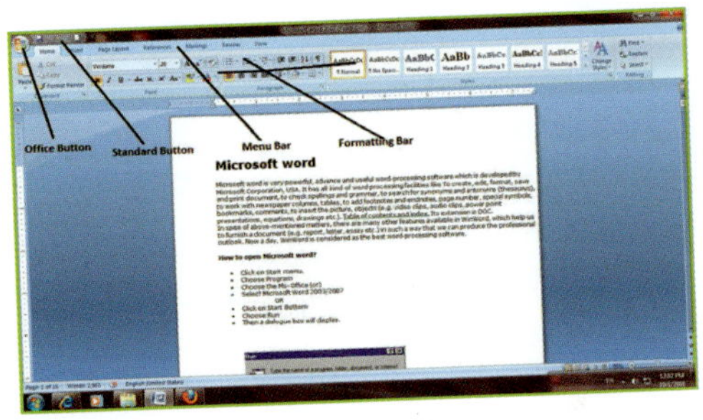

	a)	print a file
	b)	open a file
	c)	copy a text
	d)	scroll up and down

	e)	save a file
	f)	use a snipping tool
	g)	use the Internet
	h)	draw a chart

Today's Illiterates
Formerly, an illiterate was someone who could not read and write. Today we must also be able to understand what the many icons in our computer programmes mean. Often it is learning-by-doing and of course you are no computer illiterate.

A What do the icons above mean? Match them with the right computer commands, which are not in the correct order here.

B Match each of the pictures above with something you can do when using your computer. Hints: *play "shoot-em-up" games - edit films - use word-processing programs - chat with friends and family*

C What do you like best when you work with your computer? Say why you do.

D Ask your classmates what they do with their computers and what they like best. Compare your answers.

10.1 The Negative Side: Facebook, a Curse or a Blessing?

Those party pictures can come back to haunt you

The party last summer was wonderful: We had ghetto blasters with our favourite music and to share the costs, everybody brought a bottle. So there was a large variety of drinks – whisky, sherry, gin, alcopops, wine and much more. Well, I tried as many drinks as I could and I cannot remember what happened then. Somebody took this photo – and placed it on Facebook, with my name under it. I was really shocked!

Somebody must have found it very funny to upload my photo to the Internet, but I could not really laugh at the "joke" as everybody can see those photos. The Internet is a public resource. If you think about who "everybody" is, you will feel quite embarrassed.

Imagine your parents or your teachers seeing you as drunk as you were at that party. Okay, they may grin or tell you off, but they will probably have forgotten it after one or two weeks. But the Internet never forgets, as other people can copy and paste stuff on websites or message boards and save it for later. Even if you erase the photo from a server or platform yourself, somebody might well have copied it and placed it on another site.

So it is possible that even potential employers may see those photos. Believe it or not, an increasing number of employers weed out applicants for a job by surfing the web. You do not need much imagination to realise how they might come to a decision about your application …

10.2 The Positive Side: Facebook, a Platform for Protest

An Egyptian protester sleeps on the pavement in Cairo's Tahrir Square under graffiti that reads Facebook

Nobody wants to live in a dictatorship where the press is censored and free speech is suppressed. These days, social networks like Facebook have made it harder for dictators or totalitarian systems to silence the views of the people.

Take Egypt, for example.

The social network Facebook gave activists a chance to organise demonstrations there.

So it can be a means of organising political opposition and even help to overthrow dictators. One such dictator was Hosni Mubarak, the former president of Egypt. Facebook played an important role in the Egyptian uprising which began on January 25th 2011 and forced Mubarak to step down after 30 years in power.

In countries like Egypt, which are ruled by authoritarian regimes such as Mubarak's, it is very difficult and dangerous to organise protests. Such governments do not hesitate to arrest and beat up people who take part in political meetings or join political groups. The social networks give opposition groups a space where they can meet and organise. Thousands of people have been online all over Egypt and even the poorest areas have had access to the Internet through shared connections.

True, totalitarian governments may block Internet access, but whenever soldiers or police officers act violently, the many small cameras in mobile phones among the crowd can film that violence and protesters are able somehow to get it onto TV or the video-sharing site YouTube. And as injustice no longer remains undiscovered, Facebook can be of real help to people in their fight for democracy. The comment which one Egyptian posted online expressed exactly the importance of social media: "While people were the force, Facebook was the tool."

(Adapted from READ ON, Nr. 649, April 2011)

The Negative Side: Facebook, a Curse or a Blessing?

A Vocabulary – What is this? Find the words in the text.

1. a radio which can play music very loud, it is often used outdoors _______
2. a drink made of lemonade and alcohol _______
3. a social Internet platform _______
4. something you write to a friend via Internet _______
5. If someone criticises you severely he _______
6. information available for everyone _______
7. a place where old people are looked after _______
8. something that God gave the people _______
9. something the devil gave the people _______
10. a place on the Internet _______
11. to get rid of applicants who employers think are not right for the job _______
12. someone who drinks to get as drunken as possible _______

B Get dictionaries, share out the work and look for unknown words. Then answer your classmates' questions on the words you looked up and ask them questions about the meanings of words you do not understand. Write the new words into your vocabulary book and learn them.

> Some helpful phrases
> What is the meaning of .... in line ..., please?
> Could you tell me the meaning of ... in line ..., please?
> I do not understand the word ... in line .... What does it mean, please?

PRODUCTION

C You read the article about Facebook on an Internet site. Write a newspaper article about it in German for your German school magazine.

D Read the text 10.1 again and then complete the following if-clauses appropriately.

You can be sure that if you **do** this correctly and use the right tenses, your English teacher **will give** you a good mark.

1. If you try all the different drinks at a party, ...
2. If you see a nasty photo of yourself on the Internet ...
3. If you want to erase the photo, ...
4. If your parents see that awful photo on the Internet, ...
5. If employers see a nasty photo of you on the Internet ...
6. If you are looking for a job as an old people's nurse, ...
7. If people are not aware of the dangers of facebook, ...

E Imagine the girl in the photo on page 102 is your friend. You saw her photo on the Internet. Write a letter to her. (Think of what you would like to tell her.)

The Positive Side: Facebook, a Platform for Protest

PRODUCTION

A Surf the Internet and collect some information on the positive aspects of social networks like Facebook. Present your findings to the class.

B Make sure you understand the most important words in the text. Look them up in a dictionary. You will be more effective and faster if you share out the work and consult each other.

Understanding Difficult Grammatical Constructions

If you really want to understand a text, it is often not enough just to look the words up in a dictionary. You also need to understand grammatical constructions. Here is some help. Use it to translate the following terms:

the press is censored and free speech is suppressed (lines 4-6)	simple present passive is formed by am, are or is + past participle of verb Compare: It is done = Es wird getan
facebook has made it harder for dictators (lines 6 to 8)	present perfect simple to show visible effects of something that happened in the past have/has + past participle
a way of organising (line 16)	gerund after prepositions; translate it either as an infinitive or as a verbal noun Compare: the way of working = die Art zu arbeiten

MEDIATION

C Write a newspaper article in German about the text "The Positive Side: Facebook, A Platform for Protest".
You do not need to translate the English newspaper article word for word, but your German readers should be given a clear idea of the text.

D Study the grammar box on page 107 again and use the right constructions in the following exercise.

1. Now the Egyptians think they _____ no longer suppressed by a dictator.
2. An Egyptian says, "I _____ just filmed how the police clubbed a demonstrator."
3. Yesterday five men _____ arrested by the police.
4. When the police shot into the crowd, we were afraid of ____ (lose) our lives.
5. Many of us are looking forward to ____(have) a new government.
6. When ____ (to be arrested) many demonstrators offered resistance.
7. A man _____ (who was named Ali) filmed the violent soldiers.
8. That film ______ (post) on the YouTube site yesterday.

10.3 Facebook for Grandma and Grandpa – Why Not?

Some young people think that the older generation will never understand social networks on the Internet. That is nothing but a silly prejudice. There are already very committed young people who go to retirement homes and teach senior citizens how to use computers, mobile phones and even social networks like Facebook. And both young and old enjoy it very much.

PRODUCTION

A **Don't you think this is a brilliant idea, helping older people to stay in touch with others by the Internet?**

1. Think of arguments why a social network like Facebook can be good for the elderly.
2. Develop a PowerPoint presentation which you could present in an old people's home to motivate the residents to have a go on Facebook.

The Gerund

After prepositions (by, instead of, for ...) the following verb takes the ing-form.
We call that the gerund.

Example:
A cell phone can be used **for (take + ing)** digital photographs quickly.
A cell phone can be used **for taking** digital photographs quickly.

> The spelling rules for the verbs in the progressive and gerund are the same. You can look them up on page 8.

A **Try using the gerund yourself. Form sentences with the help of the prepositions in the box. The prepositions are not in the correct order.**

> in - for - for - for - from - by - to - to - instead of - about

1. I really look forward ... (see) the brandnew computer in your home.
2. ... (calculate) nutritional values per hand, you can use a computer programme. You'll be much faster.
3. ... (design) individual invitation cards for your party, you can search the web for free cliparts.
4. ... (use) spread-sheet programmes, you can do your budgeting much faster.
5. Dictionaries on the Internet are very good ... (translate) words from one language into another.
6. More and more old people are interested ... (go) to computer courses at evening schools.
7. If you think ... (send) news to all your friends at once, put them as message on Twitter.
8. I look forward ... (hear) from you.
9. We still have a lot to do. We are far ... (finish) the project.
10. I apologize ... (come) late.

B **Gerund or Infinitive? Some verbs require the gerund (ing-form), others the infinitive.**

1. As the sun refused ... (shine), Peter preferred ... (spend) some time at his computer.
2. He enjoyed ... (chat) with an old friend and suggested ... (meet) up in the next holidays.
3. The two friends chose ... (meet) in Blackpool, where Peter's grandparents happen ... (stay).
4. The grandparents offered the two young men ... (use) their yacht.
5. Peter hopes ... (get) his licence for sailing yachts next week.
6. His friend recommended ... (do) a sailing course, too.

→ See also: page 175 "Gerunds: Using Verbs as Nouns - Gerundien: Verben können als Substantive benutzt werden"

10.4 A Morning in Caren's Life in the Year 2020

It is 6 o'clock in the morning. The alarm clock rings, the bedroom curtains open, the computer screen turns itself on. "Good morning, Caren, you have to get up now," a voice says. Caren opens her eyes.
"Music," Caren says and at once the radio programme is started. Caren is a nineteen-year-old woman who lives in a flat in York.
Suddenly the radio programme is interrupted by a voice: "It is 6:15 a.m. - you are late, Caren." Caren finally gets up and presses a few keys on the bedroom terminal to end the wake-up-programme. Then she keys in orders to open the window for three hours. "The only thing I still need is a robot to turn back the bed clothes in the morning," she thinks.

In the bathroom the temperature has already been increased to 23 °C.
"Light," Caren says as she enters the room - and the light is switched on by invisible hands. Caren has to hurry up because the water in the shower is started at 6:30 a.m. She works as a cook in a hospital, so she always has to be in time.
At exactly 6:30 a.m. the shower is started and five minutes later the water is stopped. "I must change the showering time to ten minutes," Caren thinks as she leaves the shower.

It is 7 o'clock now and Caren enters the kitchen. The coffee is ready, and the toaster has just been started. A look into the fridge tells Caren that she has to order some food. So she turns on the kitchen computer and goes online. First she compares the prices of the three grocers in town, and finally she orders things like milk, bread, cereals, a cucumber, tomatoes, a cabbage, potatoes, onions, a dressing and ham.
While Caren is having breakfast, the computer tells Caren that she has got mail: "You've got a message". Caren starts the programme to exchange messages and immediately her friend's face appears on the screen. "I'm sorry, Caren," her friend Maggie says, "I can't come over this evening. My mother is ill and I want to visit her. I'll call you later to make a new appointment."
In the meantime it's 7:30 a.m. Before Caren leaves, she programmes the washing machine to start itself in the afternoon. Then she runs to her car whose engine has already been started.

A

Read the text on the left carefully and answer the following questions in complete sentences.

1. Which information do you get about Caren?
2. What does Caren do in the morning?
3. What does the computer network do
   - in the bedroom,
   - in the bathroom,
   - in the kitchen?
4. Would you like to have a morning like this? Give reasons for your answer.

B

Look for words in the text that fit these definitions:

1. A piece of cloth which hangs from the top of a window.
2. A set of rooms for living in.
3. To stop an action from continuing.
4. You press a control for an electrical device such as light or a radio.
5. A device used for washing your full body.
6. A shopkeeper who sells regular food such as flour, sugar and tinned food.

C

Look for definitions for the following words.

1. alarm clock
2. bathroom
3. invisible
4. hospital
5. fridge
6. milk

D

Find out the nouns of the following verbs.

1. to enter
2. to visit
3. to live
4. to open

E

What are the verbs of the following words?

1. comparison
2. appearance
3. interruption
4. thoughts

F

A puzzle – Here you have nine pictures and eighteen words. Look at the pictures and match each picture with two words from the list.

Example: *picture number 6 + flat screen + output device*

flat screen	pictures
smartphone	printer
hard disk drive	processor
input device	output device
keyboard	flatbed scanner
loudspeakers	sounds
motherboard	space bar
mouse	storage device
paper	touch screen

3

6

4

7

8

1

2

5

9
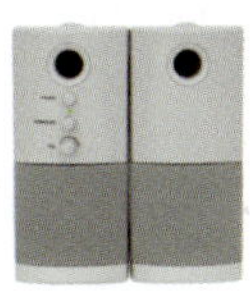

Passive Voice

Caren's dreams have become true – she has got a robot. Now she can be lazy …
The housework is done by the robot: The meals are cooked, the rooms are cleaned and much more.

Active sentence: ***The robot cooks the meal.***

We show that someone/something does something.
(subject)

Passive sentence: ***The meal is cooked by the robot.***

We tell what has happened to the subject.
It is not so important to know who does it.
→ For rules see page 173

How do you form sentences in the passive voice?
Have a look at what happens to the different parts of the sentence when you put it in the passive voice:

1. Active: The robot cooks **the meal**.
   Passive: **The meal** is cooked by the robot
   → The **object** of the active sentence is now the subject.

2. Active: The robot **cooks** the meal.
   Passive: The meal is **cooked** by the robot.
   → The **verb** of the active sentence is put into the third form (past participle, see page 164). You also need a **form of *to be*** in front of the verb. The tense of the sentence stays the same. (*to be* + past participle)

3. Active: **The robot** cooks the meal.
   Passive: The meal is cooked **by the robot**.
   → The former **subject** is now the object, and you add the preposition *by*.

When we use the passive voice, who or what causes the action is often unknown or unimportant:
A lot of money was stolen. The window was broken.

A Simple present sentences – The verbs in brackets have to be put in the simple present. Then you have a correct passive sentence in the simple present.

Example:
clean/cleans (active) – is cleaned (passive)
see/sees (active) – is seen (passive)

1. The coffee (cook) at 7 o'clock.
2. The kitchen (clean) after breakfast.
3. The laundry (wash) every Monday.
4. The flowers (water) very often.
5. The windows (polish) once a week.
6. The carpets (hoover) when it is necessary.

B Simple past sentences – The verbs in brackets have to be put in the simple past.

Example:
painted (active) – was/were painted (passive)
wrote (active) – was/were written (passive)

1. This house (build) in 1985.
2. The trees (plant) in 1987.
3. The bathroom (paint) last year.
4. The roof (repair) two weeks ago.
5. The neighbour house (sell) some weeks ago.
6. The cars (damage) last night.

C Rewrite the following sentences. However, instead of using somebody/they/people, form a passive sentence.

Example:
active: Somebody cut my flowers yesterday.
passive: My flowers were cut yesterday.

1. Somebody stole my bike yesterday.
2. Someone repaired my computer screen last week.
3. People use computers for a lot of things.
4. They bought 50 personal computers to improve education.
5. Someone invented the scanner.
6. They took my article to be a part of the homepage of our school.

D Put these active sentences into the passive voice. Use simple present or simple past.

Example:
active: Caren prepares breakfast.
passive: Breakfast is prepared by Caren.

1. The computer network controls all electrical devices.
2. The software made the mistake.
3. Peter copied all files.
4. The virus destroyed the hard disk.
5. Caren uses the Internet regularly.
6. The programmer made a backup.

E This is the hospital where Caren works. When you are in a hospital as a patient, a lot of things happen to you. Some weeks ago Caren's boyfriend Bob had a bad accident. He lost consciousness.

Hospital

Write a story about the things that happened after Bob had lost consciousness. The following list of expressions will help you. Use the passive as often as possible. Use the simple past.

to call an ambulance
to take someone to the hospital
to take someone to the emergency room
to examine
to control blood pressure
to take the temperature
to make a blood test
to give an injection
to lift someone onto the operating table
to operate on someone
to take someone to the patients' room

10.5 How to Work with a Nutritive Programme

Now we are back in reality. Caren really works as a cook in a hospital. Her task is to prepare the meals for those patients who need a special diet because of their illness or because they have to lose weight. Before Caren can start to prepare the meals she has to choose the right food and the amount of food. In order to do this quickly and correctly Caren uses the computer. Now have a look at one part of Caren's work:

First Step
Caren needs information about the patient like age, weight, height, illness. When she keys these data in, the nutritive programme tells her at once how many kilojoules and nutrients this patient needs a day.

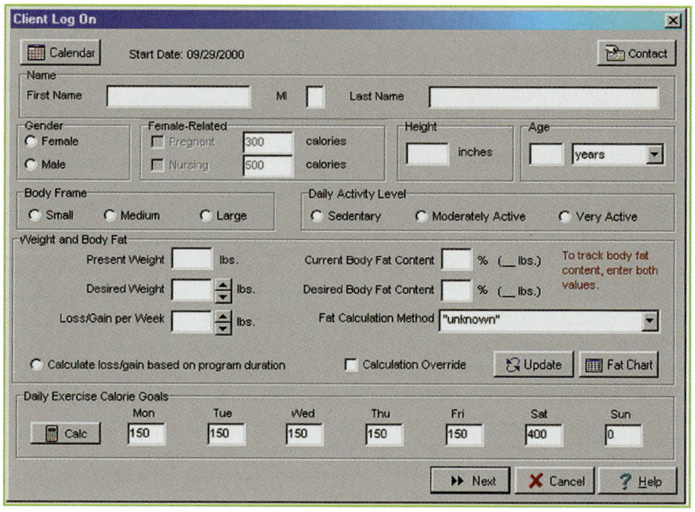

Second Step
After that Caren keys in all the meals with all the food the patient gets a day. Therefore she has to know the exact amounts of all food the patient gets a day, divided into five meals. The programme then calculates the exact amount of kilojoules and nutrients the meals contain.

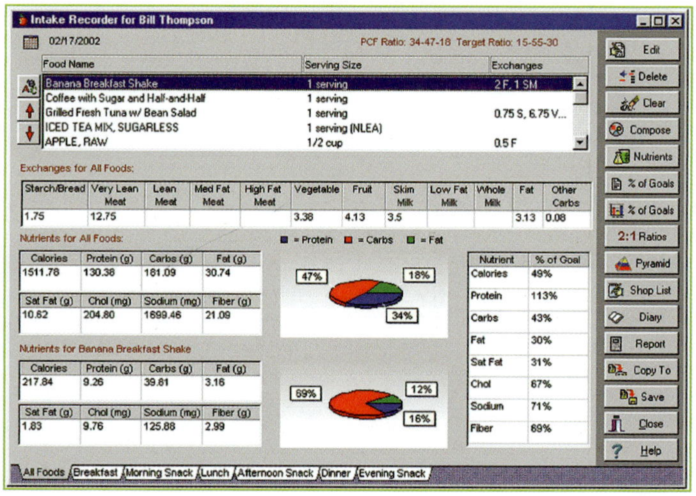

Third Step
When Caren wants to know if her planned meals guarantee the correct supply of energy and nutrients, she activates the file which compares the nominal value with the actual value.
The programme shows the results for the indicated person on the screen. Now Caren knows if the suggested meals are alright or if she has to improve something.

Past Perfect or Simple Past?

This evening Caren is very late. Her boyfriend is already waiting for her at home.
He sees at once that Caren had a bad day and asks Caren what had happened. Caren says: "In the morning I wanted to make the necessary calculations for a few new patients but the computer didn't start the programme. After the technician ***had repaired*** the computer, I keyed in the data of the patients and the meals I wanted to cook, but I was already late now.
After the computer ***had done*** the necessary calculations I prepared lunch in only one hour ..."

When do you use the past perfect?
Sometimes there is more than one thing that happened in the past. In that case we use the *past perfect* to tell about things that had happened ***before*** other things in the past.

past perfect in the morning 8:30 a.m.	past in the morning 9:00 a.m.	present in the evening 8:00 p.m.
The technician repaired the computer.	Caren keyed in the data.	Caren tells about it.

After the technician ***had repaired*** *the computer, Caren* ***keyed*** *in the data.*
→ For rules see pages 167/169

A Caren has had some terrible days before ... Look at these sentences. Put in the right tense: past perfect or simple past.

Example: When Caren (finish) work she (drive) home. – When Caren *had finished* work she *drove* home.

1. Caren (feel) tired because she (work) a lot.
2. When she (eat) something she (go) to bed.
3. She (just go) to bed when the phone (ring).
4. When Caren (wake up) the following morning she (see) that she (forget) to switch off the lights.
5. When she (arrive) at the station the train (already leave).
6. So she (call) a taxi and in the taxi she (notice) that she (forget) her money.
7. In the hospital her colleagues (tell) her that her boss (ask) for her twice.

B A nice weekend for Caren – Rewrite these sentences. Use the past perfect and connect the sentences with 'after'.

Example: Caren had breakfast. Then she went shopping. – *After* Caren *had had* breakfast she went shopping.

1. Caren bought new shoes and then she drank coffee with a girlfriend.
2. She drank coffee with a girlfriend and then she visited her mother.
3. She drove home and took a bath.
4. She dressed and then she waited for her boyfriend.
5. Bob arrived and they went to a party.
6. She woke up late on Sunday and prepared for the meeting with her uncle.
7. They had an excellent meal in a good restaurant and then they went for a walk.

Vocabulary

illiterate [ɪ'lɪt.ər.ət]	someone who cannot read or write	Analphabet/-in
10.1 The Negative Side: Facebook, a Curse or Blessing?		
public resource ['pʌb.lɪk rɪ'zɔːs]	sth. everybody can use	eine öffentliche Quelle
(to) tell s.o. off [tel]	to criticise s.o.	jemanden ausschimpfen
embarrassed [ɪm'bær.əst]	to feel uneasy	verlegen
(to) copy and paste ['kɒp.i ənd peɪst]	(comp.) to double sth.	kopieren und einfügen
10.2 The Positive Side: Facebook, a Platform for Protest		
dictatorship [dɪk'teɪ.tə.ʃɪp]	a government that wants people to obey	Diktatur
(to) suppress [sə'pres]	to end sth. by force	unterdrücken
uprising ['ʌpˌraɪ.zɪŋ]	revolution	Aufstand
(to) force [fɔːs]	to make s.o. do sth. against their will	zwingen
injustice [ɪn'dʒʌs.tɪs]	a situation in which there is no fairness	Ungerechtigkeit
violence ['vaɪə.lənt s]	extreme force; to hurt people	Gewalt
(to) censor ['sent .sər]	to control and "correct" sth., e.g. news	zensieren
(to) overthrow [ˌəʊ.və'θrəʊ]	to remove a government from power	stürzen
former ['fɔː.mər]	in an earlier time	frühere/r
(to) step down [step daʊn]	to quit one's office	zurücktreten
to remain undiscovered [rɪ'meɪn ʌndɪ'skʌv.ərd]	sth. is not noticed	unentdeckt bleiben
violent ['vaɪə.lənt]	using force to hurt	gewaltsam
10.3 Facebook for Grandma and Grandpa - Why Not ?		
prejudice ['predʒ.ʊ.dɪs]	an unfair opinion (without knowing enough)	Vorurteil
committed [kə'mɪt.ɪd]	loyal; motivated	engagiert
10.4 A Morning in Caren's Life in the Year 2020		
(to) interrupt [ˌɪntə'rʌpt]	to stop someone in doing something	unterbrechen
invisible [ɪn'vɪzəbl]	something or someone you can't see	unsichtbar
an appointment [ə'pɔɪntmənt]	you arrange to see a person at a particular time	Verabredung
handheld (or PDA) [hændheld]	Personal Digital Assistant	Kleincomputer für die Handfläche
motherboard ['mʌðəbɔːd]	the "heart" of the computer	Hauptplatine
(to) invent [ɪn'vent]	you are the first person to build or make it	erfinden
consciousness ['kɒnʃəsnɪs]	if you lose consciousness you are no longer awake	Bewusstsein
blood pressure [blʌd 'preʃə]		Blutdruck
an injection [ɪn'dʒekʃn]	someone puts a liquid into blood with it	Spritze
10.5 How to Work with a Nutritive Programme		
nutritive ['njuːtrətɪv]	relating to the food you eat	Ernährungs-
weight [weɪt]	your heaviness, measured in kilos/pounds	Gewicht
height [haɪt]	the measurement from bottom to top	Größe
nutrients ['njuːtrɪəntz]	substances that help humans, animals, plants to grow and to live	Nährstoffe
(to) guarantee [ˌgærən'tiː]	you are certain that something will happen	garantieren
nominal value ['nɒmɪnl 'væljuː]	the amount of nutrients you should eat	Bedarfszahl, Sollwert
actual value ['æktʊəl 'væljuː]	the amount of nutrients you actually eat	Zufuhr, Istwert

Unit 11 Dangerous Model of Beauty?

A Mark three aspects that are important for you when someone wants to be your friend:

honest	humorous	tastefully dressed	good-looking
generous	sportive	slim	well-educated
intelligent	wealthy		

B Which of the persons in the pictures would you like to meet?
Give reasons for your answer (for example, which person is good-looking, which one seems to be strange).

C Think about what is important for you to like a person.

11.1 People Like Us

"My name is Susan. I'm sixteen and I live in a semi-detached house in a suburb of Philadelphia, USA. I still go to school. My girlfriends say that I am a lively girl. That may be true, although I very often feel sad. That's because I am overweight. I don't dare to wear tight clothes, and I never go swimming. My best friend Pam always says that I'm a little crazy about my figure, but last year when I was on holiday in France with my parents the boys called me 'the plump American girl'. I could go on a diet but my problem is that I can't stop eating and I love sweets and fast food. The doctor told me to stop eating so much and he also said I had to do some sports. I will try to and perhaps then I'll succeed in finding a boyfriend.
All my girlfriends always talk about their boyfriends. Even Pam told me last week that she had met a boy named Mark. She said she had known him only a little while but she was already hopelessly in love with him. The only boy that is interested in me is my brother Christopher. He is six! He always asks me to play with him."

Susan

"I am Lisa. I'm 18 years old and I'm a trainee instructress. My friends say that I'm a good-looking girl but because I'm not interested in clothes, parties and especially in boys they think I'm not quite normal.
Okay, I prefer horses to parties, I mostly wear jeans and trainers and I don't eat meat, but I like boys! I must admit that I haven't told them that I got to know a very nice student. I met him near my hometown Cambridge where he was doing biological studies. We soon noticed that we are both environmentalists and vegetarians because we love nature and animals.
He told me that he condemned fast food and ready-to-serve-meals. So do I! I like to eat salad, vegetables and cereals and even if I have a problem with chips (I love them). I don't have to care about my weight.

Lisa

"Hallo, I'm Clark and I'm seventeen years old. I work as a trainee cook in a big hotel in Edinburgh. I've rented a furnished room near the hotel. My family lives in a small village near Inverness and this is the first time that I'm my own master. I like Edinburgh because you can meet a lot of interesting people there. In summer this town is crowded with tourists and you can meet a lot of nice girls. In my spare time I usually go to a leisure centre where I do body-building. My parents say that they don't like my hobby but I want to get a perfectly trained body. When I was at school the girls always laughed at me because I was very small, but now they look at me admiringly. Lately my boss asked me if I wanted to become the 'Schwarzenegger of Scotland'. It's important for me to watch my diet. I need a high amount of protein so I have to buy special drinks and pills. Oh, next week I'll take part in a competition. If I win, I'll be very proud."

Clark

A

Complete the information sheet about the three young people.
Draw a chart like this:

	Susan	Clark	Lisa
age job home hobby problems			

B

Now write a report about the three young people using the information above.

C

Answer the following questions in complete sentences.

1. Why does Susan often feel sad?
2. What does she love to eat?
3. What does Susan think is the reason that boys aren't interested in her?
4. Why does Clark like Edinburgh?
5. What do you think – why does Clark want to win a competition in body-building?
6. Why do Lisa's friends think that she is different from other people?
7. What do Lisa and the student have in common?

D

Find the opposites of these words in the text "People Like Us".

happy – slim – town – winter – unfurnished – empty – boring – to cry – unimportant – low – ugly

E

On the left side here you find some words from the text. On the right there are their dictionary definitions. However, they are not in the correct order. Can you find the matching pairs?

1. suburb
2. weight
3. crowded
4. nutrition
5. trainers
6. vegetarian

a) heaviness which can be measured in units such as kilos, pounds or tons
b) full of people
c) special shoes that people wear for running or jogging
d) an area of town which is not close to the centre
e) someone who doesn't eat meat
f) the process of providing and receiving food necessary for health and growth

F

Which of these foods would Susan, Clark and Lisa like to eat?
Name the foods. Look on page 121 for help.

Reported Speech

Changes in the Reported Speech – Personal Pronouns

Example:
direct: *Clark says: "**I am** feeling ill."*
➜ reported: *Clark says that **he is** feeling ill.*

A Read what Susan, Pam and Christopher say and then write sentences starting with *She/He says that …* or *They say that …*

1. Susan: "I am sixteen and I live in Philadelphia, USA."
2. Pam: "I met a nice boy."
3. Christopher: "I like to play with the computer."
4. Susan: "I am overweight."
5. Susan/Pam: "We want to go to the cinema."
6. Christopher: "I want to come with you."

Changes in the Reported Speech – Possessive Pronouns

Example:
direct: *Clark says: "**My** room is near the hotel."*
➜ reported: *Clark says that **his** room is near the hotel.*

B Report what Clark and the girl say and write sentences starting with *He/She says that…*

1. Clark: "My name is Clark."
2. Girl: "My name is Kate."
3. Clark: "I'm interested in your training programme."
4. Girl: "Your body looks perfect so your own programme must be very good."
5. Clark: "We can put our training programmes together."

Changes in the Reported Speech – Tenses

Tenses I

When the reporting verb is in the simple present, there is no change of tense in the words reported.

Example

direct: *Lisa says: "I* ***like*** *horses."*

➜ reported: *Lisa says that she* ***likes*** *horses.*

C **Read what Lisa and Mark say and then write sentences starting with *She/He says that …***

1. Lisa: "I often eat salad."
2. Mark: "I also prefer vegetarian food."
3. Lisa: "I will never eat meat."
4. Mark: "I saw a transport of pigs yesterday."
5. Lisa: "I can't understand people who eat meat."
6. Mark: "Most people don't think about the animals."

Tenses II

When the reporting verb is in the simple past or past perfect tense, the words reported are viewed in a different perspective and the tenses are changed accordingly.

- Present tense ➜ past tense

Example

direct: *Mark said: "I* ***study*** *biology."*

➜ reported: *Mark said that he* ***studied*** *biology.*

D **Read what Lisa and Mark said and then write sentences starting with *She/He said that …***

1. Mark: "I'm cooking a vegetable soufflé."
2. Lisa: "It smells good."
3. Mark: "I prefer to cook vegetarian meals."
4. Lisa: "I like that because I never eat meat."
5. Mark: "The soufflé is ready."
6. Lisa: "I'm very hungry."

- Past Tense/Present Perfect ➜ Past Perfect

Example

direct: *Susan said: "I* ***bought*** *a pair of jeans."*

➜ reported: *Susan said that she* ***had bought*** *a pair of jeans.*

E **Put the following sentences into the reported speech. Use different reporting verbs like *answer*, *tell* and *remark*.**

1. Pam: "Mark and I went to a party."
2. Susan: "I have never been to a party."
3. Pam: "We met some interesting people."
4. Susan: "I haven't met interesting people for ages."
5. Pam: "We danced and chatted the whole night."
6. Susan: "I have never been to such a nice party."

- Will Future ➜ Conditional I (would)

Example

direct: *Clark said, "I* ***will train*** *every day."*

➜ reported: *Clark said that he* ***would train*** *every day.*

F **Put the following sentences into the reported speech.**

1. Clark: "I will train two hours every day"
2. Trainer: "I will help you."
3. Clark: "I will buy special drinks to get enough protein."
4. Trainer: "I will give you some good pills."

G Read what Clark below thinks and write sentences starting with *He said that …*

➜ You can look on page 173 as well, there you will find some grammar information in German.

11.2 Eating Habits

We spend a lot of the daytime with eating, but usually we don't think much about it. We eat what our parents give us or what advertisements tell us to eat or we eat together with friends. But do we think about our health and our appearance when we choose our food?

A Now think about your eating habits and write down at most two answers to each of these questions.

1. The theme nutrition is …
   - boring
   - interesting
   - it doesn't matter to me
2. When I eat I care for …
   - the calories
   - the taste
   - the nutritional value
   - getting enough to eat
3. I eat what …
   - the others eat
   - I like
   - is healthy for me

4. Food should be …
   - cheap
   - healthy
   - tasty

5. I eat fast food …
   - often
   - seldom
   - never
6. I eat vegetables and salad …
   - daily
   - nearly daily
   - seldom
7. I mainly drink …
   - coke
   - juices
   - mineral water
   - coffee, tea

8. Which of the following statements is true?
   - I eat when feel bored.
   - I count the calories and I'm afraid of becoming fat.
   - I only eat because it's necessary.
   - I like to eat
   - I eat when I feel sad.

B Compare your result with that of your class neighbour.

C Try to find out what eating habits the other members of your class have. Ask questions like this: *Who thinks that the theme nutrition is boring, interesting or doesn't matter to them?* Count the number of persons.

D Write a report about your own eating habits. Start like this: **PRODUCTION**
I'm not interested in nutrition. When I eat I only care for …

E Work in pairs. Tell your partner about your eating habits. Then tell all the other pupils in your class what your partner has just told you. **INTERACTION**

Example:
Student A told me that she ate fast food very seldom.

Vocabulary Concerning Eating and Drinking

You should eat a lot of the following foods:

Vegetables

Fruits

Cereals

Drinks

Food you should eat regularly, but not too often:

Dairy Products

Meat

These foods you probably like to eat but you shouldn't:

Sweets

Fast Food

11.3 What to Eat

Last week Susan went to her doctor to talk to him about her weight problem. The doctor asked a lot of questions. He wanted to know if she ate regularly and if she ate at least five meals a day. He also wanted to know how often she ate meat, sweets, fruit and vegetables. He was even interested in getting to know how her meals were cooked.

After that he gave her a leaflet containing rules what to eat and what not to eat.
In the leaflet there was also information about how to prepare meals.

In the end the doctor showed her the following picture:

It's easy to eat right. Just follow the guidelines of the food pyramid to guarantee a healthy, balanced and tasty diet.

PRODUCTION

Here is a suggestion for a food project, maybe even in combination with your classes in Lernfeld 4, 5 and 6: Create a picture for your classroom walls where you combine the German words for food with the matching English vocabulary. It would look best if you included pictures of food as well. Ask your teacher about a project like that.

In the leaflet that the doctor gave to Susan she found the following explanations:

Grain group (eat 6 oz. every day*):
Food made from wheat, oats, barley, rice or another cereal grain is a grain product. Bread, pasta, flours and breakfast cereals are some examples. Grains supply food energy in form of complex carbohydrates (starch) and are also a source of protein, B-vitamins, minerals and fibre. Grains are divided into two subgroups: whole grains and refined grains. At least ½ of all eaten grains should be whole grains.
1 oz. = 1 slice of bread; 1 ounce of ready-to-eat cereal; 1 cup cooked cereal, rice or pasta

Vegetable group (eat 2 ½ cups every day*):
Any vegetable or 100 % vegetable juice counts as a number of this group. Vegetables provide vitamins, are excellent sources of fibre and are naturally low in fat. For maximum nutrients over a week try to consume from all subgroups: dark green vegetables (broccoli, spinach), orange vegetables (carrots, pumpkin), beans and peas, starchy vegetables (potatoes) and all other vegetables (tomatoes, cucumbers).
1 cup = 1 cup of raw or cooked vegetables or vegetable juice, or 2 cups of raw leafy greens

Fruit group (eat 2 cups every day*):
Any fruit or 100 % fruit juice is part of the fruit group. Fruits are low in fat and calories and are a good source of natural sugar, fibre, and vitamins. Select fresh fruits and fruit juices, and frozen, canned or dried fruits. Avoid fruit processed with heavy syrups and sugar-sweetened juices.
1 cup = 1 cup of fruit or 100 % fruit juice, or ½ cup of dried fruit

Milk, yogurt and cheese group (eat 3 cups every day*):
All fluid milk products and many foods made from milk are considered part of this group. Milk and its products are a good source of the mineral calcium. They also provide protein and vitamins. However dairy products may be high in saturated fats and cholesterol and some are sweetened. A tip is to choose low-fat products.
1 cup = 1 cup of milk or yogurt, 1 ½ ounces of natural cheese or 2 ounces of processed cheese

Meat, poultry, fish, dry beans, eggs and nuts group (eat 2 ½ oz. every day*):
Meat is a major source of protein, as well as iron, zinc, and vitamin B12. These nutrients can also be found in foods like eggs, dry beans and nuts. Meat alternatives also include tofu products. Fish is the most important source of iodine. Most meat and poultry choices should be lean or low-fat.
1 oz. = 1 ounce of meat, poultry or fish, ¼ cup cooked dry beans, 1 egg, 1 tablespoon of peanut butter, or 1/2 ounce of nuts or seeds

Oils (5 - 7 teaspoons*):
Oils are fats that are liquid at room temperature. Oils come from many different plants and from fish. Most oils are high in mono-unsaturated fats or poly-unsaturated fats, and low in saturated fats. Solid fats are solid at room temperature, like butter. They come from animal foods or from vegetable oils. They contain more saturated fats. You should prefer fats which are mono-unsaturated or poly-unsaturated.

* = The amount you need to eat depends on your age, sex and level of physical activity.
(source: United States Department of Agriculture)

Weights to calculate meals: US/GB/D

US		GB		D
		1 ounce	=	28.35 grams
16 ounces	=	1 pound	=	0.454 kilograms
14 pounds	=	1 stone	=	6.356 kilograms
112 pounds	=	1 hundred-weight	=	50.8 kilograms

A Describe the food pyramid on page 122.

B Make a list: What amounts of the suggested foods can a person eat a day?

Example: *You can eat 3 slices of bread, 2 ounces of ready-to-eat cereals and ½ cup of rice to meet the first group.*

PRODUCTION

C Create a table containing the six groups of the food pyramid and write down the nutrients.

Group	Nutrients

D Write down as many rules about a healthy diet as you can think of.

There are a lot of new words and vocabulary in this unit. If you don't understand some of the words and you don't find them in the vocabulary in the back of this book, then look them up in an English-English dictionary. See page 152 for information and exercises.

Vocabulary

11.1 People Like Us		
honest ['ɒnɪst]	telling the truth	ehrlich
generous ['dʒenərəs]	more than expected	großzügig
wealthy [welθɪ]	to have a lot of money	reich
tasteful [teistfʊl]	attractive, elegant	geschmackvoll
slim [slɪm]	thin and well-shaped body	schlank
suburb [ˌsʌbɜːb]	an area of a town that is not near to the city	Vorort
overweight ['əʊvəweɪt]	you are too fat	Übergewicht
tight clothes [taɪt]	clothes that fit close to your body	engsitzende Kleidung
plump [plʌmp]	rather fat	mollig
(to) succeed in [sək'siːd]	to manage to do it	gelingen
environmentalist [ɪnˌvaɪərən'mentəlɪst]	someone who wants to protect nature and prevent pollution	Umweltschützer/-in
vegetarian ['vedʒɪ'teərɪan]	someone who doesn't eat meat	Vegetarier /-in
to condemn [kən'dem]	to say that something is very bad	verurteilen
ready-to-serve meals ['redɪ tʊ sɜːv miːlz]	meals that are already prepared when you buy them	Fertiggerichte
crowded [kraʊdɪd]	full of people	überfüllt
leisure centre ['leʒə 'səntə]	a large building where you can do different activities or sports	Freizeitzentrum
(to) chat [tʃæt]	to talk in a friendly way	plaudern
11.2 Eating Habits		
advertisement [əd'vɜːtɪsmənt]	an announcement in a newspaper, on TV etc. to encourage people to buy something	Werbung
appearance [ə'pɪərəns]	the way you look	Aussehen
nutritional value [njuː'trɪʃnl 'væljuː]	the quality of food, i.e. the amount of proteins, vitamins, minerals etc.	Nährwert
juice [dʒuːs]	a drink made out of fruit	Saft
11.3 What to Eat		
grain [greɪn]	the small, hard seeds of food plants like wheat	Getreide(-korn)
(to) provide [prə'vaɪd]	give something to someone	bereitstellen; hier: liefern
source [sɔːs]	the place or item from which you get something	Quelle
wheat, barley, oats [wiːt] ['bɑːli] [əʊts]	these are different cereals	Weizen, Gerste, Hafer
fibre ['faɪbə] (British English)	fiber (American English)	Ballaststoff
starchy foods [stɑːtʃɪ fuːds]		stärkereiche Lebensmittel
starch [stɑːtʃɪ]		Stärke
whole grain [həʊl greɪn]	the complete grain	Vollkorn
refined grain [rɪ'faɪnd greɪn]	superfine flour	ausgemahlenes Getreide
(to) select [sɪ'lekt]	to choose	auswählen
leafy greens ['liːfɪ griːn]		grünes Blattgemüse
syrup ['sɪrəp]		Sirup
saturated fats ['sætʃəreɪtɪd fæts]	compare: unsaturated fats	gesättigte Fettsäuren
dairy products ['deərɪ 'prɒdəkts]	products made from milk	Milchprodukte
iodine ['ɑrəʊdiːn]	element found in sea water	Jod
lean [liːn]	with only a little fat	mager

Unit 12 Problems in Life

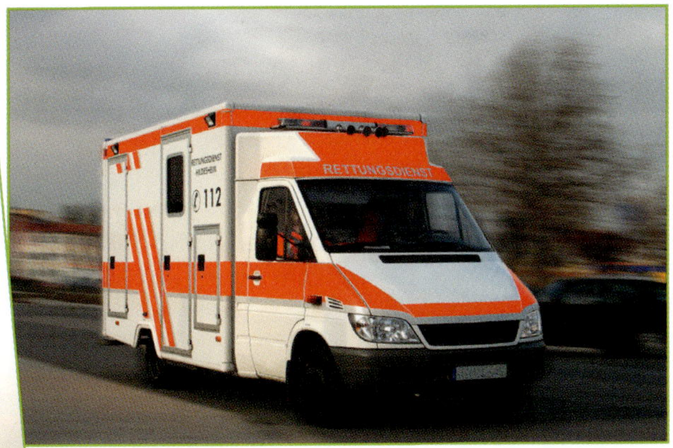

A Look at the pictures. What do you think are people afraid of?

B Is there anything you are afraid of? What do you do against your fear?

12.1 Being Ill

Mark is ill. He has had fever for two days and he has not eaten during the last two days either. Normally he can eat at least five slices of bread for breakfast – but at present he is not interested in anything. He neither cares about meals nor is he interested in TV or football. He only lies in bed and sleeps. His mother starts worrying about him. She has tried to get his temperature down with wet and cold towels wrapped around his calves and she has also given him two pills against fever, but it wasn't very successful. The fever sank only a little bit. Mark has told her that something was wrong with his stomach.

The night was restless. Mark was tossing and turning in his bed. His mother was sitting at his bed during the night and was holding his hand. She was also very tired and every now and then she had a little nap. Half sleeping, half awake she was thinking:

If I don't sleep myself, I won't manage to stay awake tomorrow.

If Mark feels better tomorrow, he will take part in his next football match.

If his temperature doesn't fall by midnight, I will call the doctor.

The doctor came at 1 a.m. He looked at Mark's tongue, looked into his eyes and asked about his temperature. When he finally pressed his thumb into the right side of Mark's stomach, the boy started to scream.

"Oops," the doctor said. "This is an emergency case. I'm pretty sure that you have got appendicitis. You must to go to hospital at once. I'll call for the ambulance."

A Working with the text – Are these sentences right or wrong? Correct the wrong ones.

1. Mark has been ill for five days.
2. Mark complained about pain in his stomach.
3. While he was ill Mark ate a lot.
4. His mother wanted to call the doctor the next morning.
5. The doctor pressed his thumb into the left side of Mark's stomach.
6. The doctor said that Mark could stay at home.

B Can you complete these sentences with words from the text?

RECEPTION

1. When your temperature is very high you have got … (5 letters)
2. When you only get bad marks at school you are beginning to … (5)
3. When you reach everything you want to you are very … (10)
4. When you go to school without breakfast you have got an empty … (7)
5. When you are unable to sleep you will spend a very … night. (8)
6. When you have a short sleep after school you take a … (3)
7. The short thick finger that is set apart from the other four of your hand is your … (5)

C Have you or one of your relatives ever been in hospital? If so, what was wrong with you or with them? Form complete sentences. The words from the box below and the pictures might help you.

appendicitis – broken leg/arm/knee – hernia – heart attack – diabetes – tonsillitis – birth of child – abuse of drugs – anorexia nervosa – infection – high temperature

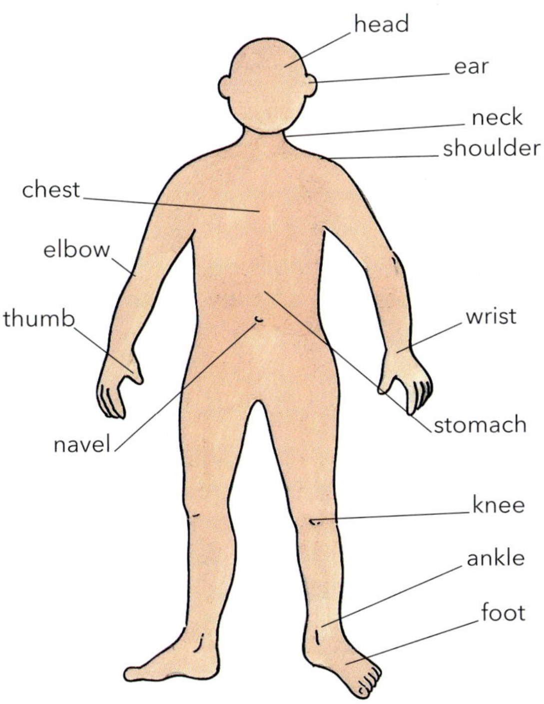

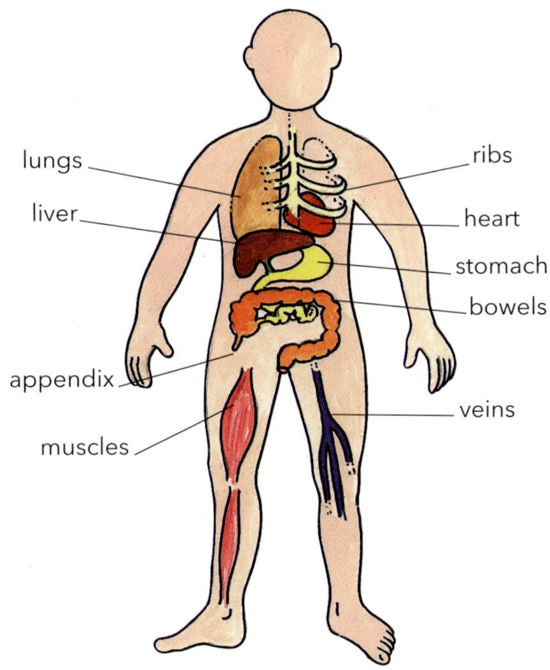

If-Clauses Type I

	If-Clause	Main-Clause
Example 1	If I **go** to the hospital,	I **will get** help.
Example 2	If the temperature **doesn't fall**,	I **will call** the doctor.

(➜ For rules see page 174)

- If-clauses have got two parts: The if-clause and the main-clause.
- The if-clause can be placed before or after the main clause.

When do you use the if-clause type I?
You use it when you are sure that something is very likely to happen.
The possibility that it will happen (or not happen, if it is a negative sentence) is about 80 per cent.

How do you form an if-clause type I?
If-clause:
You use the simple present.
Main-clause:
You can use the will-future + infinitive or won't (will not) + infinitive.

A **Now it's your turn. Use if-clauses type I to form the following sentences.**

Example:
You not live healthier/will/become ill one day.
- If you **don't live** healthier, you **will become** ill one day.

1. Susan/eat less/will/lose weight.
2. Peter/not do more sports/will/get less attractive.
3. You/will disturb the neighbours/not turn down the radio.
4. Ellen/will/break her leg/not wear proper shoes.
5. Mark/still lie in bed/won't come with us.

B **Form some more sentences of your own in which you use the if-clause type I. Work with a partner.**

C **Do you want to stay healthy? Here are some ideas what you should do. Match the two halves of these sentences that fit together. Careful, they are not in the correct order.**

1. If I brush my teeth regularly …
2. If I stop smoking …
3. If I sit down a while ..
4. If I don't drink alcohol …
5. If I don't go out into the hot sun …
6. If I sleep regularly …
7. If I do a lot of swimming …
8. If I want to become pregnant …
9. If I don't drink so much coffee …

a) … I will be less nervous.
b) … I will avoid lung cancer.
c) … I will not have to see the dentist so often.
d) … I will stop smoking and drinking.
e) … I won't be so tired at school.
f) … I will strengthen my muscles.
g) … I will get my breath back.
h) … I will avoid a sun burn.
i) … I won't die of liver cirrhosis.

If-Clauses Type II

	If-Clause	Main-Clause
Example 1	If I **owned** a house,	I **would have** a garden, too.
Example 2	If I **had** € 2,000,	I **could go** to Spain for three months.
Example 3	If I **were** you,	I **would tell** my parents.

(→ For rules see page 174)

When do you use the if-clause type II?
You use an if-clause type II when you doubt that something is going to happen.
The possibility that it is going to happen is about 20 per cent.

How do you form an if-clause type II?
If-clause:
You use the simple past in the if-clause.
(However, that does not mean that you talk about the past!
It is only the tense you are using.)
Main-clause:
You use would or
could or
might + infinitve in the main-clause.

Tip

You never ever use would in the if-clause!

A Now it's your turn. Use if-clauses type II to form the following sentences.

Example:
Sue/have swimming-pool/swim every day.
- If Sue **had** a swimming-pool, she **would swim** every day. But she has none.

1. I /have driving licence /invite you to a nice trip in the car.
2. Bob finishes school/apply for a job.
3. I know her name/tell you. I forgot it.
4. I have longer holidays/be happier.
5. I like you better/you are not so loud.
6. Life be easier/I not have to do so much homework.
7. Peter be better to live with/have more friends.

If I had a swimming pool, I would ...

B Complete these first parts of if-sentences with your own examples.

1. If I left home, ...
2. If I had enough money, ...
3. I would eat a frog if ...
4. If I were a teacher, ...
5. If I lived in Spain, ...
6. I would be happy if ...
7. I would visit more countries if ...
8. My parents would shout at me if ...

If-Clauses Type III

	If-Clause	Main-Clause
Example 1	If I **had seen** you,	I **would have said** hello to you.
Example 2	If I **had not taken** a bath,	I **might have heard** the phone.

(→ For rules see page 174)

When do you use the if-clause type III?
You use an if-clause type III when something has happened that cannot be made undone anymore. The possibility that it can happen is 0 per cent.

How do you form an if-clause type III?
If clause:
You use the past perfect in the if-clause.
Main-clause:
You use would or could or might + have + past participle

A Now it is your turn. Use if-clauses type III to form the following sentences.

Jill and Joe, a young couple, have lived together in a flat for three months now. They wanted to meet Joe's friend Mark early in the morning, but they were too late. Mark had already left. Now Jill and Joe argue about this issue.

Example:
Jill: If we / leave/ earlier, we would / not be / too late.
Jill: If we **had left** earlier, we **would not have been** too late.

1. Joe: This was not my fault. We / leave/ earlier, if you / not need / so much time in the bathroom.
2. If I /know/ you need so much time, I /get up/ earlier. I did not even have a shower!
3. Jill: The bathroom was vacant. If you / not need / so much time for your breakfast, you / use / it. In the end I was waiting for you!
4. Joe: That's not true! You were reading your E-mails before we left. If you / not check/ them, we / leave/ much earlier.

B Complete the first parts of these if-clauses with your own examples. Use if-clause type III.

1. My parents would have gone mad, if ...
2. If you had listened to me, ...
3. This would have been a good idea, if ...
4. If it had not started to rain, ...
5. If I had not been too late, ...
6. If my parents had not got married, ...

Relative Pronouns

Relative Pronouns are used to connect the two parts of a relative clause. Relative clauses are used to define a noun more closely.
(→ For rules see page 174)

Example 1:
People **who** have problems need help.

Example 2:
The ambulance car, **which** stands in front of the hospital, is red.

Who and **which** are relative pronouns.
You use **who** when you talk about **persons**.
You use **which** when you talk about **things** or **animals**.

A Complete the following sentences and use who or which.

1. Mark, … was ill, was taken to hospital.
2. This is the hospital in … he lies.
3. Mark's temperature, …. was too high, didn't go down.
4. Is this the girl … you have told me about?
5. Cyberbullying is a problem … is really nasty.
6. Some girls … were attacked via the Internet felt really awful.
7. There are a lot of things … are forbidden.
8. Is this the girl … I saw last night?

We distinguish between defining and non-defining relative clauses:

Non-defining relative clauses give you some additional information, but you can understand the sentence without this information.

Example:
My sister, *who is taller than me*, has a new boyfriend. (The information *who is taller than me* is not necessary. You just as well get the message and understand what is meant:
My sister has got a new boyfriend.)

Non-defining relative clauses are separated from the rest of the sentence by commas.

Defining relative clauses give information which is necessary to understand the meaning of the sentence.

Example:
I met the girl who I had seen before. (To only say *I met the girl* does not make much sense, because you do not know which girl is meant.) Defining relative clauses do not carry a comma.

12.2 Cyberbullying

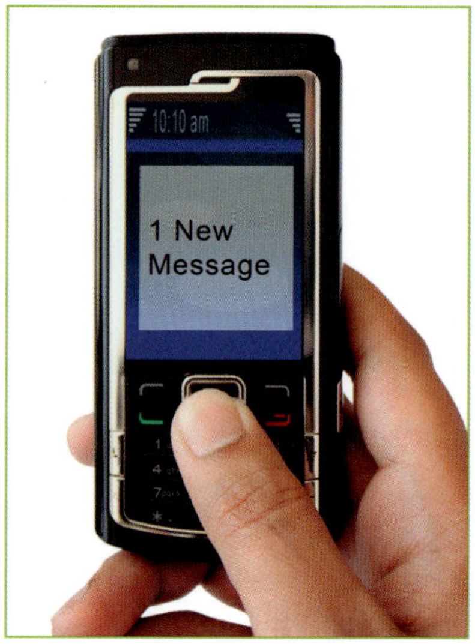

A Talk about cyberbullying. What is it? Have you heard of it? Have you or your friends ever experienced it?

INTERACTION

B Describe the pictures. Try to explain what kind of cyberbullying might take place in those situations.

Susan
Do you remember me? I'm Susan, the overweight girl from Philadelphia who thought that she would never get a boyfriend … listen to my story. Last autumn my parents and I moved to Boston. In my new class it was difficult for me to find friends. But then the most beautiful girl of the class wanted to be my friend on Facebook. We also exchanged IMs. But suddenly things changed. I got messages and E-mails all saying the same 'You're fat', 'you're ugly' and other insults which hurt me. The girl who seemed to be my friend had copied our IM-exchanges and showed them to other girls. They had a good laugh at my expense. I wanted to leave school at once, I hated them all.

Lisa
I told you about the nice student, didn't I? What he didn't tell me was that his former girlfriend (named Jean) was a girl I knew at school. And nearly all the students at the school use the same blog … Jean went online and posed as me, telling everyone how funny it was to steal her (Jean's) boyfriend and how silly she was! She stole my online identity. Then many girls in my class attacked me and told me I was mean. No one believed me.

Clark
I feel so stupid! Last summer when preparing for a bodybuilding competition, I got into a lot of trouble. I started receiving parcels which contained protein drinks. But I hadn't ordered them! More parcels were delivered containing more bodybuilding drinks and pills. I got at least 10 parcels a day and nearly went crazy … someone had stolen my online password! Then I remembered that Steven, the other trainee cook, had borrowed my mobile phone for an urgent call a while ago. I save my passwords in there.

Tip

Watch the EU video spot "Stop Cyber-Mobbing" and/or the movie "Let's fight it together".

C Describe the cyberbullying methods used in the three stories.

D Image you are a good friend of Susan. What would you advise her to do?

E Describe one blog you use. How does it work (for example registration)? What do the members talk about?

PRODUCTION

F On the Internet you need passwords everywhere. Give some rules for password protection.

Portfolio

Search the Internet for password protection tips (for example www.internetgeeks.org/blog/10-password-protection-tips-every-internet-user-must-know)

Copy them and add the list to your portfolio.

Why Do Kids Cyberbully Each Other?

1. This type of cyberbullying occurs when someone is bored or looking for entertainment. It is ego-based and usually done in a group either virtually or together in one room. Mostly the cyberbullies are female.
2. Cyberbullies like these want to show that they are more powerful than others. They try to get their way through fear or by hurting someone. Sometimes these types are actually being bullied in school. Such people act tough online, but they aren't tough in real life. Sometimes they have a lot of technical knowledge and use the Internet as a tool for bullying.

A Mean Girls

B The Power-Hungry or Revenge of the Nerds

G Which title and picture fits to which description? Characterize the two groups in your own words.

Vocabulary

12.1 Being Ill		
fever ['fi:və]		Fieber
slice of bread [slaɪs əv bred]	bread cut into smaller pieces	Brotscheibe
(to) worry ['wʌrɪ]		sich Sorgen machen
towel ['taʊəl]	you dry your wet body with a towel	Handtuch
calf; calves (pl.) [kɑ:f] [kɑ:vz]	lower part of leg	Wade
stomach ['stʌmək]	When you haven't eaten anything you have got an empty stomach	Magen
restless ['restlɪs]	giving no rest	ruhelos; schlaflos
(to) toss and turn [tɒs ænd tɜ:n]	move about continously	sich hin und herwälzen
(to) be awake [bɪ 'əweɪk]	the opposite of being asleep	wach sein
(to) stay awake [steɪ ə'weɪk]		wach bleiben
midnight [mɪdnaɪt]	12 o'clock at night	Mitternacht
tongue [tʌŋ]	the moveable organ in the mouth	Zunge
thumb [θʌm]	the short thick finger that is set apart from the other four of a hand	Daumen
(to) scream [skri:m]	to shout out loud	schreien
an emergency case [ɪ'mɜ:dʒənsɪ keɪs]		Notfall
at once [ət wʌns]	immediately	sofort
an ambulance ['æmbjʊləns]	the car that takes you to hospital	Notarztwagen
(to) complain about something [kəm'pleɪn ə'baʊt]	to express feelings of unhappiness	über etwas klagen
relative ['relətɪv]	your uncle is your relative	Verwandter, Verwandte
appendicitis [əˌpendɪ'saɪtɪs]		Blinddarmentzündung
hernia ['hɜ:njə]		Leistenbruch
heart attack [hɑ:t ə'tæk]		Herzinfarkt
tonsilitis [ˌtɒnsɪ'laɪtɪs]		Mandelentzündung
abuse [ə'bju:z]	wrong use, to use badly	Missbrauch
anorexia nervosa [ˌænə 'reksia nɜ:voʊsɑ:]		Magersucht
regularly ['regjʊlə]	if you do s.th. every day at the same time	regelmäßig
lung cancer [lʌŋ 'kænsə]	disease that comes from smoking	Lungenkrebs
(to) strengthen muscles [streŋθn 'mʌslz]	you can strengthen your muscles in a fitness centre	Muskeln stärken
breath [breθ]		Atem
liver cirrhosis ['lɪvə sɪ'rəʊsɪs]	disease of liver because of alcohol	Leberzirrhose
frog [frɒg]	an animal that lives in the water and on the land	Frosch
12.2 Cyberbullying		
cyberbully [saɪ.bə.'bʊl.i]	a person who cyberbullies	jmd., der im Internet mobbt/ schikaniert
at my expense [ɪk'spents]		zu meinen Lasten
blog [blɒg]	a website containing the writer's experiences and opinions	Internettagebuch, Weblog
ego-based		ego-basiert, um das eigene Ego drehend
tough [tʌf]	strong	rau, hart
revenge [rɪ'vendʒ]		Rache
nerd [nɜ:d]	an intelligent but single-minded person obsessed with a non-social hobby	Computerfreak, Sonderling
insult ['ɪn.sʌlt]	an offensive remark	Beleidigung

Unit 13 The Way I Want to Live

A Imagine you are ten years older than now. Where do you want to live by then?

B Think about it and then answer the question. The following words may help you:

block of flats – terraced house – detached house – rented room – village
city – suburb – bungalow – semi-detached house – hotel – boarding-house

13.1 Different Ways of Life

7:00 a.m. - At the Hanks'

"Good morning Sue, darling," Peter says as he returns to the bedroom, "the shower is yours now." Sue stays in bed another five minutes because her work as a doctor's assistant starts later than Peter's. In the meantime Peter has already dressed. "Your new suit looks great," Sue murmurs out of bed, "your superior will be very pleased with your perfect styling." "I hope so," Peter answers, "next week they'll make the decision about my promotion. Is there anything for breakfast in the house?" "I'm afraid not," Sue answers, "please stop at a coffee shop to have breakfast." "Okay, bye, darling." "Bye, Peter, and don't forget to get your old suit and your shirts from the cleaner's."

1:00 p.m. - At the Hanks'

As Peter enters the canteen he remembers that it's his job to go shopping and to fetch the laundry from the cleaner's this evening. "I'll go to Quinnsworth," he says to himself, "my favourite pizza is on sale there." At the counter Peter chooses chicken, French fries and a salad. His colleagues have already finished their lunch, and so he looks for a quiet place to enjoy his chicken. "It's a pity that Sue doesn't like to cook," Peter thinks while eating, "all these ready-to-serve meals we buy cost a lot of money and here I also have to pay a lot of money. But I'm glad to get such delicious meals here."

7:00 a.m. - At the Johnsons'

"Mum, where are my socks?" eight-year-old Brian asks. Caroline, who is just preparing breakfast, tells him and waits for the next question. "Mum, I can't find my maths book." Like nearly every morning Brian can't find his things, but because her husband Charles left home half an hour earlier, Brian is the only one she has to take care of at the moment. Caroline takes two cutlets out of the freezer and starts to peel the potatoes. She has to hurry up because she has to begin her work at the nursery school earlier this morning. "Please Brian, hurry up, there are only ten minutes left for your breakfast," she shouts. "Hi, Mum. I'm not hungry," Brian answers as he comes into the kitchen. "No, Brian, I at least want you to eat some cereals."

1:00 p.m. - At the Johnsons'

Caroline is cleaning the carrots she has bought on her way home. She is thinking about what to do in the afternoon. Because it's Monday she has to do the laundry but she wants to visit her mother afterwards. "When Charles returns at 4 o'clock he'll have time to check Brian's homework and to warm up his lunch," she thinks as she puts the potatoes and the carrots onto the cooker, "and I have to make an appointment with my hairdresser urgently," she says to herself. Ten minutes later Brian returns from school. "I'm the best long jumper in my class," he shouts proudly, "and now I'm as hungry as a wolf."

9:00 p.m. – At the Hanks'

Peter and Sue are sitting in the living-room now. Peter is watching TV and Sue is chatting on the Internet. Their flat is very modern, especially their living-room. The last five years they've spent a lot of money on buying the newest computer, TV-set and so on. Both of them enjoy these modern forms of communication and they are 'online' most of their evenings. Only at weekends they go out into the city to meet friends and have fun. Sometimes they drive to a nearby holiday park. "If I get the promotion, there won't be time to have a holiday this year," Peter says suddenly. "Oh Peter," Sue's reaction sounds angry, "but we are planning to travel to France with Roy and Tina." "I'm very sorry, but at the moment the job is more important. Think of the high costs we have every month. We urgently need the higher wage."

9:00 p.m. – At the Johnsons'

Caroline and Charles are sitting in the living-room. Charles works for a big motor company. His job is a hard one so he always comes home very tired in the evening. His wife Caroline is a little bit disappointed about this sometimes, because she wants to talk about lots of things with him. At the moment they are making plans for the weekend. "What about a cycling tour?" Caroline asks. "Yes, good idea," Charles answers, "but I've promised Brian to go to the football match with him." "Okay, but don't forget the invitation in the evening." They are invited to a big birthday party at one of their friends. Charles isn't too happy about this invitation because that certainly means dancing and chatting the whole evening.

RECEPTION

A **Read the texts about the two families. You will then notice that all these following statements are false. Rewrite them to turn them into true statements.**

1. Peter has his breakfast at home.
2. Peter wears a new suit because he has got a promotion.
3. Charles and Caroline have got two children.
4. Bob gets a cutlet and potatoes for breakfast.
5. Peter returns home for lunch.
6. Peter and Sue only spend a small amount of their housekeeping money on foods.
7. Every Friday morning Caroline does the laundry.
8. Caroline has bought frozen carrots.
9. Caroline's and Charles' flat is very modern and has got a lot of electrical appliances.
10. Susan doesn't mind staying at home during her holiday this year.
11. Charles likes chatting in the evening.
12. Caroline and Charles often use all modern means of electronical communication.

B **There are many differences in the lives of the Hanks and the Johnsons, especially in their way of household management. Write down the differences.**

Example:
Caroline prepares the meals for her family herself.
– Sue doesn't like to cook.

C **Think about the advantages and the disadvantages of these two ways of household management. Write them down in a chart like this:**

	advantages	disadvantages
The Hanks		
The Johnsons		

PRODUCTION

D **Imagine you manage your own household. What do you spend your money on? Make a list of the possible costs a household of two persons has.**

Different Tenses Training

A Put the verbs in brackets into the given tense.

1. Sue (to chat/present progressive) with a girl from Ireland.
2. Peter (to love/simple present) series like 'Star Trek'.
3. The prices for petrol (to increase/ present perfect) enormously.
4. Last year Charles (to be/simple past) in the hospital for two weeks.
5. The doctor (to tell/simple past) him to do a lot of sports.
6. After Caroline (to iron/past perfect) the shirts she (to telephone/simple past) her girlfriend.
7. The weather (to be/will-future) nice next week.
8. Peter and Sue (to travel/going-to-future) to Spain.

B Form questions – Ask for the underlined words.

1. Peter buys a <u>new suit</u> each year.
2. Sue is having <u>a shower</u> at the moment.
3. <u>Caroline</u> has worked as a nursery nurse for ten years now.
4. The pizza Peter had bought tasted <u>awful</u>.
5. The children were playing <u>outside</u> when the accident happened.
6. Ryan and Sally will marry <u>next year</u>.
7. The students are going to write <u>a test</u> tomorrow.
8. Charles had danced with Caroline <u>five</u> times.

C Negatives – Form negative sentences with the words and the tenses given.

1. Sue/to dance last night ➜ simple past
2. The dog/to chase/the cat ➜ past perfect
3. Brian/to be good/at long jump/ yesterday ➜ simple past
4. The girls/to chat/when the teacher came in ➜ past progressive
5. We/to get/a hot summer ➜ will-future
6. The car/to be repaired/yet ➜ present perfect
7. Peter/to get/his promotion ➜ going-to-future
8. Caroline/to cook/a meal just now ➜ present progressive
9. Charles/to go/to the cinema often ➜ simple present

INTERACTION

D A game – Choose a noun or pronoun and a verb out of the first two boxes and then a tense out of the third box. Tell this your neighbour or any other person in the class. He or she has to form a sentence with those words in the right tense.

Noun/Pronoun

The teacher – He – We
The car – The dog
The horse – I – She – The
You – The girl – It

Verb

to jump – to write
to eat – to watch – to laugh
to drive – to want
to take – to run – to like
to hate – to drink

Tense

simple present – will-future
simple past – present progressive
going-to-future – present perfect
past progressive – past perfect

13.2 Are You an Environmentalist?

Test your knowledge and your behaviour concerning our environment. Answer the questions spontaneously and most important: Be honest. Write down your answers (example: 1 A). You can find the solutions on the next page.

1. How many litres of air does a human being breathe a day?
   A 1.000 litres
   B 15.000 litres
   C 50.000 litres

2. At what time of the day is the most energy spent?
   A 8 a.m. - 12 p.m.
   B 13 p.m. - 5 p.m.
   C 8 p.m. - 12 a.m.

3. You go by means of public transport or by bike …
   A as often as possible
   B only sometimes
   C never

4. The destruction of the tropical rain forests supports the greenhouse effect …
   A by around 40 per cent
   B by around 15 per cent
   C not at all

5. Suppose the bottle bank and the recycling containers are three kilometres away from your home. Then you would bring the waste there …
   A by bike
   B by car
   C You would put the waste into your regular dustbin.

6. Organic farming is less harmful to the environment. When you go shopping you prefer organic foods …
   A always
   B sometimes
   C You have never thought about that.

7. If each smoker in Berlin should throw away his non-returnable lighter, how many tons of rubbish would that amount to?
   A 1 ton
   B 3 tons
   C 33 tons

8. How much water does everyone flush down the toilet per day?
   A 10 litres
   B 15 litres
   C 50 litres

9. Which gas increases the greenhouse effect mostly?
   A carbondioxide
   B methan
   C CFC

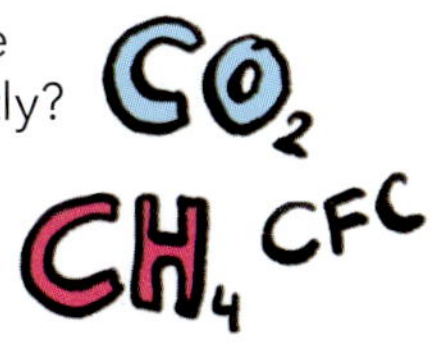

10. You are in a traffic jam with your car. What do you do?
    A You stop the engine.
    B You let the engine run.
    C You let the engine run because when you start the engine again, more harmful gases will be released.

11. You write your letters on recycled paper …
    A always
    B sometimes
    C You always take completely white paper.

12. A car that needs 11 litres at a speed of 130 kmph needs how many litres at a speed of 170 kmph?
    A 13 litres
    B 15 litres
    C 18 litres

13. There are a lot of films about environmental themes on TV. You …
    A watch those films regularly.
    B are not interested in such films.
    C try to get information about environmental themes by other media as well.

14. How much energy can you save if you lower your room temperature by 1 degree Celsius?
    A 1 per cent
    B 3 per cent
    C 6 per cent

15. In inner city traffic bikers should breathe by nose because they absorb less harmful gases that way. How much less?
- A About 20 per cent less
- B About 50 per cent less
- C About 90 per cent less

16. You buy drinks in returnable bottles …
- A always
- B sometimes
- C seldom, because you don't like to bring them back

17. Because of the destruction of the rain forests a lot of species of plants and animals become extinct. How many per day?
- A 10 species
- B 50 species
- C 70 species

18. You can go to school by bike, by car or by means of public transport. What do you do?
- A I prefer to go by car.
- B I surely go by means of public transport.
- C Whenever possible I go by bike.

19. Low-energy light bulbs use less electric current. How much energy do they save?
- A 20%
- B 80%
- C 50%

20. You use the full capacity of the washing machine …
- A sometimes
- B always, because you want to save energy and water
- C You have never thought about that.

	1	2	3	4	5	6	7	8	9	10	11	12	13	14	15	16	17	18	19	20
A	1	3	3	1	3	3	1	3	3	3	3	1	3	1	1	3	1	1	1	2
B	3	1	2	3	2	2	1	2	1	2	2	1	1	1	1	1	3	3	3	3
C	1	1	1	1	1	1	3	1	1	1	1	3	3	3	3	1	1	2	1	1

Have a look at the chart and add all of your points. The result will tell you how much you care about our environment.

20–30 Points

You must admit that you aren't interested in environmental things. You have never seriously thought about these things. You want to believe that all the so-called environmental problems are exaggerated. But sometimes you aren't quite sure because you notice the consequences of all the environmental sins. You are worried about the rise of temperature and the increasing number of allergies. But you don't take action. That is not the right way - get information about these themes and change your behaviour. Even little steps help.

31–45 Points

Your environmental consciousness is rather marked - you are aware of the problems. But you find it difficult to do without the beloved comfort. You excuse yourself with the lack of time and you say that one person alone cannot change anything.
Try to be more consequent, even if that means spending more time selecting rubbish or going by bike. Understand that as a consumer you can influence retailers, producers and the products they sell.

46–60 Points

Congratulations. You are an expert in environmental themes. You are involved in environmental things and you do a lot in your daily life to protect the environment. Maybe you are even a member of an environmental organization. Continue like this and try to improve the environment. Even if you sometimes feel a little discouraged because of all the disasters and the consequences they have, be sure that more and more people will think like you do.

Mixed Tenses Training

A Present and Past

Put the verbs into the correct form: simple present, present progressive, simple past or past progressive.

1. We can't go out now. It is ________ (to rain) cats and dogs.
2. Susan usually _______ (to do) the laundry on Monday but she _______ (not do) it last Monday.
3. Yesterday evening a lightning _____ (to strike) the neighbour's house while we _______ (to watch) TV.
4. What's that noise? Who _______(to mow) the lawn?
5. Tom _______ (not go) to work yesterday. He didn't feel well.
6. Where ________ (come from)? Is he English?
7. Look, what _______ those boys_____ (play)?
8. "Charles has bought a new car." "Oh, has he? When _______ (to buy) it?"

B Present and Past

Choose the correct one of the two alternatives in each of the sentences and write it down.

Example:
Charles ***has worked*** *for the motor company for ten years now.*

1. He earns/is earning a lot of money there.
2. Last year he has got/got a promotion.
3. Caroline has always worked/ had always worked as a nursery nurse.
4. Sometimes she hates/hated her job.
5. Some days ago while the children washed/ were washing the dishes she saw that a boy hit a little girl with his fist.
6. The boy said that the girl doesn't want/ didn't want to clean his plates.

C Past Tenses

Put the verbs into the correct form: simple past, past progressive or past perfect.

1. Yesterday evening Sandy _____ (to go) to the cinema to meet Paul. When she _____ (to arrive) there, Paul _____ (already/wait) for her. His bus _____ (to arrive) early.

2. Last night when I _____ (lie) in bed and _____ (read) a book I suddenly _____ (hear) a noise. I _____(get up) and _____ (to go) to the window to see what it was. Outside I _____ (to see) that a car _____ (damaged) our fence.

3. I _____ (to meet) Joyce and Ron yesterday as I _____ (to walk) through the city. They _____ (to be) at the job centre where they _____ (to ask) for an odd job. We _____ (to decide) to go to a café for a drink.

13.3 My Decisions as a Consumer

A magazine carried out an opinion poll about reasons for consumers' selection of foods. They interviewed a lot of people in a supermarket. Their question was: "Can you tell us which aspects were decisive that you have put these foods into your trolley?"
Here are some of the answers they got:

Jane: "Ron and I have invited friends for dinner. We want to sit outside and enjoy the evening. So we were looking for dishes which are tasteful and look nice, for example …"

Mark: "I only chose products that don't do any harm to the environment. I prefer foods with no or only little packaging, like fresh fruit and vegetables. I only bought vegetables today which were produced in an environmentally-friendly way, grown with no pesticides for example."

Gina: "Jim and I are vegetarians because we are against the mass production of animals. We hate the way they are transported and how they are treated. We think that meat makes us ill, and that is why we bought …"

Sue: "I've got a hard job and so I chose food that is easily and quickly prepared. I also have to look at the price. So I've chosen …"

George: "I'm convinced that a healthy diet keeps my body fit. Therefore I pay attention to the nutritive value of the food. It should contain a high amount of vitamins, minerals, fibres and carbohydrates and only a little fat. I've bought …"

A Write down all the reasons for the people's selection of food.

1. Jane and Ron chose food which …
2. Mark …
3. …

B The reasons for the decisions can be for example the following aspects:

> ecological value - look - nutritive value - psychology (opinion, experience) - practical value - price - taste

Sort these terms to the shopping behaviour of the people above.

1. Jane and Ron …
2. Mark …
3. …

C Write down examples for food that you might find in the trolley of …

1. Mark
2. Sue
3. George

D Think of other reasons to prefer or reject food and write them down.

INTERACTION

E Which of the aspects mentioned are important for your own buying of food? Talk about it with a classmate.

There are a lot of reasons for the selection of food and drinks. As a consumer you take influence on the offer of supermarkets and retailers. Remember for example the mad-cow-disease and the consequences this disease had on the sales of beef. Another example is organic foods. The consumers demand those products and because of this, the range of organic goods has increased enormously during the last years. Here are some aspects you should think about when you go shopping:

Ecological Standard

Different aspects must be mentioned here. Firstly you should not buy products with a lot of packaging and you should avoid non-returnable bottles or cans for drinks.
Secondly you should consider that organic products are less harmful to the environment and that they are usually safer and more nutritious than conventionally grown products. The third aspect to be mentioned here is that you as a consumer should prefer products which were harvested or produced in an area close to you. This is one step to reduce the rush of traffic.

Nutritive Value

Healthy food contains only a little fat, sugar, energy and salt. It contains a lot of vitamins, minerals, fibres and complex carbohydrates instead. You should eat fresh food often and avoid things that have been manufactured intensively.

100 gm	energy kJ	fat gm	fibre gm	carbohydrate	water gm
boiled potatoes	209	+	2	15	79
chips	1140	13	4	31	44

Psychological Aspect

Many people don't eat meat because of factory farming for the production of meat. In those places the animals are crated, crammed or confined in small spaces. They are often kept in conditions of utter deprivation and are treated as little more than production machines. Farm animals are being pushed to their natural limits to maximise production here. Ask at the counter of your store where the meat is from and how the animals were reared.

Social Aspect

Our love of cheap foods and fashion is often not good for the people who produce or make it. Clothes for example are produced in factories in developing countries, often with bad working conditions and very low pay for the workers. Aid agencies or social movements like *FairTrade* care for the payment of fair prices and for social and environmental standards in the production of goods in those countries. You can help by buying foods (e.g. coffee, cocoa, sugar, tea, bananas, honey) which are certified by *TransFair*.

FAIRTRADE

F Interpret the chart.

PRODUCTION

G Make a list of rules that should be followed when we go shopping.

Example: *Always buy drinks in returnable bottles.*

H Comment: Factory farming is necessary to produce cheap meat. Do you agree or not? Give reasons for your answer.

The Future

Simple Present with a Future Meaning
We use the simple present when we talk about timetables, programmes (public transport, cinema etc.).
Example: *The lesson ends in ten minutes.* *The train arrives at 10:30 a.m.*

Present Progressive with a Future Meaning
We use the present progressive to say what we have already arranged (future arrangements).
Example: *She is meeting my mother this afternoon.*

Going-To-Future
We use this future form to say what we have decided or intended to do,
Example: *I'm going to travel to France next week.*
and to describe something that is very likely to happen.
Example: *Look at the black clouds! It is going to rain.*

Will-Future
We use *I will* or *I'll* when we spontaneously decide something at the moment of speaking,
Example: *I'll cut next lesson.*
and we also use *will* when we predict a future happening which is not clearly foreseeable.
Example: *Perhaps he'll stay the whole week.*

A

Simple Present with a Future Meaning – A friend of yours wants to travel by plane for the first time. Look at the timetable and explain to him what the numbers mean. Answer in full sentences.

Flight Number	Destination	Time of Departure	Boarding Time	Gate
148	Paris	8:15 a.m.	7:30 a.m.	B13
234	Munich	11:30 a.m.	10:45 a.m.	A10
569	Atlanta	3:20 p.m.	2:30 p.m.	C1
450	Shanon	5:00 p.m.	4:15 p.m.	A15
963	Brussels	6:15 p.m.	5:45 p.m.	B8

Example:
Flight number 148 to Paris leaves at 8:15 a.m.
The stewardess checks your boarding ticket at 7:30 a.m. at gate B13.

B

Present Progressive with a Future Meaning – Your friend Robert wants to go out with you but you are very busy. Look at your schedule for the next days and explain to him why you have no time.

Robert: "I want to go out with you on Monday."
You: "Sorry, but I'm going to the hairdresser's then."
Robert: "Hmh, and what about Tuesday?"
You: "Not Tuesday, I ..."
Robert: "And Wednesday evening?"
You: "..."
Robert: "Your last chance is Thursday!"
You: "..."

Monday	Tuesday	Wednesday	Thursday
5:30 p.m. hairdresser	tennis	learn German	help Grandma

C

Different ways of expressing future – which is correct?

Example:
"Did you phone grandmother?"
– "Oh no, <u>I'll phone</u> her later."

1. The train from York <u>is going to arrive/arrives</u> at 10:30 a.m.
2. I can't help you this evening. <u>I'm working/I'll work</u> at Harrods.
3. "Look, the sun is shining." – "Oh great, <u>I go/I'll go</u> to the beach."
4. "Do you have any plans for your future?" – "<u>I am studying/I am going to study biology</u>."
5. We are going to the cinema this evening. The film <u>is beginning/begins</u> at 8:15 p.m.
6. <u>I am not working/don't work</u> tomorrow.
7. "Are you going out this evening?" – "No, <u>I will watch/am watching</u> TV."
8. I'm very hungry. <u>I will buy/am buying</u> a hamburger.

D

Read the following sentences and complete them, using will or going to.
➜ For rules see also page 169

1. The bell rings. You open the door. The neighbour wants to speak to your father. You say: "Just a moment. I … (get him)."
2. It's a hot day. You have decided to go swimming. You tell your friend: "It's very nice today. I … (have a swim)."
3. You have lost your purse. Your friend says: "Don't worry. You … (surely find it)."
4. You have got an invitation from a man you don't know very well. Your girlfriend asks: "What have you decided about Mr Johnson's invitation? " You answer: "I … (meet) him."

Vocabulary

boarding house ['bɔ:dɪŋ haʊs]	a house where people stay for a short time	Pension
13.1 Different Ways of Life		
to murmur ['mɜ:mə]	to say something very quietly	murmeln
superior [su:'pɪərɪə]	someone who has more authority on the job	Vorgesetzter
promotion [prə'maʊʃn]	you get a more important job	Beförderung
urgently [ɜ:dʒənt]	when something has to be dealt with as fast as possible	dringend
wage [weɪdʒ]	the money you get for your work	Lohn
cutlet ['kʌtlɪt]	a small piece of meat usually fried of grilled	Kotelett
to peel [pi:l]	to remove the skin of vegetables or fruit	schälen
cooker ['kʊkə]	large mostly electrical device in the kitchen used for cooking food; a stove	Herd
long jumper [lɒŋ 'dʒʌmpə]	an athlete who tries to jump as far as he can	Weitspringer
proudly [praʊd]	you feel glad about something good you have done	stolz
to promise ['prɒmɪs]	to say that you will do something definitely	versprechen
behaviour [bɪ'heɪvjə]	the way a person behaves	Verhalten
13.2 Are You an Environmentalist?		
means [mi:ns]		Mittel
destruction [dɪ'strʌkʃn]	the act of destroying something	Zerstörung
to support [sə'pɔ:t]	to help something/someone to succeed	unterstützen
greenhouse effect [gri:nhaʊs ɪ'fekt]		Treibhauseffekt
distant ['dɪstənt]	far away	entfernt
to destroy [dɪ'strɔɪ]	to ruin completely	zerstören
ozone layer ['əʊzəʊn 'leɪə]		Ozonschicht
CFC [si:efsi:]		Fluorchlorkohlenwasserstoff
lighter ['laɪtə]	a small device which produces a flame	Feuerzeug
non-returnable [nɒn rɪ'tɜ:nabl]	things that can only be used once	Wegwerf-, Einweg-
traffic jam ['træfɪk dʒæm]	a long line of cars that can't move because the road is blocked	Verkehrsstau
species ['spi:ʃi:z]	class of plants or animals	Art, Spezies
to become extinct [ɪk'stɪŋkt]	no living members exist anymore	aussterben
capacity [kə'pæsɪtɪ]	the quantity of things	Fassungsvermögen
to admit [əd'mɪt]	you say that something is true	zugeben
to exaggerate [ɪg'zædʒəreɪt]	you make the thing you are talking about seem better, bigger or worse than it actually is	übertreiben
sin [sɪn]	a bad and immoral behaviour	Sünde
algae ['ældʒi:]	green, slimy plants which live in the water	Algen
to apologize [ə'pɒlədʒaɪz]	to say 'Sorry'	sich entschuldigen
opinion poll [ə'pɪnjan paʊl]	when several people are asked about their opinion	Meinungsumfrage
13.3 My Decisions as a Consumer		
trolley ['trɒlɪ]	a small cart where you put things in when you are shopping	Einkaufswagen
harm [hɑ:m]	bad influence	Schaden
pesticides ['pestɪsaɪds]	chemicals which farmers put on their crops to kill animals	Pestizide
to convince [kən'vɪns]	to make sure that something is necessary	überzeugen
ecological value [ˌi:kə'lɒdʒɪkl 'vælju:]		ökologischer Wert
to deny [dɪ'naɪ]	you say that it is not true	verneinen, ablehnen
retailer [ri:teɪlə]	a person or a business that sells goods to the public	Einzelhändler
mad cow disease [mæd kaʊ dɪ'zi:z]		Rinderwahnsinn, BSE
organic foods [ɔ:'gænɪk fu:ds]	foods grown without chemicals	biologisch-dynamisch erzeugte Lebensmittel
to harvest ['hɑ:vɪst]	to cut or pick crop, fruit or vegetables when they are ripe	ernten
to crate [kreɪt]		in Verschlägen halten
to cram [kræm]		mästen
to confine ['kɒnfaɪn]	to keep someone in prison	einsperren
utter deprivation ['ʌtə ˌdeprɪ'veɪʃn]		völlige Entbehrung
to rear [rɪə]	to bring someone up	aufziehen
factory farming ['fæktərɪ 'fɑ:mɪŋ]	when animals are reared in an unnatural way in narrow stables	Massentierhaltung
to predict [prɪ'dɪkt]	to say what will happen in the future	vorhersagen
destination [ˌdestɪ'neɪʃn]	the place to which someone/something is going	Bestimmungsort, Bestimmung
aid agency [eɪd 'eɪdʒənsɪ]		Hilfswerk, Hilfsorganisation
developing countries [dɪ'veləpɪŋ 'kʌntrɪ]	the opposite of industrialized countries	Entwicklungsländer

Role Play

There are some texts in your Englishbook which you could use for a role play. Have a look at the text about scenes in the life of Ryan, for example – page 49 ff.
If you want to do role-playing, there are several steps you should follow:

Step One
Decide which text you want to use for your role play.

Step Two
Find out how many actors you need for this.
In our example you need an actor who plays Ryan. Then you need a waitress and some colleagues of the hotel staff. Somebody has to play the boss.

Step Three
Decide who wants to play which role.
Important: Only choose pupils who want to play. Nobody should be forced to play.
If you are not sure, why not just try it? You will at least make an interesting experience.

Step Four
Can you think of some material or items you might use to make your play more lively?
Maybe you have got some plastic plates at home – why not bring them to school?
Or – what can you use instead of porridge?

Step Five
Form three or four groups – one group for each actor that will take part in the role-playing later on.
Go through the text again.
Each group has to form ideas what the actor could say. Make a list of those ideas.
You are free to add something or to leave something out when you are playing your role.
This list is only a help for the actor.

Step Six
Give the actors some time to coordinate their parts and to learn their roles.

Step Seven
Have you got anything you need? Start and play.
Do it as freely as you can.
The pupils who are not playing should observe the play and write down everything they notice.

Step Eight
The role play is over. Discuss what you have seen or heard. How did the actors feel?
What was good? What could have been better?

Step Nine
You can play it again, this time with other actors.
Compare the actors to each other.

Planning a Project

A good way to learn, to use and to present your knowledge of the English language is a practical project. The following method will help you to do this.

Example:
An English Breakfast
Breakfast is more than just eating food for most British people. It is a part of their way of life. Why not bring this aspect of British life into your school?
Such a project must be planned well, therefore here are five steps to help you. First it is important to find out if this project is suitable for your lessons. The following guide may be of some help to you.

Steps	Questions	Examples
Step One - Setting Aims	What are your reasons for doing such a project?	• use of the English language for vocational reasons • completing vocational knowledge • learning by practical experience • learning to organise something yourself

Step Two - Collecting Ideas	Which kind of lessons can be included in the project?	• nutrition (well-balanced nutrition, fibre)
		• practical domestic science (laying a table)
		• mathematics (calculation of energy in food, of costs)
		• English
		  • collecting English menus (letters, e-mails, telephone, Internet)
		  • informing/presenting (teachers, students, parents, other interested people)

	Who are your guests?	• teachers who speak English • a group of students • parents
	How can you create a British atmosphere?	• decorating the tables (blue and red napkins) • decorating the walls (posters with landmarks of Great Britain) • English newspapers
Step Three - Making Decisions	Prepare a plan of work: - What has to be done? - Who has to do it? - On what date has the task to be completed?	• Each student writes down what he or she expects from the project. • What food is going to be offered? • setting dates • calculating the costs
Step Four - Checking the Management	How are the plans carried out?	• presenting the project to the public • organising the layout of the room • carrying the plans through • creating a page for a school chronicle
Step Five - Looking at the Results	Was the project a success?	• Did all the students fulfill their tasks? • Was it worthwhile to invest work, time and money in the project? • Experiences which have been learned and can be used for future projects? • Reactions of the guests? • Maybe even an evaluation with a video camera?

Renoir
RESTAURANT

Breakfast

From the Serve-Yourself Buffet

Chilled Juices
Orange • Apple
Assorted Yoghurts
Grapefruit Segments
Poached Figs in Syrup

Cereals Served with Chilled Milk
Cornflakes • Muesli • Fruit & Fibre (Ballaststoffe)

Brown Soda Bread • Crispy Rolls • Croissants
Brown or White Toast

Waiter Service to Your Table

Country Style Breakfast:
Bacon, Sausage, Pudding, Fried Egg, Sauté of Mushrooms

Or

Grilled Filet Of Plaice (Scholle)

Or

Continental Plate
Cheese, Ham, Salami, Sliced Tomato

Barry's Tea • Hot Chocolate • Coffee

£10.25 Adults ***£7.00 Children***

Example of a breakfast menu

Applying for a Job: a To-Do-List

When you want to apply for a job, there are several steps to follow. Use this checklist to make sure you make a good impression on your potential employer.

Letter of Application
- ❑ Write to a named person.
- ❑ Identify the position for which you are applying.
- ❑ Say where you saw the job advertised.
- ❑ Express briefly why you are seeking a job.
- ❑ Write why you think you are the right person to do the job.
- ❑ Say what interests you about the job.
- ❑ Show that you got actual information from the organisation's or company's web pages.
- ❑ Revise and edit your text so that it is clear and convincing.
- ❑ Write your letter of application on a single sheet of A4.

Enclosure
- ❑ Include copies of all qualifications from secondary school onwards.
- ❑ Include references from previous employers.
- ❑ Make sure the application is fully completed before submitting the documents.

CV (Curriculum Vitae)
- ❑ Provide information on your personal and professional development.
- ❑ Your CV must be in strict reverse chronological order, leaving no gaps unaccounted for.
- ❑ The CV should include a passport-sized photograph. (But be careful, this rule may soon be abolished.)
- ❑ Mention your hobbies only if they are relevant for the job.
- ❑ Sign your CV at the bottom.

Before the Interview
- ❑ There are several questions which frequently come up. Be prepared for them.
- ❑ Prepare at least three questions to ask the interviewer.

At the Interview
- ❑ Be punctual!
- ❑ Do not speak too quickly.
- ❑ Do not interrupt the interviewer.
- ❑ Use the interviewer's name regularly throughout the conversation.
- ❑ Use the company's name a few times.

In General
- ❑ Ask someone to check your application before you send it.
- ❑ Online applications are getting more and more popular. Here you send your application by e-mail with pdf-enclosures. In this case, make sure that the formatting is readable by all IT packages.
- ❑ Use a normal typeface such as Times New Roman or Arial. Do not use underlining or italics.

Having a Discussion

We are all individuals and we all think differently about politics, religion, environment, leisure activities and so on. Consequently we very often discuss when we have a talk. But often discussions end in a quarrel.
Here are some rules to have a good discussion.

Preparations

1. Find one person to be the chairman of the discussion.
2. Form small groups. Only in groups with less than five people all participants have the chance to take part in the discussion equally.
3. Sit down in a circle so that all participants can see each other.
4. You might set a speaking time and give one person the task to be the time controller.

How to Do It

1. The guide should start the discussion with a question or an example. Then he or she should call on the speakers.
2. The participants should listen to all arguments and put up their hand if they want to talk. Never interrupt a speaking person.
3. As a speaker you shouldn't talk too long, and you should concentrate on your main thoughts. Always be objective and never become personal in your arguments.
4. The guide can summarize arguments from time to time and should make sure that the theme of the discussion is not lost.

Useful Expressions for Discussions

Here are some expressions to use for your arguments in a discussion:

Introducing the Topic
There are many points of view …
There are several questions to think about …
It is important to say …

Stating Points
I think …
In my opinion …
I am of the opinion …
My view is …

Stating Alternatives
On the other hand …
However …
Although …

Stating Results
As a result …
Because of this …

Closing the Discussion
It is clear that …
It seems that …

How to Work with an English-English Dictionary

A dictionary can be a real friend. It can for example help you
1. to pronounce a word correctly,
2. to spell a word correctly or find irregularities,
3. to find out what type of word or word class it is,
4. to find out what meaning(s) a word has,
5. to find the right preposition,
6. to find the noun if you have the verb.

These are just some examples. For more information, consult the first pages of a good dictionary.

Pronunciation

The pronunciation is given behind the word. If you understand the special signs, called "Received Pronunciation" or "RP" in short, then you know how to pronounce a word correctly. To find out, look at this pronunciation table.

Consonants	
Symbol	Keywords
p	pen
b	back
t	ten
d	day
k	key
g	get
f	fat
v	view
θ	thing
ð	then
s	soon
z	zero
ʃ	ship
ʒ	pleasure
h	hot
x	loch
tʃ	cheer
dʒ	jump
m	sum
n	sun
ŋ	sung
w	wet
l	let
r	red
j	yet

Vowels		
	Symbol	Keywords
short	ɪ	bit
	e	bed
	æ	cat
	ɒ	dog (BrE)
	ʌ	but
	ʊ	put
	ə	about
	i	happy
	u	actuality
long	i:	sheep
	ɑ:	father
	ɒ:	dog (AmE)
	ɔ:	four
	u:	boot
	ɜ:	bird
diph-thongs	eɪ	make
	aɪ	lie
	ɔɪ	boy
	əʊ	note (BrE)
	oʊ	note(AmE)
	aʊ	now
	ɪə	real
	eə	hair (BrE)
	ʊə	sure (BrE)
	uə	actual
	iə	peculiar

A Read the words on the left and train the consonants and the vowels.

B Now get dictionaries from the school library and try to find out how you spell these words correctly:
1. domestic
2. bursar
3. apron
4. recipe
5. alternative

C Look at the balloon. The signs there are **RP**. Can you read what the policeman says?

Special signs
ı| separates British and American pronunciations, British on the left, American on the right
/'/ shows main stress
/ˌ/ shows secondary stress
. divides syllables

Spelling Rules and Other Irregularities

Look for the following words. The dictionary may inform you about spelling and other irregularities.

1. one fly, two ???
2. You pay today, he ??? yesterday.
3. acceptable, ???-ly
4. information, plural ???
5. one box, two ???
6. one cactus, two ???
7. four, fourteen, 40 = ???

Finding out the Type of Word or Word Class

The words in the dictionary are sometimes followed by abbreviations like adj, adv, conj, n, prep, v. What do those abbreviations mean? Can you make a list of the abbreviations and the meanings? The abbreviation can be important for the meaning of a word. Try to translate the following words, **but be careful and look at the word class or you will make mistakes!**

1. fast, adj
2. fast, v
3. fast, n
4. open, adj
5. open, v
6. open, n
7. saw, v (from see)
8. saw, n
9. saw, v

Finding out the Right Meaning of a Word

If you look up a word you do not understand, the dictionary can give you

- one or more definitions behind the word,
- example sentences in which the word is used in a context,
- pictures.

There may be new words which you do not understand either. Don't worry: If you learn vocabularies on a regular basis, you will get better day by day. Now try to find the German meanings of these words:

1. ladle, n (soup)
2. mustard, n (spice)
3. spice, v (food)
4. whisk, n (cream)
5. iron, v (clothes)
6. iron, n (for clothes)
7. sheet, n (bed)

Finding out the Right Preposition

Sometimes we cannot just translate the German preposition into English. Verbs, nouns or adjectives may take **other** prepositions in English. Your dictionary informs you about the right preposition. Try to find the right propositions in the following text.

Mary has always been fond …[1] Jack. She was interested …[2] getting to know him since she first met him …[3] school. When school was over, she was looking …[4] to seeing him the next day. He felt a great admiration …[5] her as well. They fell in love …[6] each other and she soon longed …[7] spend the rest of her life …[8] him. When they left school, he finally popped the question and she said "Yes, I will." Now she is married …[9] him and they are happy ever after.

Finding Other Types of Words (Word Classes)

It can happen that you know the verb and look for the noun or the adjective. This is not that easy:

Example:
You *invest* money in a project and this is an ??? (*invest**ment***, n). Did you know that? Well, if you didn't, here the dictionary can help you as well. Can you find the right words?

1. employ, v (n = ?)
2. cook, n (v = ?)
3. ladle, n (v = ?)
4. contraceptive, n (adj = ?)
5. spice, v (n = ?)
6. duster, n (v = ?)
7. automatic, adj (adv = ?)

Preparing a Quiz

… is team work!

Would you like to prepare a quiz? In English? That would even be more fun. Well, what do you need for this?

Preparations

Before you can have an interesting quiz, you need…

- prizes,
- lots of questions on different subjects,
- material to make the questions more interesting for everybody,
- rules to say
  - what is allowed,
  - what is forbidden,
  - how you can score points,
- things with which you can measure points,
- funny games which the candidates must play if they do not know the right answer.

Form teams to prepare the quiz.

Prizes

- You could collect some money and buy something.
- You could prepare things in your cooking lessons: cakes, tarts, cookies, pots of jam or make other things yourselves.
- You could look for sponsors.

Questions on Different Subjects

It may be difficult to choose subjects you have not talked about in your English lessons. It could be fun to think about subjects presented in this book. Examples:

- kitchen tools
- furniture
- types of homes
- food and spices
- jobs
- computer items
- cosmetics

but there can also be

- general knowledge (capital of France?)

Material

You can ask questions or just show things ("What is this?") or you can use pictures, charts or maps.

Rules

The quiz will be boring if someone takes a long time for thinking. You could have rules like:

- the fastest team wins
- there is a time limit (not more than 30 seconds for answering)
- wrong answers mean that the other groups get one point
- Decide: Are candidates allowed to speak German? What if they do?
- Decide: Are candidates allowed to use their hands and feet for explaining?
- What if someone else helps?

Things for Measuring Points

Everybody wants to see at any time how many points the teams have scored already and how much time is left to answer the question. You could

- prepare number boards,
- write on the blackboard,
- use score cards (from gym hall?),
- use a large stopwatch, if available.

Funny Games If Candidates Cannot Answer

Use your fantasy!

When everything has been prepared, form teams and select a quizmaster and an assistant. Make sure that the team members did not develop the questions they are being asked themselves!

Talking Game

Talking Game

This game is an exercise in talking to people and using the English language by speaking as much as possible.
Two students form a team, one student is partner A, the other is partner B. Partner A reads his own part A out loud, while partner B looks up his B-part on page 159.
Together they answer the questions and work on the exercise given in the game.

Partner A

Game 1A
(partner B takes Game 1B)

On the Phone
Who is that speaking, please? – This is …
Dictate these names to partner B.
1. Carol
2. Mary
3. Jason
4. Jim
5. Maureen
6. Laura

Sometimes it is hard to understand people's surnames and write them correctly.
In that case you may ask: "How do you spell that, please?"
Dictate the following surnames to partner B. Spell the names if he or she asks you to do so.
→ For spelling, refer to page 165
1. Hartnett
2. Kelly
3. Gordon
4. Meyrick
5. Pembroke
6. Crown
7. Brown
8. Marsh

Now write down what partner A dictates you. If you do not know how to write the name or surname, you can ask him or her to spell it.

Game 2A
(partner B takes Game 2B)

Asking for Information about People
You need some information about these people – ask partner B to give it to you. Do that in full sentences.

- Stephen Miller:
  a) age?
  b) job?
  c) hobbies?
  d) address?
  e) phone number?
  f) e-mail address?
- Sara Celtenham:
  a) age?
  b) job?
  c) hobbies?
  d) address?
  e) phone number?
  f) e-mail address?
- Jodie Baker:
  a) age?
  b) school she goes to?
  c) future plans?
  d) part-time job?
  e) wage?

Now partner B asks you to give him/her information about the following people. Always answer in full sentences.

- Jack Smart:
  a) 22,
  b) cook,
  c) go-cart racing, chess, cinema,
  d) 14 Cheltenham Road, Norwich
  e) 832770,
  f) smart.jack@att.uk (@ = at) (. = dot)
- Liz Hornsby:
  a) 19,
  b) hotel clerk,
  c) riding, parties, books,
  d) 27 St David's Road, Bristol,
  e) 7321113
  f) none
- Use the information of yourself/ of a friend/of someone you know.

Talking Game

Game 3A
(partner B takes Game 3B)

Where Is My Recipe?
You want to make an apple crumble, but you forgot some of the ingredients and how much you need of them. You phone partner B and ask him to get the missing information. And how exactly do you have to prepare it?

Ingredients
?? g apples

?? g soft brown sugar
1/2 teaspoon of ??? (spice)
?? of orange juice

For the Crumble
?? plain flour
50g ???
75 g ???
(which is sugar, which is butter?)
a pinch or a pint (??) of salt

Cook the apples in a ??? with ??? until ???. Spread the crumble out with a ??? but do not press it down.
Bake the crumble for about ??? to ??? minutes. It will be ready when ???. The oven setting should be ??? °C, gas mark ???. Serve the crumble with ??? or ???. Now partner B rings you up. He does not exactly remember what he needs for "Pumpkin Gnocchi", the meal you brought home with you from your last holidays in Italy. Of course, now you can help him.

Ingredients
1 kg pumpkins
200 g flour
1 egg
crushed nutmeg
1 pinch of salt

For the Sauce
700 g chopped tomatoes
1 chopped onion
6 chopped basil leaves
olive oil
a pinch of salt

Peel the pumpkin, prepare the dough.
Cut it into pieces and bake it at 160 to 180 °C for 40 minutes.
Fry the onions briefly in 2 tablespoons of oil, add the tomatoes and cook for 30 minutes. Oven setting: medium. Stir while cooking. Pass through a sieve and bring it to boil again.
Add the sauce and the basil shortly before you serve the dish.

Game 4A
(partner B takes Game 4B)

Going for an Interview
You have read an advertisement that a hotel is looking for a trainee cook. Now you phone the hotel (partner B) and want to know more about the job:

- job?
- working hours?
- working time?
- shift work?
- working days per week?
- weekends off?
- pay?
- college?
- holidays?
- clothing?
- time of training?
- promotion prospects?

Now your old people's home is offering a job for a trainee old people's nurse. You are interviewing a young woman who has some questions on the job. Please give her the information she wants.

- Job: helping old people to get along with their problems

Examples:
- *bring them their breakfast every morning*
- *tidy up their rooms*
- *give them the medicine the doctor prescribed …*
- working hours: from 7 a.m. to 4 p.m.

Talking Game

- night shift: yes, once a week, from 7 p.m. to 7 a.m.
- days off: 1 day per week
- work at weekends: once a month
- pay: £80 per week for a start, later up to £120 per week at end of training
- holidays: 24 working days per year
- college: once a week, on Tuesdays
- length of training: 3 1/2 years

Game 5A
(partner B takes Game 5B)

A Survey of a Market Research Institute
You (partner A) are working for a Market Research institute. The management of a department store want to get more information about their customers. So you ask the people (partner B) after they leave the store.

You want to find out:
- what the customer bought,
- how old she is,
- if she remembers what items she can buy in this store,
- what she thinks about the information she can get in this store,
- if the shop assistants are friendly and helpful,
- the reason why she can go shopping in the morning.

Now you are interviewed by partner B. Here are your details - tell the interviewer that ...
- it took some time until you found what you were looking for,
- you go there perhaps once or twice a month,
- you think it's quite agreeable; your suggestion: a larger variety of clothes for young people,
- as to the special offers, yes;
- it took you some 30 minutes to find what you were looking for,
- the shop assistant helped you quite a lot and gave you some good advice.

Game 6A
(partner B takes Game 6B)

Buying Electrical Household Equipment
You have the technical information about a washing machine. Your partner has also got some information about another washing machine. Try to find out which of the two machines is better, can hold more washing, is more economical etc.

Ask your partner for his technical data and then form sentences like: *"My washing machine needs less electricity than yours."* You can use adjectives like: *much, easy to handle, wide, high, long, economic, little, slow, fast.*

This list of adjectives is neither complete nor in the right order!

Super Wash 2000	
amount of washing	5 kg
control	fully automatic
spin drier speeds	400 to 1800 rpm
Consumption Data at 60 °C	
water	39 litres
power consumption	0.89 kWh
washing programmes	3
dimensions (height, width, length)	85 by 60 by 60 cm
price	£299.-

Discuss which washing machine you would prefer to buy.

You also want to buy a freezer. You have collected the technical data about the "Eco-Arctic Super" and partner B has collected information about the "Freezer Freak 2001 S". Ask each other for the technical data, then form sentences and compare the freezers.

Talking Game

Eco-Arctic Super	
capacity	176 litres
control	fully electronic
warning	acoustic door and temperature alert
power consumption	208 kWh per year
defrosting	not mentioned in brochure
dimensions (height by width by length)	126 by 65.5 by 65cm
price	£495.–

Game 7A (partner B takes Game 7B)

Getting and Giving Information about a Flat

You are a flat hunter. Phone a landlord (partner B) and try to get more information about the flat he advertised in the newspaper. Please speak in full sentences or the landlord will not give you the flat!

- carpets on the floor?
- get ground plan of the flat?
- see the flat?
- type of heating?
- extra rooms like cellar or attic?
- telephone outlet?
- place for drying washed clothes?
- next bus stop?
- shopping facilities near?

Now you are the one who offers a flat and you have to answer questions on the phone. These are the answers:

- there is a hall, a bedroom, a living-room, a bathroom, a kitchen and a balcony
- kitchen and the bathroom: tiled; all the other rooms: stripped floor
- any time, give me a ring before you come
- £250 pcm
- no, extra costs for heating
- former lodger: £30 per month
- washing machine, dishwasher: just call a plumber; telephone: yes
- parking space: right in front of the house (if lucky)
- shopping centre: five minutes by bus

Game 8A (partner B takes Game 8B)

Getting an Idea of Computer Devices

Give a definition of a computer device to your partner. Partner B has a list of words which match your definitions, but they are not in the correct order. Decide if he gave you the wrong or the right term. You could say: "Yes, I think that's right" or "No, I think it's a …"

- I need this for drawing something on the monitor.
- This is used for getting pictures into the computer.
- … a device for storing information on it and carrying it with you
- … for storing large programmes
- … surf … the Internet
- … type … letters
- … watch … input data
- … calculate nutritional values
- … design kitchens

Now you would like to know what the following things are for. Ask partner B for his information. He has a list of explanations which are not in the correct order, however. So do not believe everything he tells you!

- … What is a mouse (for)?
- … a DSL modem … ?
- … a printer … ?
- … a text processing programme … ?
- … a DVD … ?
- … a file directory?
- … multi-tasking?
- … a layout?
- … a preview?

Talking Game

Game 9A
(partner B takes Game 9B)

Reported Speech Memory Game
Read the following sentences out loud to partner B. For the first one (*"I often go to a beauty farm"*) he must answer: *"You said learning English was great fun."*
When you read your second sentence, he must put your first sentence into reported speech.

Now start reading and give him some time to think.

1. I often go to a beauty farm.
2. I never eat pork.
3. Do you want to give up smoking?
4. You will be happier if you eat carrots.
5. Why do you eat hamburgers?
6. Stop making a fool of me!

Here are sentences that are already in reported speech - now do it the other way around.

1. You said that learning English was great fun.
2. You said you had eaten …
3. You said you couldn't …
4. You asked me if …

Partner B

Game 1B
(partner B takes Game 1A)

On the Phone
Who is that speaking, please? - This is …
Write down what partner A dictates you.
Then you dictate these names to your partner.

1. Liz
2. Sue
3. Michael
4. Peter
5. Jean
6. Samantha

Sometimes it is hard to understand people's surnames and write them correctly.
In that case you may ask: "How do you spell that, please?"

Write down what partner A dictates. If you do not know how to write the name or surname, you ask him or her to spell it.
Now dictate the following surnames to partner B. Spell the names if he or she asks you to do so.
→ For spelling, refer to page 165.

1. Parker
2. Hewlett Packard
3. Lewis
4. Marleybone
5. Banks
6. Studebaker
7. Joyce
8. Yeats

Game 2B
(partner B takes Game 2A)

Asking for Information about People
Your English friend rings you and needs some information about these three people. Please help him/her, but you must answer in full sentences.

- Stephen Miller:
  a) 24
  b) baker
  c) skating, hockey, judo
  d) 18 Bardwell Square, Stratford on Avon
  e) 2214731
  f) Steph.Miller@iol.uk (@ = at)
- Sara Celtenham:
  a) 29
  b) domestic bursar
  c) tayloring, shopping, mountain climbing
  d) 49 Butcher's Lane, Liverpool
  e) 8877794
  f) Celtysar.ham@att.uk

Talking Game

- Jodie Baker:
  a) 16
  b) Brunel College
  c) old people's nurse
  d) babysitting
  e) £2 per hour

Now you need some information about three other people. Ask partner B to give it to you. Do that in full sentences.

- Jack Smart:
  a) age?
  b) job?
  c) hobbies?
  d) address?
  e) phone number?
  f) e-mail address?
- Liz Hornsby:
  a) age?
  b) job?
  c) hobbies?
  d) address?
  e) phone number?
  f) e-mail address?
- Ask for partner A's own data or for A's friend or for someone he/she knows.

Game 3B
(partner A takes Game 3A)

Where Is My Recipe?
Your friend (partner A) phones you. She wants to make an apple crumble, but she has lost the recipe. Of course, you can help her.

Ingredients
900 g apples
50 g soft brown sugar
1/2 teaspoon of ground cinnamon (spice)
2 tablespoons of orange juice

For the Crumble
175 g plain flour
50g sugar
75 g butter
(which is sugar, which is butter?)
a pinch of salt (or do you want to kill your guests?)

Cook the apples in a saucepan with the orange juice, cinnamon and brown sugar until soft.

Spread the crumble out with a fork but do not press it down.

Bake the crumble for about 20 to 30 minutes. It will be ready when the top has browned a bit. The oven setting should be 200 °C, gas mark 6.

Serve the crumble with hot custard or ice cream.

When you visited partner A last time, she had brought a new recipe from Italy – "Pumpkin Gnocchi". You do not exactly remember what you need for making pumpkin gnocchi. Parts of the paper on which you wrote the recipe are now unreadable. So you phone her to get the missing information.

Ingredients
?? kg pumpkins
?? g flour
1 ???
crushed ???
1 pinch of ???

For the Sauce
?? g chopped tomatoes
1 chopped ???
6 chopped ???
olive ???
??? salt

Peel the pumpkin, prepare the dough. Cut it into pieces and bake it at ??? °C for ??? minutes.

Fry the onions briefly in 2 tablespoons of oil, add the tomatoes and cook them for ??? minutes. Oven setting: ??? Stir while cooking. Pass through a sieve and bring it to boil again.

Add the sauce and the basil (when?).

Talking Game

Game 4B
(partner A takes Game 4A)

Going for an Interview
You have published an advertisement saying that your hotel is looking for a trainee cook. Now a young man/woman is sitting in front of you and wants to know more about the job. Please answer his/her questions.

- job: helping to prepare the various meals in the hotel kitchen
- working hours: 8 hours per day, 40 hours per week
- working time:
- two shifts: morning shift - 6 a.m. to 2 p.m., late shift - 6 p.m. to 2 a.m.
- working days per week: 5 days
- weekends off: every other weekend
- pay: £100 per week for a start, later up to £150 per week at end of training
- college: once a week, on Wednesdays
- holidays: 4 weeks per year
- clothing: provided by the hotel
- time of training: 3 to 5 years
- promotion prospects: junior cook usually after three years, it depends on how well you are doing

Now you are looking for an apprenticeship as a trainee old people's nurse. In an interview, you ask them (partner A) some questions about the job. Remember that someone who has no questions may be seen as an idiot …

- job?
- examples?
- working hours?
- night shift?
- free days?
- work at weekends?
- pay?
- holidays?
- college? How often?
- length of training?

Game 5B
(partner A takes Game 5A)

A Survey of a Market Research Institute
When you (partner B) leave a department store, an interviewer (partner A) wants to ask you some questions. You are friendly and answer them, as you can win "half a washing machine or something." This is what you can answer - but in full sentences!

- you found a pullover, a T-shirt and a pair of socks,
- you are ??? years old,
- they mainly sell clothes, toys, books, household equipment and food,
- some shop assistants: no idea; others: informed quite well,
- some shop assistants seem to prefer chatting to helping customers; they kill you with looks when you ask questions,
- you work the night shift this week.

Now you interview partner A. Promise him that he can win a long distance flight from Heathrow to Gatwick.

Try to find out:
- if he found what he was looking for,
- how often he goes shopping in this department store,
- what he thinks about the offers in this store,
- if he thinks the prices are okay,
- if he had problems to find what he was looking for,
- how good the advice was which the shop assistants gave him.

Talking Game

Game 6B
(partner A takes Game 6A)

Buying Electrical Household Equipment
You have some technical information about a washing machine. Your partner has also got some information about another washing machine. Try to find out which of the machines is better, can hold more washing, is more economical etc.

Ask your partner for his technical data and then form sentences like: "*My washing machine needs less electricity than yours.*"

You can use adjectives like: *much, easy to handle, wide, high, long, economic, little, slow, fast.*

This list of adjectives is neither complete nor in the right order!

Cleaning Mate 2020 de Luxe	
amount of washing	4,5 kg
control	half automatic
spin drier speeds	600 to 1500 rpm
Consumption Data at 60 °C	
water	49 litres
power consumption	0.95 kWh
washing programmes	4
dimensions (height, width, length)	85 by 60 by 60 cm
price	£286.-

Discuss which washing machine you would prefer to buy.

You also want to buy a freezer. You have collected the technical data about the "Freezer Freak 2001 S" and partner A has collected information about the "Eco-Arctic Super". Ask for the technical data, then form sentences and compare the freezers.

Freezer Freak 2001 S	
capacity	225 litres
control	fully electronic
warning	acoustic door and temperature alert
power consumption	329 kWh per year
defrosting	quick defroster system
dimensions (height by width by length)	155 by 66 by 66 cm
price	£595.-

Game 7B
(partner A takes Game 7A)

Getting and Giving Information about a Flat
You are a landlord who offers a flat. Someone phones you (partner A) and wants to know more about the flat. You give him the information he needs. Since you want him to come and rent the flat, be friendly and answer in full sentences!
These are the answers to his questions:

- in the bedroom and in the living room; lino in the hall, tiled floors in kitchen and bathroom
- come and measure yourself
- tomorrow afternoon?
- gas central heating
- a 2-square metre partition in the cellar
- no problem!
- small place in the attic, buy a drier
- just round the corner
- a five-minute walk to a supermarket

Talking Game

Now you are a flathunter yourself and you ask the landlord questions about a flat you are interested in:

- number of rooms?
- type of floor covering in the rooms?
- see the flat? when?
- rent - how high?
- rent exclusive or inclusive of heating charges?
- heating costs on the average?
- outlets for washing machine, dishwasher, telephone?
- parking space - where?
- shopping facilities near?

Game 8B
(partner A takes Game 8A)

Getting an Idea of Computer Devices
Partner A gives you a definition of a computer device. You have a list of words that go with the definitions, but the list is not in the correct order. Find the terms which match his definitions.

1. I think that is … a spread-sheet programme
2. … a hard disk or a DVD
3. … a flatbed scanner
4. … a mouse
5. … a monitor or flat screen
6. … a drawing programme
7. … a keyboard
8. … a DSL modem
9. … a USB flash drive

Partner A has heard some computer terms which he doesn't understand. He wants to know what they mean. Make sure that you are the expert who can explain. Here is a list of explanations, which is not in the correct order, however.

1. It's for getting your work on a sheet of paper.
2. … something you can see before you infix it into your file
3. … kind of a "bookcase" in which you for example store letters of the same type
4. … for large programmes which you can buy in computer shops
5. … an operation modus in which you can quickly change from one programme to another
6. … how you arrange text and pictures
7. … it connects your computer to the Internet
8. write … letters and design … a nicer layout
9. … for moving the cursor more quickly

Game 9B
(partner A takes Game 9A)

Reported Speech Memory Game
What did partner A say? For the first statement, you answer: "You said learning English was great fun."

When partner A gives you his second statement, you report what he said in his first sentence etc.

1. You said that learning English was great fun.
2. You said you often …
3. You said you never …
4. You asked me if …

Now do it the other way around.

1. I ate two rolls this morning.
2. I simply cannot reduce my weight.
3. Have you ever eaten fat bacon?
4. All my friends are too fat.
5. When did you eat your last bar of chocolate?
6. Start thinking!

Present Progressive (Verlaufsform der Gegenwart)

Aussagen und Verneinungen			
I	am		
He/She/It	is	(not)	baking a cake.
We/You/They	are		

Die Verlaufsform der Gegenwart wird immer mit einer von Form von *to be* gebildet. An das Verb wird ein *-ing* angehängt.

Die Verlaufsform wird immer dann gewählt, wenn eine Handlung noch im Verlauf ist, d.h. zum Zeitpunkt des Sprechens noch nicht abgeschlossen ist. – *I am preparing the meal.* Die Verlaufsform wird ebenfalls angewendet, wenn eine Handlung vorübergehend ist, aber nicht unbedingt zum Zeitpunkt des Sprechens stattfindet. – *I am working in an ice-cream parlour this week.*
Signalwörter: *at the moment, (just) now, look*
Verneinte Sätze werden gebildet, indem an die Form von *to be* ein *not* angehängt wird.

Ja-/Nein-Fragen			Kurzantworten	
Am	I		Yes, I am	No, I am not.
Are	you	baking a cake.	Yes, you are.	No, you are not.
Is	he/she/it		Yes, he/she/it is.	No, he/she/it is not.
Are	we/you/they		Yes, we/you/they are.	No,we/you/they are not.

Um Fragen zu bilden, wird die jeweilige Form *am/is/are* mit dem Subjekt getauscht.
In der Kurzantwort wird jeweils die Form von *to be* aus der Fragestellung wiederholt.

Simple Present (Einfache Gegenwart)

Aussagen			Verneinungen		
I/You	walk		I/You	do not (don't)	
He/She/It	walks	home.	He/She/It	does not (doesn't)	walk home.
We/You/They	walk		We/You/They	do not (don't)	

Das Simple Present drückt aus, dass etwas regelmäßig geschieht bzw. regelmäßig nicht geschieht: *I go to school; I don't work at home;* etc.
Tatsachen werden ebenfalls in Simple Present ausgedrückt: *Peter lives in London*.
Diese Zeit wird auch verwendet, um auszudrücken, welchen Beruf, welches Hobby oder welche Fähigkeit jemand hat.
In den Aussagesätzen wird das Verb nicht verändert; bei *he/she* und *it* wird jedoch ein *-s* (*walks*) bzw. *-es* (*goes*) angefügt. Endet das Verb mit *o, s, sh, ch, x*, wird *-es* angehängt. (Regel: *He, she, it* → s muss mit.)
Signalwörter: *always, usually, sometimes, never* etc.
Verneinte Sätze werden mit *do not/don't* bzw. *does not/doesn't* gebildet. Das Verb wird nicht verändert.

Ja-/Nein-Fragen		Kurzantworten	
Do	I live in London?	Yes, I do.	No, I don't.
	you live in London?	Yes, you do.	No, you don't.
Does	he/she/it live in London?	Yes, he/she/it does.	No, he/she/it doesn't.
Do	we/you/they live in London?	Yes, we/you/they do.	No,we/you/they don't.

Bei Ja-/Nein-Fragen wird *do* (bzw. *does* bei *he/she/it*) an den Satzanfang gestellt.
Die höfliche Antwort sollte niemals nur 'yes' oder 'no' lauten. Es muss stets heißen: *Yes, I do* bzw. *No, I don't*.

Der Gebrauch von "to do"

Wann wird *to do* verwendet?

- bei Verneinungen – *I don't like Peter.*
- bei Fragen – *Do you live in London?*

Do/does erscheint nur im Simple Present bzw als *did* im Past Tense.

- *Does Peter like you?*
- *Did you go to school yesterday?*

Ausnahmen:

- *To do* erscheint nicht in Fragesätzen, wenn eine Form von *to be* vorhanden ist.
  - *Are you at home?*
  - *Why is he so late?*
- *To do* wird nicht verwendet, wenn bereits ein Hilfsverb wie *can, must, may, will, shall* vorhanden ist.
  - *Can I come home later? No, you can't.*
  - *Must I really stay at home tonight? Yes, you must.*
- To do wird ebenfalls nicht verwendet, wenn nach dem Subjekt gefragt wird (wer oder was?).
  - *Who stays at home? Peter.*

Simple Past (Einfache Vergangenheit)

Bei regelmäßigen Verben wird ein *-ed* an das Verb gehängt (open → open**ed**)
Bei unregelmäßigen Verben wird die zweite Verbform benutzt (break → **broke**)
(→ Vgl. Liste der unregelmäßigen Verben auf Seite 164 f.)

Aussagen		
I/You/ He/She/It/ We/You/They	**opened**	a bottle.
I/You/ He/She/It/ We/You/They	**broke**	a plate.

Verneinungen werden mit *did not/didn't* gebildet. Das nachfolgende Verb erscheint daraufhin wieder in der Grundform.
Das Simple Past wird gebraucht, um auszudrücken, dass eine Handlung völlig abgeschlossen ist.
Signalwörter: last year, last month, two weeks ago, in 2010 etc.

Verneinungen		
I/You/ He/She/ It/ We/You/They	**did** not (didn't) **open**	a bottle.
I/You/ He/She/ It/ We/You/They	**did** not (didn't) **break**	a plate.

Achtung: An *he/she/it* wird im Simple Past kein -s angehängt!

Ja-/Nein-Fragen				**Kurzantworten**
Did	I/you/he/she/it	**open**	a bottle?	Yes, I did. No I didn't
	we/you/they			
	I/you/ he/she/it	**break**	a plate?	Yes, we did. No we didn't
	we/you/they			

Bei Ja-/Nein-Fragen wird *did* an den Satzanfang gestellt.
Die Antwort lautet: *Yes, I did* oder *No, I didn't*.
Handelt es sich um Informationsfragen (when, why, were, how often etc.) wird das jeweilige Fragewort an den Anfang des Satzes gestellt: *When did you break the plate?*
Die Verwendung von *did* entspricht den Regeln der Verwendung von *do* bzw. *does*.

Past Progressive (Verlaufsform der Vergangenheit)

Aussagen und Verneinungen				
I	**was** (wasn't)	frying	meatballs	at that time.
You	**were** (weren't)			
He/She/It	**was** (wasn't)			
We/You/They	**were** (weren't)			

Das Past Progressive wird mit der zweiten Form von *to be* (= *was/were*) bzw. bei der Verneinung mit *wasn't/weren't* gebildet. An das Verb wird ein *-ing* angehängt.

Past Progressive wird immer dann benutzt, wenn es sich um eine Handlung handelt, die in der Vergangenheit im Verlauf war. Das Ergebnis ist unwichtig.

Ja-/Nein-Fragen					Kurzantworten
Was	I he/she/it	frying	meatballs	at that time?	Yes, I was. No I wasn't.
Were	you				Yes, you were. No you weren't.
Were	we/you/they				Yes, we were. No we weren't.

Bei Ja-/Nein-Fragen wird *was* bzw. *were* an den Satzanfang gestellt.

Present Perfect (Das Perfekt)

Aussagen und Verneinungen				
I You	**have**	(not)	**been**	to Ireland yet.
He/She/It	**has**			
We/You/They	**have**			

Das Present Perfect wird mit have (have not) bzw. has (has not) und der dritten Verbform gebildet.
Bei regelmäßigen Verben wird dazu ein -ed an das Verb gehängt. *work* → *worked*
Bei unregelmäßigen Verben wird die dritte Form des Verbs genommen. *go* → *gone*
→ Vgl. hierzu die Liste der unregelmäßigen Verben auf S. 164.

Das Present Perfect wird benutzt, um auszudrücken, dass eine Handlung oder ein Zustand in der Vergangenheit begonnen wurde und nun bis in die Gegenwart oder darüber hinaus andauert oder Auswirkungen auf die Gegenwart hat.
So kann z. B. ein sichtbares Ergebnis vorliegen: *I have painted my fence. Now it is blue.*

Das Present Perfect wird auch verwendet, um auszudrücken, dass sich etwas einmal, mehrmals oder nie <u>bis zum Zeitpunkt des Sprechens</u> ereignet hat: *I haven't been to Ireland yet.*
Signalwörter: so far, up to now

Ja-/Nein-Fragen				Kurzantworten	
Have	I you	worked	on the projekt?	Yes, I have. Yes, you have.	No, I haven't. No, you haven't.
Has	he/she/it			Yes, he/she/it has.	No, he/she/it hasn't.
Have	we/you/they			Yes, we/you/they have.	No, we/you/they haven't.

Past Perfect (Vollendete Vergangenheit)

Past Perfect					Past Tense		
After	I/you				I/you		
	he/she/it	**had**	**seen**	the accident	he/she/it	**called**	the police.
	we/you/they				we/you/they		

Das Past Perfect wird mit had (*had not/hadn't*) und der dritten Form des Verbs gebildet.

Das Past Perfect wird verwendet, um auszudrücken, dass zwei Handlungen aufeinander folgen. Beide haben in der Vergangenheit stattgefunden.
Die zeitlich weiter zurückliegende Handlungen wird in Past Perfect ausgedrückt:
After I ***had seen*** …. (= erste Handlung)
Die darauf folgende Handlung wird in Past Tense ausgedrückt: … *I* ***called*** *the police.*
(= zweite Handlung)
Signalwörter: when, after

Die Anwendung dieser Zeit entspricht dem deutschen Plusquamperfekt.

Future (Zukunft)

Es gibt mehrere Möglichkeiten, zukünftiges Geschehen oder zukünftige Handlungen auszudrücken. Die beiden wichtigsten sind die **Going-To-Future** und die **Will-Future**.

- Going-To-Future

Das Going-To-Future wird mit *am/are/is* + *going to* + der Grundform des Verbs gebildet.

Aussagen und Verneinungen				
I	am	going to	see	the doctor.
You	are			
He/She/It	is			
We/You/They	are			

Das Going-To-Future wird dann verwendet, wenn man etwas in naher Zukunft geplant hat oder es zu tun beabsichtigt (bzw. es nicht zu tun beabsichtigt):
I ***am*** *(not)* ***going*** *to tell you what I know.*

Das Going-To-Future wird ferner bei einem wahrscheinlich eintretenden zukünftigem Ereignis benutzt – wenn man es bereits vorhersehen oder erahnen kann:
The chair ***is going to*** *break if you don't stop moving on it.*

- Will-Future

Das Will-Future wird mit *will* (*will not/won't*) + der Grundform des Verbs gebildet.

Aussagen und Verneinungen			
I/You	will	see	the doctor.
He/She/It			
We/You/They			

Das Will-Future wird verwendet, um einen spontanen Entschluss zum Ausdruck zu bringen:
You are not able to do your homework? I ***will help*** *you.*

Das Will-Future wird ferner verwendet, um ein künftiges Geschehen auszudrücken, das der Sprecher nicht beeinflussen oder nicht klar vorhersehen kann: *What* ***will*** *the world* ***be*** *like when I'm 64?*

Das Will-Future wird auch verwendet, um eine Vermutung über ein zukünftiges Ereignis auszudrücken:
I'm sure you ***will be*** *able to understand these explanations.*

Die Verwendung der Simple-Form und der Progressive-Form bei verschiedenen Verbgruppen

Jedes Verb kann in der Simple-Form verwendet werden. Die meisten Verben können sowohl in der Simple-Form als auch in der Progressive-Form (mit *-ing*-Endung) erscheinen. Das zweite sind vor allem Verben, die Tätigkeiten (z. B. *read, play, sing*) ausdrücken.

Folgende Verben können in der Regel nur in der Simple-Form verwendet werden:
Alle Formen von *to be, have (got), mean, look, seem, sound, need, want, like, dislike, love, hate, agree, doubt, remember, understand*

Verben der Sinneswahrnehmung (z. B. *hear, see, smell, taste, feel*) erscheinen in der Simple-Form: *This soup tastes good.* (= *Sinneswahrnehmung*)

Aber: *Smell, taste* und *feel* können auch Tätigkeitsverben sein und dann in der Progressive-Form erscheinen: *I am tasting the soup.* (= *aktive Handlung*)

Some und Any

Aussagen	Verneinungen	Fragen	Angebote/Bitten
I need **some** bread, butter and **some** tomatoes.	There isn't **any** butter left.	Is there **any** bread left? No, there isn't.	Can I have **some** cheese then, please?
No, you can't. **Somebody** must have eaten all our food, I'm afraid.	I haven't seen **anybody** in this house except you and me.	Can you think of **anybody** who is keen on our food?	No, you can't. But I can offer you **some** peanuts.
I want **something** real to eat!	But there isn't **anything** left!	Why isn't there **anything** to eat in the house?	What about **some** fast food?

Some und *any* können sowohl bei zählbaren (z. B. *tomatoes*) als auch bei nicht zählbaren (z. B. *butter*) Begriffen stehen.
In Fragen und Verneinungen wird *any* verwendet.
Some wird in Aussagesätzen verwendet.
Some erscheint lediglich dann in Fragen, wenn man eine Bitte aussprechen oder etwas anbieten will.
Wie *some* und *any* werden auch die Zusammensetzungen *somebody, something* und *anybody, anything* verwendet.

Personal Pronouns (Personalpronomen)

Bei den Personalpronomen unterscheidet man zwischen Subjektpronomen, Objektpronomen, den besitzanzeigenden Fürwörtern und den rückbezüglichen Fürwörtern.
Pronomen ersetzen ein Hauptwort.

Nach dem Hauptwort wird mit „Wer oder was?" gefragt. Man kann z. B. sagen: *Peter is nice.*
(Peter ist das Hauptwort.)
Man kann ebenfalls sagen: *He is nice.*

Subject Pronouns (Subjektpronomen)			
Einzahl		Mehrzahl	
I	ich	we	wir
you	du	you	ihr
he/she/it	er/sie/es	they	sie

Ein Objekt ist der Satzteil, mit dem beschrieben wird, auf wen oder was eine Handlung oder ein Zustand ausgerichtet ist.
- I like **Peter**. (Wen mag ich?) I like **him**.
oder: I like **my room**. (Was mag ich?) I like **it**.

Object Pronouns (Objektpronomen - direktes Objekt)			
Einzahl		Mehrzahl	
me	mir, mich	us	uns
you	dir, dich	you	euch
him	ihm, ihn	them	sie, ihnen
her	ihr, sie		
it	ihm, es		

Besitzanzeigende Fürwörter geben an, wem oder zu wem etwas gehört.
- This is **my** room. Is this **your** handbag?
Possessive Pronouns I stehen immer zusammen mit einem Hauptwort.

Possessive Pronouns I (besitzanzeigende Fürwörter)			
Einzahl		Mehrzahl	
my	mein	our	unser
yours	dein, Ihr	your	euer, eure
his	sein	their	ihr
hers	ihr		
its	sein		

Possessive Pronouns II stehen anstelle eines Hauptworts.
Man kann z.B. sagen: - This room is my room.
Oder: This room is **mine**.
- Is this handbag your handbag?
Oder: Is this handbag **yours**?

Man verwendet die Possessivpronomen II, wenn man das vorausgegangene Hauptwort nicht noch einmal wiederholen will.

Possessive Pronouns II (Possesivpronomen)			
Einzahl		Mehrzahl	
my	mine	our	ours
yours	yours	your	yours
his	his	their	theirs
hers	hers		
its	its		

Reflexivpronomen werden benutzt, um auf das Subjekt des Satzes zurückzuverweisen.
- She enjoyed herself. (Sie amüsierte sich.)
- The children can take care of themselves.
(Die Kinder können auf sich selbst aufpassen.)

Reflexive Pronouns (rückbezügliche Fürwörter)			
Einzahl		Mehrzahl	
me	myself	we	ourselves
you	yourself	you	yourselves
him	himself	they	themselves
her	herself		
it	itself		

Adjectives (Adjektive - Wiewörter)

Adjektive beschreiben Eigenschaften oder Merkmale. Sie beschreiben, wie etwas ist:
*The **pretty** girl oder The girl is **pretty**.*

Die Steigerung von Adjektiven
Wie Adjektive gesteigert werden, hängt von der Endung und der Silbenzahl des Adjektivs ab. Die beiden Steigerungsstufen heißen Komparativ und Superlativ.

Bei einsilbigen Adjektiven wird *-er/-est* angehängt. Wenn ein einsilbiges Adjektiv auf einen Konsonanten (Mitlaut) endet, wird dieser verdoppelt: *hot - hotter - (the) hottest*

Zweisilbige Adjektive, die auf *-er, -ow, -le, -re* und *-y* enden, werden ebenfalls mit *-er/-est* gesteigert.
Das *-y* wird zu *-i*: *pretty - prett**ier** - (the) prett**iest***

Die meisten Adjektive mit zwei und mehr Silben werden mit *more/most* gesteigert.
Das Adjektiv selbst verändert sich dann nicht: *expensive - **more** expensive - **most** expensive*

	Adjektiv	Komparativ	Superlativ
Einsilbige Adjektive	nice	nicer	(the) nicest
Adjektive, die auf *-y, -er, -ow, -le* oder *-re* enden	pretty	prettier	(the) prettiest
Adjektive mit zwei und mehr Silben	expensive	more expensive	(the) most expensive
Unregelmäßige Adjektive	good	better	(the) best
	bad	worse	(the) worst
	much/a lot of/some/many	more	(the) most
	far	further	(the) furthest

Vergleiche von Dingen oder Personen
Vergleiche können mit *-er/more … than* oder (*not*) *as … as* gebildet werden:
I am taller ***than*** *Peter but I am* ***not as tall as*** *Fred.*
Butter is ***more*** *expensive* ***than*** *milk.*
Cheese is ***as*** *expensive* ***as*** *butter.*

Adverbs (Adverbien – Umstandswörter)

Adverbien beschreiben, unter welchen Umständen etwas geschieht oder nicht geschieht. Die wichtigsten sind die Häufigkeitsadverbien und die Adverbien der Art und Weise.
Adverb (lat.): dem Verb hinzugefügt

- **Adverbs of Frequency (Häufigkeitsadverbien)**

Häufigkeitsabverbien sind z. B. *always, usually, regularly, seldom, never*

Achtung: Im Gegensatz zum Deutschen stehen die Häufigkeitsadverbien vor dem Vollverb.
Deutsch: *Ich trinke immer Kaffee.* (↑ Verb ↑ Adverb) Englisch: *I always drink coffee.* (↑ Adverb ↑ Verb)

Aber: Bei den Formen von *to be* stehen diese Adverbien – genauso wie im Deutschen – nach dem Hilfsverb: *Peter is never ill.*

- **Adverbs of Manner (Adverbien der Art und Weise)**

Adverbien der Art und Weise beschreiben beispielsweise Tätigkeiten genauer.
In der Regel werden diese Adverbien durch ein Anhängen von *-ly* an das Adjektiv gebildet:
successful – successfully *quick – quickly*
Endet das Adjektiv bereits auf *-y*, wird *-ily* angehängt: *easy – easily*

Man kann die Art und Weise z. B. wie jemand schreibt durch diese Adverbien genauer umschreiben: *He writes slowly. He writes quickly.*

Keine Regel ohne Ausnahmen!
- Die Adverbien *hard, early* und *fast* sind identisch mit den Adjektiven und werden nicht verändert:
  He is a ***hard*** *worker, he works* ***hard****.*
- Das Adverb von *good* ist *well*: *She writes well.*
- Nach den Verben *be, feel, look* und *seem* folgen keine Adverbien, sondern Adjektive:
  You look good.

Hier wird ein Zustand beschrieben.

The Passive Voice (Das Passiv)

Ein Aktivsatz drückt aus, wer oder was eine Handlung durchführt: *The robot …*, *Caren …* Das Subjekt des Aktivsatzes wird zum Objekt des Passivsatzes.

Aktivsatz		
The robot	**cooks**	the meal.
Caren	**started**	the toaster.
↑ Subjekt		↑ Objekt

Ein Passivsatz hebt die Person oder die Sache hervor, mit der etwas geschieht: *The meal …*, *the toaster …*

Wer oder was die Handlung veranlasst hat, ist oft unbekannt oder uninteressant.

Das Passiv wird mit einer Form von *to be* + der dritten Form des Verbs gebildet.

Passivsatz		
The meal	**is cooked**	by the robot.
The toaster	**was started**	(by Caren).
↑ Subjekt (ehemaliges Objekt)		↑ Objekt (ehemaliges Subjekt)

Reported Speech (Indirekte Rede)

In der indirekten Rede wird einem Dritten erzählt, was jemand gesagt, geschrieben oder gedacht hat.

Direkte Rede	Indirekte Rede
Susan: **I'm** too fat. The boys don't like **me**.	Lisa: Susan thinks that **she** is too fat and that the boys don't like **her**.

- Die Verschiebung der Zeiten

Wenn das einleitende Verb wie im obigen Beispiel im Simple Present steht (thinks), ändern sich die Zeiten in der Umwandlung von der direkten zur indirekten Rede nicht.
In allen anderen Fällen müssen in der indirekten Rede andere Zeiten als in der direkten Rede verwendet werden, vgl. Tabelle:

Direkte Rede		Indirekte Rede
Simple Present I **eat** too much chocolate.	›	Simple Past She said that she **ate** too much chocolate.
Present Progressive Mark **is cooking** a soufflé.	›	Past Progressive Carol told me that Mark **was cooking** a soufflé.
Past Tense We **bought** a pullover.	›	Past Perfect She said that they **had bought** a pullover.
Present Perfect We **have** never **been** to London.	›	Past Perfect We were told that they **had** never **been** to London.
Will-Future I **will train** every day.	›	*Would* + Grundform des Verbs He remarked that he **would train** every day.

- Veränderungen der Personalpronomen

I, you (Singular)	›	he, she
we, you (Plural)	›	they

- Veränderungen der Possessivpronomen

my, your (Singular)	›	his, her
our, your (Plural)	›	their

Relative Pronouns (Relativpronomen)

Mit Relativpronomen werden Relativsätze eingeleitet. Relativsätze haben die Funktion, ein Substantiv näher zu beschreiben.
Die Pronomen *who* oder *that* beziehen sich auf Personen, *which* oder *that* auf Tiere und Dinge.
Im Zweifelsfall ist immer *that* das richtige Relativpronomen.

Personen	Tiere und Dinge
Mark, **who** was ill, had to go to the hospital.	The ambulance, **which** came to Mark's house, took him to the hospital.

Who, which oder *that* können entfallen, wenn sie die Stelle des Objekts im Relativsatz einnehmen: *This is the hospital (that/which) Mark went to yesterday.*
– *This is the hospital Mark went to yesterday.*

If-Clauses Type I (Bedingungssätze Typ I)

If-Sätze des Typs I beschreiben Bedingungen, unter denen etwas sehr wahrscheinlich erfüllt wird oder sehr wahrscheinlich nicht erfüllt wird. Die Eintritts-wahrscheinlichlichkeit des Gesagten liegt bei ca. 80 Prozent.

If-Satz	Hauptsatz
If I **don't sleep** now,	I **will be** tired tomorrow.
If Mark's temperature **falls**,	I **will not call** the doctor.

Im If-Satz steht das Simple Present, im Hauptsatz steht das Will-Future.
Der Hauptsatz kann dem If-Satz auch vorangestellt werden: *I will be tired tomorrow, if I don't sleep now*. Der If-Satz wird vom Hauptsatz durch ein Komma getrennt.

If-Clauses Type II (Bedingungssätze Typ II)

If-Sätze des Typs II beschreiben Bedingungen, unter denen etwas vielleicht eintreten könnte oder auch nicht eintreten könnte. Die Wahrscheinlichkeit, dass dieses geschieht bzw. nicht geschieht liegt bei ca. 20 Prozent.

If-Satz	Hauptsatz
If I **had** a car,	I **would invite** you for a trip
If Gina **passed** her exam,	she **could work** as a student nurse.

Im If-Satz steht das Simple Past – es hat hier aber nichts mit der Vergangenheit zu tun –, im Hauptsatz steht *would, could* oder *might* + Grundform des Verbs.

Achtung: Im If-Satz darf niemals *would* stehen!

If-Clauses Type III (Bedingungssätze Typ III)

If-Sätze des Typs III beschreiben Bedingungen, unter denen etwas hätte eintreten oder auch nicht eintreten können. Dies ist jedoch nicht geschehen. Die Wahrscheinlichkeit des Eintretens liegt nur noch bei 0 Prozent.
→ Er ist nicht zum Konzert gegangen, folglich hat er sie auch nicht getroffen.

If-Satz	Hauptsatz
If I **had been** to the concert,	I **would have** met you
If the bus-driver **had seen** the traffic light,	he **would not have killed** the dog.

Im If-Satz steht das Past Perfect, im Hauptsatz steht *would, could* oder *might* + *have* + die dritte Form des Verbs.

Gerunds: Using Verbs as Nouns (Gerundien: Verben können als Substantive benutzt werden)

Die *ing*-Form eines Verbs kann als Substantiv benutzt werden: *Das Schwimmen …*
Diese Form kann dann sowohl als Subjekt als auch als Objekt des Satzes verwendet werden.

ing-Form als Subjekt	ing-Form als Objekt
Swimming is fun for most people.	Some people don't like swimming.

→ Für Ausnahmen bei der Bildung der *ing*-Form vgl. Seite 170, "Die Verwendung der Simple-Form und der Progressive-Form bei verschiedenen Verbgruppen".

Quantifiers (Mengenangaben)

Many	= viele	much	= viel
a few	= einige wenige	a little	= (ein) wenig
more	= mehr	less	= weniger
fewer	= weniger(e)	more	= mehr
a lot of	= recht viele		

Many people waste much time for earning a little money, but who counts time and money?

Zählbar	Nicht zählbar
Many girls believe cooking is fun.	They believe that there is not **much** work to do.
Only **a few** girls think that it is an awful job.	They think there is only **a little** to do.
There are **more** girls who like cooking.	Women who stay at home earn **less** money than those who go out to work.
There are **fewer** girls who don't like it.	Usually men earn **more** money than women.
A lot of men think to keep a household isn't difficult.	

Must/Have to (müssen)

Sowohl ‚*must*' als auch ‚*have to*' bedeuten *müssen*. Es gibt jedoch Unterschiede in der Bedeutung.

Must
‚*Must*' drückt eine dringende Verpflichtung aus, die a) von einem selbst oder b) von anderen Personen ausgeht, und die man unbedingt einhalten sollte.
Zu a) *I must get my hair cut. / I must see the doctor.* (Verpflichtung, die man sich selbst auflegt, und die man unbedingt einhalten will)
Zu b) *You must go to the Empire State Building when you are in New York.* (dringende Empfehlung, die von anderen Personen ausgeht)

‚*Must not*' bedeutet nicht, dass man etwas nicht muss, sondern dass etwas nicht erlaubt ist.
You must not walk over the grass. (Sie dürfen nicht über den Rasen laufen.)
‚*Must*' bzw. ‚*must not*' wird nur in der Gegenwart (Present Tense) benutzt. In der Vergangenheit (Simple Past) wird aus ‚*must*' – ‚*had to*'.

Have to
‚*Have to*' ist allgemeiner gehalten und weniger dringlich in der Aussage als ‚*must*'. Es handelt sich meistens um Anordnungen oder Anweisungen, die ganz allgemein einzuhalten sind.
When you are in Britain, don't forget that you have to drive on the left.

Bei Fragen wird die Umschreibung mit ‚*do*' gebildet.
Do I have to wear a special cloth for that event?

Grundwortschatz

Diese Liste enthält zirka 750 Grundwörter, die in Living Together als bekannt vorausgesetzt werden. Nicht aufgeführt, jedoch vorausgesetzt sind internationale Wörter (Taxi, Fax, TV usw.) und einige sehr elementare Wörter, wie Pronomen, Zahlen und Tage.

a lot	viel/e, sehr
a. m.	vor 12:00 Uhr mittags
about	über, etwa, circa
above	über, oben, obenstehend
accident	Unfall
address	Adresse
advantage	Vorteil
adventure	Abenteuer
after	nach
afternoon	Nachmittag
again	wieder
against	gegen, an
age	Alter
air	Luft
airport	Flughafen
all	alle
alone	alleine
along	entlang, weiter, vorwärts
also	auch, außerdem
always	immer
America	Amerika
American	Amerikaner/-in, amerikanisch
angry	verärgert
animal	Tier
(to) answer	beantworten, auch als Substantiv: Antwort
any	irgendetwas, irgendwelche
anyone	jemand, jeder
anything	etwas
apple	Apfel
arm	Arm
(to) arrive	ankommen
(to) ask	fragen, bitten
at	in, an, bei, auf, zu … hin
at home	zu Hause
at once	sofort

at the moment	im Augenblick
aunt	Tante
Austria	Österreich
Austrian	Österreicher/-in
autumm, auch: fall	Herbst
away	weg
awful	schrecklich
back	Rücken, auch: zurück
bacon	Schinkenspeck
bad(ly)	schlecht, schlimm
bag	Sack, Packung, Tasche
baker	Bäcker/-in
banana	Banane
bank	Bank, auch: Ufer
bath	Bad, auch: Badewanne
bathroom	Badezimmer
(to) be	sein
(to) be able to	können
(to) be right	Recht haben
beach	Strand
beautiful	schön
because	weil
bed	Bett
bedroom	Schlafzimmer
beef	Rindfleisch
beer	Bier
before	bevor, zuvor
(to) begin	anfangen, beginnen
beginning	Anfang
behind	hinter, hinten
below	unter, unten
between	zwischen
bicycle	Fahrrad
bike	Fahrrad (Kurzform)
bird	Vogel
birthday	Geburtstag
black	schwarz

blood	Blut
boat	Boot, Schiff
body	Körper
book	Buch
both	beide
bottle	Flasche
box	Kästchen
boy	Junge
boyfriend	fester Freund
branch	Ast
bread	Brot
(to) break	brechen, kaputt machen
breakfast	Frühstück
bridge	Brücke
(to) bring	bringen, mitbringen, holen
Britain	Großbritannien
British	britisch
brother	Bruder
brown	braun
(to) build	bauen
bus	(Linien-)Bus
but	aber, sondern, als
butcher	Fleischer/-in
(to) buy	kaufen
by	bis, durch, per, von, an … vorbei
cake	Kuchen, Torte, Gebäckstück
calculator	Taschenrechner
can	können
cannot = can not	nicht können
car	Auto
careful	vorsichtig, sorgfältig
(to) carry	tragen
book	Buch
both	beide
bottle	Flasche
box	Kästchen
boy	Junge

boyfriend	fester Freund
branch	Ast
bread	Brot
(to) break	brechen, kaputt machen
breakfast	Frühstück
bridge	Brücke
(to) bring	bringen, mitbringen, holen
Britain	Großbritannien
British	britisch
brother	Bruder
brown	braun
(to) build	bauen
bus	(Linien-)Bus
but	aber, sondern, als
butcher	Fleischer/-in
(to) buy	kaufen
by	bis, durch, per, von, an ... vorbei
cake	Kuchen, Torte, Gebäckstück
calculator	Taschenrechner
can	können
cannot = can not	nicht können
car	Auto
careful	vorsichtig, sorgfältig
(to) carry	tragen
class	(Schul-)Klasse, Unterricht
classroom	Klassenraum, Klassenzimmer
clean	sauber
clever	klug
(to) climb	klettern
clock	Uhr
(to) close	schließen
closed	geschlossen
clothes	Kleidung, Kleider
coat	Mantel
coffee	Kaffee
cold	kalt, auch: Erkältung
college	(Berufs-)Fachschule, Fachhochschule, Universität
colour	Farbe

(to) come	kommen
(to) compare	vergleichen
concert	Konzert
(to) continue	fortsetzen
(to) cook	kochen, als Substantiv: Koch/Köchin
corner	Ecke
difference	Unterschied
difficult	schwer, schwierig
dinner	Abendessen
dirty	schmutzig
(to) do	tun, machen
doctor	Arzt, Ärztin
dog	Hund
door	Tür
double	Doppel-...
down	nach unten, hin-/herunter, unten
dress	Kleid
(to) drink	trinken, als Substantiv: Getränk
(to) drive	fahren
driver	Fahrer/-in
during	während
each	jede/r/s
ear	Ohr
early	früh
east	Osten, Ost-, nach Osten
easy (easily)	einfach, leicht
(to) eat	essen, fressen
egg	Ei
emergency	Notfall, Not-
empty	leer
English	englisch
(to) enjoy	genießen
enough	genug
Europe	Europa
European	europäisch, Europäer/-in
evening	Abend
every	jede/r/s
everyone	jede/r/s, alle
everything	alles
everywhere	überall, überallhin
example	Beispiel

(to) excuse	entschuldigen
exercise	Übung
(to) expect	erwarten
expensive	teuer
(to) explain	erklären
eye	Auge
face	Gesicht
factory	Fabrik
false	falsch
family	Familie
family name	Familienname
far	weit
farm	Bauernhof
farmer	Bauer, Bäuerin
fast	schnell
father	Vater
(to) fight	kämpfen
(to) find	finden
finger	Finger
(to) finish	beenden, abschließen
first	erste/r/s
first name	Vorname
fish	Fisch
flat	flach
flat	Wohnung
flight	Flug
floor	Etage, auch: Fußboden
fly	Fliege
(to) fly	fliegen
(to) follow	folgen
food	Essen, Nahrung, Lebensmittel
foot	Fuß
football	Fußball
for	für
(to) forget	vergessen
fork	Gabel
form	Form, Formular, als Verb: bilden
France	Frankreich
free	kostenlos, frei
French	französisch
friend	Freund/-in
from	von, aus

front	Vorderseite, Vorderteil
fruit	Obst, Frucht
full	voll
funny	komisch
furniture	Möbel
future	Zukunft
game	Spiel
garden	Garten
German	deutsch
Germany	Deutschland
(to) get	bekommen, auch: werden
girl	Mädchen
girlfriend	feste Freundin
(to) give	geben, schenken
glad	froh, glücklich
(to) go	gehen, auch: fahren
good	gut
goodbye	auf Wiedersehen
government	Regierung
granddad	Opa
granddaughter	Enkelin
grandfather	Großvater
grandma	Großmama
grandmother	Großmutter
grandparents	Großeltern
great	toll
green	grün
group	Gruppe
(to) grow	wachsen
guest	Gast
guitar	Gitarre
hair	Haar
hairdresser	Friseur/-in
half	Hälfte
ham	Schinken
hand	Hand
happy	glücklich, zufrieden
(to) have	haben
head	Kopf
health	Gesundheit
healthy	gesund
(to) hear	hören

heart	Herz
heavy	schwer
height	Höhe
hello	hallo
help	Hilfe, helfen
here	hier
high	hoch
holiday	Ferien, Urlaub, auch: Feiertag
home	Zuhause
(to) hope	hoffen
horse	Pferd
hospital	Hospital, Krankenhaus
hot	heiß, warm
hotel	Hotel
hour	Stunde
house	Haus
how	wie
how many	wie viele
how much	wie viel
hungry	hungrig
husband	(Ehe-)Mann
ice	Eis
ice-cream	Speiseeis
idea	Idee, Gedanke, Vorstellung
if	wenn, falls
ill	krank
important	wichtig
impossible	unmöglich
in	in, auf, hinein, herein
industry	Industrie
interesting	interessant
into	in … hinein
Italy	Italien
jacket	Jacke, Jackett
job	Arbeit, Aufgabe
joke	Witz, Scherz
just	nur, gerade
key	Schlüssel
(to) kill	töten, umbringen
kilometre	Kilometer
kitchen	Küche
knife	Messer

(to) know	kennen, wissen
label	Aufkleber, Etikett
lamb	Lamm
lamp	Lampe
language	Sprache
large	groß
last	letzte/r/s
late	spät
(to) laugh	lachen
lazy	faul
(to) learn	lernen
(to) leave	abreisen, weggehen, verlassen
left	linke/r/s, links
leg	Bein
lesson	(Schul-)Stunde
(to) let	lassen
letter	Buchstabe, auch: Brief
(to) lie	lügen, auch: liegen
life	Leben
lift	Aufzug
like	wie
(to) like	mögen, gern haben
line	Linie, Zeile
(to) list	auflisten
(to) listen	zuhören
(to) listen to	hören, sich anhören
little	klein, wenig
(to) live	leben, wohnen
long	lang
(to) look	sehen, schauen
(to) look at	sich anschauen
(to) look for	suchen (nach)
(to) lose	verlieren
lot	Menge
loud	laut
(to) love	lieben
low	niedrig
lucky	Glücks-, glücklich
lunch	Mittagessen
mad	verrückt
magazine	Zeitschrift, Magazin

mail	Post
(to) make	tun, machen, bilden
man	Mann
manager	Leiter/-in
many	viele
margarine	Margarine
(to) marry	heiraten
match	Streichholz
may	dürfen, können
maybe	vielleicht
meaning	Bedeutung, Sinn
meat	Fleisch
(to) meet	(sich) treffen, (sich) begegnen
middle	Mitte
mile	Meile
milk	Milch
million	Million
minute	Minute
(to) miss	verpassen, auch: vermissen
mistake	Fehler
moment	Moment
money	Geld
month	Monat
moped	Moped, Mofa
morning	Morgen
mother	Mutter
mountain	Berg
mouth	Mund
(to) move	(sich) bewegen
much	viel
music	Musik
must	müssen
name	Name
nearly	beinahe, fast
necessary	notwendig, nötig
neck	Hals
(to) need	brauchen
neighbour	Nachbar
nervous	nervös
never	nie, niemals
new	neu
newspaper	Zeitung
next	nächste/r/s

nice	schön, nett
night	Nacht
nobody	niemand
noise	Lärm
none	keine/r/s
nonsense	Unsinn
normal	normal, üblich
north	Norden, Nord-
nose	Nase
not	nicht
nothing	nichts
(to) notice	bemerken
now	nun, jetzt
o'clock	(fünf usw.) Uhr
odd	ungerade
of	von
(to) offer	anbieten, Angebot
office	Büro
often	oft, häufig
old	alt
on	auf, an
onion	Zwiebel
only	nur
(to) open	offen, aufmachen
opinion	Meinung
opposite	gegenüber, Gegenteil
or	oder
other	andere/r/s
out	draußen, hinaus, heraus
over	über
(to) own	besitzen
p. m.	nach 12:00 Uhr mittags
page	Seite
(to) paint	streichen, malen
pair	Paar
palace	Palast
pan	Pfanne, Topf
paper	Papier
parent	Elternteil
park	Park
(to) park	parken
part	Teil
party	Party, Fest

passport	(Reise-)Pass
(to) pay	bezahlen
pea	Erbse
peace	Frieden
pen	Füllfederhalter, Kugelschreiber
pence	Pence (ehem. britische Währung)
people	Leute, Menschen
perhaps	vielleicht
person	Mensch, Person
phone	Telefon, als Verb: anrufen
photo	Foto
phrase	Redewendung
piano	Klavier
picture	Bild
piece	Stück, Teil
place	Platz, Ort
plan	Plan, planen, vorhaben
plane	Flugzeug
plate	Teller
(to) play	spielen
please	bitte
(to) please	gefallen
pleased	froh, erfreut
police	Polizei
policeman	Polizist
policewoman	Polizistin
pop music	Popmusik
number	Nummer, Zahl
post	Post
poster	Plakat
postman	Briefträger
postwoman	Briefträgerin
potato	Kartoffel
pound	Pfund (Sterling) (ehem. britische Währung)
present	Geschenk
pretty	hübsch
problem	Problem
(to) produce	herstellen
programme	Programm
progress	Fortschritt
pub	Wirtshaus, Kneipe

pullover	Pullover
pupil	Schüler
(to) put	setzen, stellen, legen
quarter	Viertel
queen	Königin
question	Frage
quick(ly)	schnell
quiet	ruhig
quite	ziemlich
railway	Eisenbahn
rain	Regen, als Verb: regnen
(to) read	lesen
reason	Grund
red	rot
(to) remember	sich erinnern, daran denken
rent	Miete
(to) rent	mieten
(to) repair	reparieren
(to) repeat	wiederholen
rest	Pause
rice	Reis
rich	reich
(to) ride	reiten
right	rechts, auch: richtig
river	Fluss
road	Straße
roll	Brötchen
roof	Dach
room	Zimmer, Raum, Platz
round	rund, um (… herum)
(to) run	laufen, rennen
sad	traurig
safe(ly)	sicher
salad	Salat
sale	Verkauf, Ausverkauf
salt	Salz
same	gleiche/r/s, der-, die-, dasselbe
sandwich	Sandwich
(to) say	sagen

school	Schule
science	Wissenschaft
sea	Meer
season	Jahreszeit
second	zweite/r/s
second	Sekunde
secret	geheim
(to) see	sehen
(to) seem	scheinen
(to) sell	verkaufen
(to) send	senden, schicken
sentence	Satz
serious	ernsthaft
ship	Schiff
shop	Laden, Geschäft
shopping	einkaufen
short	kurz, klein
(to) shout	rufen, schreien
(to) show	zeigen
shower	Dusche
(to) shut	schließen
side	Seite, Rand
sight	Anblick, auch: Sehvermögen
silly	dumm
since	seit
(to) sing	singen
sister	Schwester
(to) sit	sitzen
size	Größe
(to) sleep	schlafen
slow(ly)	langsam
small	klein
(to) smile	lächeln
(to) smoke	rauchen
snow	Schnee
so	also
sofa	Sofa
soft	leise, weich
some	einige, etwas
somebody	jemand
someone	jemand
something	etwas
sometimes	manchmal
son	Sohn

soon	bald
sorry	traurig
south	Süden, Süd-
(to) speak	sprechen, reden
spoon	Löffel
real	echt, wirklich
square	Quadrat
(to) stand	stehen
(to) start	beginnen
station	Bahnhof
(to) stay	bleiben, übernachten
still	immer noch
(to) stop	(an)halten
story	Erzählung, Geschichte
stranger	Fremde, Fremder
street	Straße
strong	stark
student	Student/-in
suddenly	plötzlich
sugar	Zucker
suitcase	Koffer
summer	Sommer
sun	Sonne
supermarket	Supermarkt
sure	sicher, freilich
surname	Nachname
survey	Umfrage
sweets	Süßigkeiten
(to) swim	schwimmen
Switzerland	Schweiz
table	Tisch, Tabelle
(to) take	nehmen, bringen
(to) talk about	sprechen (über)
tall	groß
tax	Steuer
tea	Tee, (frühes) Abendbrot
teacher	Lehrer/-in
telephone	Telefon
television	Fernsehen, Fernseher
(to) tell	sagen, erzählen
temperature	Temperatur
terrible	schrecklich

than	als
(to) thank	danken, sich bedanken
thank you, thanks	danke
that	dies, der, die, das, jene/r/s
then	dann
there	dort, dorthin
there are	es gibt
these	diese
thick	dick
thief	Dieb
thin	dünn
thing	Sache, Ding
(to) think	denken, glauben, meinen
this	dies, diese/r/s
those	jene
through	durch … hindurch, durch
ticket	(Fahr-)Karte, Ticket
time	Zeit, Mal, Uhrzeit
timetable	Fahrplan, Stundenplan
tired	müde
to	zu, nach, in, um zu
today	heute
toe	Zehe
together	zusammen
tomorrow	morgen
tonight	heute Abend
too	zu, auch
town	Stadt
traffic	(Straßen-) Verkehr
train	Zug
tram	Straßenbahn
(to) translate	übersetzen
transport	Vekehrsmittel
(to) travel	reisen
tree	Baum
trouble	Schwierigkeiten
trousers	Hose
true	richtig, wahr
(to) try	probieren, versuchen
tube	U-Bahn

typical	typisch
ugly	hässlich
uncle	Onkel
under	unter
(to) understand	verstehen, begreifen
unhappy	unglücklich
unit	Lektion
until	bis
unusual(ly)	ungewöhnlich
up	oben, nach oben
US(A)	die Vereinigten Staaten (von Amerika)
(to) use	verwenden
usual(ly)	gewöhnlich
vegetable	Gemüse
very	sehr
visit	Besuch, als Verb: besuchen
(to) wait (for)	warten (auf)
waiter	Kellner
waitress	Kellnerin
(to) walk	Spaziergang, (zu Fuß) gehen
wall	Wand, Mauer
(to) want	wollen
warm	warm
(to) wash	(sich) waschen
watch	Armbanduhr
(to) watch	(zu)sehen, beobachten
water	Wasser
way	Weg, Art und Weise
(to) wear	tragen
weather	Wetter
week	Woche
weekend	Wochenende
(to) welcome	willkommen heißen
well	gesund
west	Westen, West-
what	was, welche/r/s
wheel	Rad
when	wenn, als, wann
where	wo, wohin

which	welche/r/s
while	während
white	weiß
who	wer, der, die
whom	wen, wem
why	warum
wife	Ehefrau
(to) win	gewinnen, siegen
wind	Wind, als Verb: spulen
window	Fenster
wine	Wein
winter	Winter
with	mit
without	ohne
woman	Frau
wonderful	wunderbar, wundervoll
word	Wort
work	Arbeit, arbeiten, funktionieren
world	Welt
(to) write	schreiben
wrong	falsch
year	Jahr
yellow	gelb
yesterday	gestern
young	jung
zoo	Zoo

sth. = something s.o. = someone, somebody
AmE = American English BrE = British English

Vokabel	Erstes Vorkommen	Übersetzung
abbreviation	(unit 6)	Abkürzung
ability	(unit 4)	Fähigkeit
(to) abolish	(activity)	abschaffen
absorbency	(unit 3)	Aufnahmefähigkeit
accomodation	(unit 6)	Unterkunft
(to) account	(activity)	klären
acrylic	(unit 3)	Acryl
actor (male), actress (female)	(activity)	Schauspieler/-in
(to) adapt	(unit 9)	anpassen
adjoining	(unit 9)	angrenzend
admiration	(activity)	Bewunderung
(to) admit	(unit 13)	zugeben
advantageous	(unit 6)	nützlich
advice	(unit 4)	Rat
(to) agree	(unit 3)	zustimmen
aim	(activity)	Ziel
algaes	(unit 13)	Algen
almonds	(unit 11)	Mandeln
ambulance	(unit 12)	Notarztwagen
amount of washing	(talking games)	Wäschemenge
anorexia nervosa	(unit 12)	Magersucht
apartment (AmE); flat (BrE)	(unit 6)	Wohnung
(to) apologize	(unit 13)	entschuldigen
appearance	(unit 11)	Aussehen, auch: Auftreten
appendicitis	(unit 12)	Blinddarmentzündung
application	(unit 5)	Bewerbungsschreiben
(to) apply	(activity)	anwenden
appointment	(unit 10)	Verabredung
apprenticeship	(unit 8)	Ausbildung
(to) arrange	(unit 9)	für etwas sorgen
assistance	(unit 9)	Hilfe
assorted	(activity)	verschiedene, eine Auswahl von
at least	(unit 6)	wenigstens
at my expense	(unit 12)	zu meinen Lasten
at once	(unit 12)	sofort
(to) attend	(unit 1)	etwas besuchen, an etwas teilnehmen
attic	(talking games)	Bodenkammer, Dachboden
autism	(unit 9)	Autismus
awful	(unit 4)	furchtbar, entsetzlich
(to) ban	(unit 12)	verbannen
bar	(unit 3)	Strich, Balken
bargain	(unit 3)	Gelegenheitskauf
basil leaves	(talking games)	Basilikumblätter
bath salts	(unit 7)	Badezusatz, Badesalz
(to) be ambitious	(unit 5)	ehrgeizig sein
(to) be awake	(unit 12)	wach sein
(to) be confused	(unit 6)	verwirrt sein
(to) be confused	(unit 1)	verwirrt sein
(to) be curious	(unit 4)	neugierig sein
(to) be disabled	(unit 8)	behindert sein
(to) be disappointed	(unit 4)	enttäuscht sein
(to) be divorced	(unit 2)	geschieden sein
(to) be excited	(unit 8)	aufgeregt sein
(to) be hygienic	(unit 8)	hygienisch sein
(to) be in charge of s.o.	(unit 1)	verantwortlich sein für jmd.
(to) be lucky	(unit 2)	Glück haben
(to) be off sick	(unit 1)	krankgeschrieben sein
(to) be over	(unit 5)	vorbei sein
(to) be overweight	(unit 4)	übergewichtig sein
(to) be paralysed	(unit 8)	gelähmt sein
(to) be patient	(unit 8)	geduldig sein

(to) be proud	(unit 1)	stolz sein
(to) be ready for sth.	(unit 5)	bereit sein
(to) be sensitive	(unit 8)	sensibel sein
(to) be short of money	(unit 2)	mit dem Geld knapp sein
(to) be unable	(unit 8)	unfähig sein
(to) be unemployed	(unit 2)	arbeitslos sein
(to) be upset	(unit 4)	bestürzt sein
(to) bear in mind	(unit 6)	bedenken
(to) become extinct	(unit 13)	aussterben (Arten)
bedsitter, bedsit	(unit 6)	Wohnschlafzimmer, Einzimmerapartment
bedsore	(unit 8)	Druckgeschwür; Dekubitus
behaviour	(unit 13)	Verhalten
bills (or: extra costs, extras)	(unit 6)	Nebenkosten
bits and pieces	(unit 5)	Scherben
(to) bleach	(unit 3)	bleichen
blog	(unit 12)	Weblog, Internettagebuch
blood pressure	(unit 10)	Blutdruck
blouse	(unit 3)	Bluse
boarding house	(unit 13)	Pension
boring	(unit 2)	langweilig
(to) bottle up emotions	(unit 4)	Gefühle in sich hineinfressen
bow tie	(unit 3)	Fliege
brackets	(unit 5)	Klammern
brave	(unit 4)	tapfer (nicht: brav)
(to) break up with s.o.	(unit 4)	eine Freundschaft beenden
breath	(unit 12)	Atem
(to) breed	(unit 2)	züchten
brickwork	(unit 6)	Mauerwerk
(to) brush	(unit 12)	bürsten
bucket	(activity)	Eimer
button	(unit 9)	Knopf
by 10 p.m.	(unit 6)	bis (spätestens) 22:00 Uhr

by 6 o'clock	(unit 5)	bis (spätestens) sechs Uhr
calf (sg.), calves (pl.)	(unit 12)	Wade
canned	(unit 11)	in Dosen verpackt
capacity	(unit 13)	Fassungsvermögen, Kapazität
cardigan	(unit 3)	Strickjacke
(to) care for s.o.	(unit 3)	jmd. pflegen
carpenter	(unit 4)	Zimmermann, Zimmerfrau
carpet	(unit 6)	Teppich
(to) carry out	(activity)	durchführen
(to) cause	(unit 3)	verursachen
cellar	(talking games)	Keller
(to) censor	(unit 10)	zensieren
CFC	(unit 13)	FCKW = Fluorchlorkohlenwasserstoff
change	(unit 3)	Wechselgeld
(to) chat	(unit 11)	plaudern
cheese platter	(unit 6)	Käseplatte
chef	(unit 5)	Koch/Köchin, Küchenchef/-in
cheque	(unit 3)	Scheck
chlorine	(unit 3)	Chlor, auch: chlorhaltig
chopped	(unit 11)	gehackt, zerkleinert
chopping block	(unit 5)	Hackklotz
chronicle	(activity)	Chronik
chronological	(activity)	zeitlich
city council	(unit 9)	Stadtverwaltung
classmate	(unit 4)	Klassenkamerad/-in
clatter	(unit 5)	Geklirr
cleansing agents	(unit 6)	Reinigungsmittel
Clonakilty Pudding	(activity)	(englisches Gericht)
clothes factory	(unit 2)	Textilfabrik
College of Further Education	(unit 2)	berufsbildende Schule (Bezeichnung in Great Britain)
(to) comfort	(unit 4)	trösten

(to) commit suicide	(unit 8)	Selbstmord begehen
(to) complain about sth.	(unit 12)	über etwas klagen
compress	(unit 7)	Kompresse, Wickel
(to) concentrate (on)	(unit 6)	sich konzentrieren
concrete	(unit 6)	Beton
(to) condemn	(unit 11)	verurteilen
conduct	(unit 9)	Verhalten
confidence	(unit 4)	Selbstvertrauen
connecting door	(unit 9)	Verbindungstür
consciousness	(unit 10)	Bewusstsein
(to) consider	(unit 4)	betrachten, ansehen als
consonant	(activity)	Konsonant
consumption data	(talking games)	Verbrauchsdaten
(to) contain	(unit 3)	enthalten, aufweisen
control	(talking games)	Steuerung
controversial	(list. comp.)	kontrovers
conviction	(activity)	Überzeugung
(to) convince s.o.	(unit 13)	jmd. überzeugen
cooker	(unit 13)	Herd
(to) cope with sth.	(unit 4)	mit etwas fertig werden
(to) copy and paste	(unit 10)	kopieren und einfügen
cordial	(activity)	herzlich
cost of living	(unit 9)	Lebenshaltungskosten
cottage	(unit 6)	kleines Landhaus
(to) create	(activity)	herstellen
crowded	(unit 11)	überfüllt
crushed nutmeg	(talking games)	geriebene Muskatnuss
cul de sac	(unit 6)	Sackgasse
culinary art	(unit 5)	Kochkunst
curriculum vitae (CV)	(activity)	Lebenslauf
curse	(unit 10)	Fluch
customer	(unit 3)	Kunde
cutlet	(unit 13)	Kotelett

cyberbully	(unit 12)	jmd., der im Internet mobbt/schikaniert
deaf	(unit 9)	gehörlos
death	(unit 4)	Tod
decision	(activity)	Entscheidung
(to) decorate	(activity)	schmücken, dekorieren
definitely	(unit 4)	ganz bestimmt
degree	(unit 3)	Grad
delay	(unit 7)	Verspätung
(to) deliver	(unit 1)	liefern
(to) deny	(unit 13)	verneinen, ablehnen
department store	(unit 2)	Warenhaus
deposit required	(unit 6)	Mietkaution erforderlich
(to) deserve sth./s.o.	(unit 4)	jmd./etwas verdienen (aber: Geld verdienen - to earn money)
destination	(unit 7)	Zielort
(to) destroy	(unit 13)	zerstören
destruction	(unit 13)	Zerstörung
detached house	(unit 6)	Einzelhaus, Einfamilienhaus
device	(unit 9)	Gerät
dictatorship	(unit 10)	Diktatur
(to) die	(unit 4)	sterben
dietician	(unit 1)	Diätassistent/-in
difference	(unit 4)	Unterschied
(to) direct	(activity)	lenken
disability	(unit 9)	Behinderung
disabled	(unit 9)	behindert
disabled people	(unit 9)	Menschen mit Behinderung
disadvantage	(unit 4)	Nachteil
(to) discuss	(unit 2)	diskutieren
dish	(unit 13)	Gericht
disorder	(unit 9)	Fehlsteuerung
distance	(unit 6)	Entfernung
distant	(unit 13)	entfernt
(to) distinguish	(unit 12)	unterscheiden

DIY	(unit 6)	Do it yourself, Heimwerken
DIY enthusiast	(unit 6)	Heimwerker
(to) do the garden	(unit 2)	den Garten pflegen
doctor's assistant	(unit 13)	Arzthelfer/-in, med. Fachangestellte/r
domestic bursar (or: housekeeper)	(unit 2)	Hauswirtschafter/-in
domestic science	(unit 2)	Hauswirtschaft
dressy	(unit 3)	schick
(to) drop s.o./sth.	(unit 8)	jmd./etwas fallen lassen
(to) dry-clean	(unit 3)	chemisch reinigen
dull	(list. comp.)	langweilig
(to) dust	(unit 6)	Staub wischen
ecological value	(unit 13)	ökologischer Wert
education	(unit 1)	Bildung
ego-based	(unit 12)	ego-basiert
elderly	(unit 6)	ältlich
embarrassed	(unit 10)	verlegen
emergency	(unit 9)	Notfall
employee	(unit 9)	Arbeitnehmer/-in
employer	(unit 5)	Arbeitgeber/-in
enclosure	(activity)	Anlage
(to) ensure	(unit 3)	sichern
enthusiastic	(unit 6)	begeistert
envelope	(unit 5)	Briefumschlag
environment	(unit 3)	Umwelt
environmentalist	(unit 11)	Umweltschützer/-in
equipment	(unit 6)	Ausstattung
essay	(unit 7)	Aufsatz, Zeitschriftenartikel
evaluation	(unit 8)	Auswertung, Bewertung
event	(unit 7)	Ereignis
every now and then	(unit 2)	ab und zu
exactly	(unit 8)	genau
(to) exaggerate	(unit 13)	übertreiben
exhibition	(unit 7)	Ausstellung
experience	(unit 2)	Erfahrung
(to) express	(unit 7)	ausdrücken
fabric	(unit 3)	Gewebe
fabric conditioner	(unit 3)	Weichspülmittel
facility	(unit 9)	Ausstattung
facing brick	(unit 6)	Verblender
fair pay	(unit 2)	angemessene Bezahlung
(to) feel insecure	(unit 1)	sich unsicher fühlen
fellow students	(unit 2)	Mitschüler/-in
fever	(unit 12)	Fieber
fibre	(unit 11)	Ballaststoff
fig	(activity)	Feige
fillet	(activity)	Filet
finally	(unit 4)	schließlich, endlich
fish fingers	(unit 6)	Fischstäbchen
flat-hunting	(unit 6)	Wohnungssuche
flight	(unit 7)	Flug
(to) foam with rage (ugs.)	(unit 5)	vor Wut schäumen
food	(unit 1)	Nahrung, Essen
football supporters	(unit 5)	Fußballfans
for ages	(unit 4)	seit Ewigkeiten
(to) force	(unit 10)	zwingen
(to) force one's way	(unit 5)	sich seinen Weg bahnen
formatting	(activity)	Format
former	(unit 10)	frühere/r
(to) found	(unit 8)	gründen
freedom	(unit 6)	Freiheit
fridge	(unit 6)	Kühlschrank
frog	(unit 12)	Frosch
funeral	(unit 9)	Begräbnisfeier
furnished	(unit 6)	möbliert
gap	(unit 4)	Lücke
generous	(unit 11)	großzügig
gentle	(unit 3)	sanft
geriatric home (or: old people's home, retirement home)	(unit 1)	Altersheim

geriatric nurse (or: old people's nurse)	(unit 1)	Altenpfleger/-in
(to) get a divorce	(unit 4)	sich scheiden lassen
(to) give s.o. a hand	(unit 1)	helfen
glass of (stout etc.)	(unit 7)	0,284 Liter (britische Maßeinheit)
(to) go abroad	(unit 8)	ins Ausland gehen
grades	(list. comp.)	Schulnoten
greenhouse effect	(unit 13)	Treibhauseffekt
ground plan	(unit 6)	Grundrisszeichnung einer Wohnung
(to) guarantee	(unit 10)	garantieren
guide	(activity)	Führer/-in
guideline	(unit 3)	Richtlinie
guttering	(unit 6)	Regenrinnen
hairy	(unit 2)	haarig (auch: unangenehm)
ham	(activity)	Schweineschinken
hand of a clock	(unit 5)	Zeiger einer Uhr
(to) handle a problem	(unit 4)	mit einem Problem umgehen
(to) handle sth.	(unit 3)	behandeln
(to) hang about	(unit 8)	herumlümmeln
hardness in the water	(unit 3)	Wasserhärte
harm	(unit 13)	Schaden
harmful	(unit 3)	schädlich
(to) have a bad conscience	(unit 2)	ein schlechtes Gewissen haben
(to) have arguments	(unit 8)	Streit haben
head scarf	(unit 2)	Kopftuch
heart attack	(unit 12)	Herzinfarkt
heartily	(unit 7)	herzlich
height, width, length	(talking games)	Höhe/Größe, Breite, Tiefe
hell	(unit 2)	Hölle
helpless	(unit 4)	hilflos
herb	(unit 7)	Kraut, Kräuter
herbal garden	(unit 7)	Kräutergarten
hernia	(unit 12)	Leistenbruch

hesitantly	(unit 3)	zögernd
hint	(unit 5)	Tipp, Ratschlag
hole	(unit 6)	Bruchbude (ugs.); Loch
holly	(unit 7)	Stechpalme
home remedy	(unit 7)	Hausmittel
honest	(unit 11)	ehrlich
(to) honour	(unit 9)	ehren
(to) hoover	(unit 6)	staubsaugen
hotel lounge	(unit 5)	Hotelsalon
household chores	(unit 2)	Hausarbeiten
housekeeper	(unit 1)	Hauswirtschafter/-in
housekeeping	(unit 5)	Hauswirtschaft
housewarming party	(unit 6)	Kistenparty, Einzugsparty
(to) hurt s.o.	(unit 5)	jmd. verletzen
identity	(unit 3)	Individualität
immediately	(unit 4)	sofort
impairment	(unit 9)	Beeinträchtigung
improvement	(unit 3)	Verbesserung
in brackets	(unit 5)	in Klammern
in common	(unit 2)	gemeinsam
(to) include	(unit 6)	einschließen
(to) increase	(unit 8)	zunehmen
independent	(unit 9)	eigenständig
indifference	(unit 5)	Gleichgültigkeit
ingredient	(unit 8)	Zutat
initial	(unit 7)	am Anfang, erste/r
injection	(unit 10)	Spritze
injustice	(unit 10)	Ungerechtigkeit
(to) inspire	(activity)	auslösen
instead of	(unit 4)	anstelle von
insulation	(unit 6)	Isolation
insult	(unit 12)	Beleidigung
integration	(unit 9)	Integration
intention	(unit 8)	Absicht
(to) interrupt	(unit 10)	unterbrechen
invisible	(unit 10)	unsichtbar
invitation	(unit 6)	Einladung
(to) iron	(unit 3)	bügeln

irregularities	(activity)	Unregelmäßigkeiten
IT package	(activity)	Computerprogramm
italic	(activity)	kursiv
item	(unit 3)	Sache, Gegenstand
jam	(unit 1)	Marmelade
jobseeker	(unit 7)	Arbeitssuchende/r
juice	(unit 11)	Saft
keycard	(unit 9)	Kartenschlüssel
kindergarten teacher (or: nursery nurse)	(unit 11)	Erzieher/-in
kitchenette	(unit 6)	Kochnische
knowledge	(unit 4)	Wissen
lager	(unit 7)	helles Bier
landing	(unit 6)	Trepppenabsatz
landlady	(unit 6)	Vermieterin
landlord	(unit 6)	Vermieter
landmark	(activity)	Wahrzeichen (eines Landes)
(to) last	(unit 1)	dauern, andauern
laundry	(unit 3)	(Schmutz-)Wäsche
laundry basket	(unit 6)	Wäschekorb
lavatory	(unit 6)	Toilette, Waschraum
(to) lay the table	(unit 5)	den Tisch decken
leafy greens	(unit 11)	grünes Blattgemüse
lean	(unit 11)	mager
lecturer	(unit 9)	Hochschuldozent/-in
leisure activities	(activity)	Freizeitaktivitäten
leisure centre	(unit 11)	Freizeitzentrum
lighter	(unit 13)	Feuerzeug
likely	(unit 7)	wahrscheinlich
lino	(talking games)	Linoleum
lively	(activity)	lebensnah, lebendig
liver cirrhosis	(unit 12)	Leberzirrhose
living space	(unit 6)	Wohnraum
location	(unit 6)	Ort, Wohnort
lodger	(unit 6)	Mieter
long jumper	(unit 13)	Weitspringer

(to) look tired	(unit 1)	müde aussehen
low income	(unit 8)	geringes Einkommen
(to) lower	(unit 3)	herabsetzen, verringern
lung cancer	(unit 12)	Lungenkrebs
mad-cow-disease	(unit 13)	Rinderwahnsinn, BSE
mainly	(unit 9)	überwiegend
maisonette	(unit 6)	Einliegerwohnung
majority	(unit 7)	Mehrheit
(to) make a promise	(unit 4)	ein Versprechen machen
(to) make sth. cook anew	(talking games)	etwas erneut aufkochen lassen
male nurse	(unit 1)	Krankenpfleger
mark	(unit 6)	Note
Maths	(unit 4)	Mathematik
mature	(unit 4)	reif, erwachsen
means	(unit 13)	Mittel
measurement	(unit 7)	Maßeinheit
meatballs	(unit 6)	Frikadellen
men's wear	(unit 3)	Männerkleidung
menu	(unit 1)	Speiseplan
mews	(unit 6)	zur Wohnung umgebauter Stall
midnight	(unit 12)	Mitternacht
mineral rock wool	(unit 6)	(Mineral-)Steinwolle
minimum criteria	(unit 6)	Mindestkriterien
mistletoe	(unit 7)	Mistel (-zweig)
(to) moan	(unit 5)	maulen
mobility	(unit 7)	Mobilität
molasses	(unit 11)	Melasse, Zuckersirup
monarchy	(unit 7)	Monarchie
(to) move into	(unit 6)	einziehen (in Wohnung)
(to) mow the lawn	(unit 2)	Rasen mähen
(to) murmur	(unit 13)	murmeln
mushrooms	(activity)	Pilze
napkin	(activity)	Serviette

narrow	(unit 4)	eng
national anthem	(unit 7)	Nationalhymne
nerd	(unit 12)	Sonderling
nightmare	(unit 5)	Alptraum
noise	(unit 5)	Lärm
noisy	(unit 8)	laut
non-returnable	(unit 13)	Wegwerf-
not to care about	(unit 4)	sich nicht kümmern um
nurse	(unit 1)	Krankenpflegerin
nursery nurse	(unit 8)	Kinderpfleger/-in, Erzieher/-in
nutrients	(unit 10)	Nährstoffe
nutrition	(activity)	Ernährung
nutritional value	(unit 11)	Nährwert
nutritive	(unit 10)	Ernährungs-
obituary	(unit 4)	Todesanzeige
odd job (or: part-time job)	(unit 2)	Gelegenheitsarbeit
old couple	(unit 2)	ein altes Paar
old people's home (or: geriatric home)	(unit 1)	Altersheim, Altenwohnheim
old people's nurse (or: geriatric nurse)	(unit 1)	Altenpfleger/-in
on time	(unit 7)	pünktlich
once	(unit 4)	einmal
one's own four walls	(unit 6)	die eigenen vier Wände
opinion poll	(unit 13)	Meinungsumfrage
organic foods	(unit 13)	biologisch-dynamisch erzeugte Lebensmittel
Ouch!	(unit 6)	Aua!
"out of the saucepan into the fire"	(unit 6)	"vom Regen in die Traufe kommen" (Redewendung)
(to) overthrow	(unit 10)	jmd. stürzen
overweight	(unit 11)	Übergewicht
ozone layer	(unit 13)	Ozonschicht
(to) paralyse	(unit 9)	lähmen
(to) paraphrase	(unit 4)	umschreiben
participant	(activity)	Teilnehmer/-in
partition	(talking games)	Vorschlag

(to) pass away	(unit 4)	sterben, dahinscheiden
(to) pass through a sieve	(talking games)	durch ein Sieb passieren
(to) patronise	(unit 9)	beschützen
(to) peel	(unit 13)	schälen
people with special needs	(unit 9)	Menschen mit Behinderungen
per cent (BrE), percent (AmE)	(unit 12)	Prozent
permanently	(unit 7)	dauerhaft
personally	(unit 12)	persönlich
pesticides	(unit 13)	Pestizide
pharmacy	(unit 7)	Apotheke
physical strength	(unit 8)	körperliche Stärke
piece of clothing	(unit 2)	ein Stück Kleidung
pint	(unit 7)	0,568 Liter (britische Maßeinheit)
plaice	(activity)	Scholle
plate	(unit 1)	Teller
plum pudding	(unit 7)	Plumpudding
plump	(unit 11)	mollig
(to) poach	(activity)	dünsten
(to) polish	(unit 5)	polieren
political activist	(unit 9)	politischer aktiver Mensch
porous concrete	(unit 6)	Schaumbeton
porridge	(unit 5)	Haferflockensuppe
posture	(activity)	Haltung
power consumption	(talking games)	Stromverbrauch
practical experience	(unit 7)	praktische Erfahrung
practical training	(unit 1)	Praktikumsplatz
(to) prefer	(unit 5)	vorziehen, lieber tun
presentation	(unit 7)	Darbietung, Vorstellung
(to) prevent	(unit 8)	verhindern
prevention	(unit 4)	Verhütung, Vermeidung
prewash	(unit 3)	Vorwäsche
privacy	(unit 6)	Ungestörtheit
probably	(unit 4)	wahrscheinlich

(to) promise	(unit 1)	versprechen
promotion	(unit 13)	Beförderung
(to) pronounce	(activity)	(ein Wort) aussprechen
pronounciation	(activity)	Aussprache
property	(unit 6)	Eigentum, Besitz
property type	(unit 6)	Wohnungstyp
(to) protect	(unit 3)	schützen
proudly	(unit 13)	stolz
(to) provide	(unit 11)	liefern, bereitstellen
pub	(unit 7)	Gaststätte
public	(activity)	Öffentlichkeit
public resource	(unit 10)	eine öffentliche Quelle
pure	(unit 3)	rein, pur
(to) put sth. at risk	(list. comp.)	etwas riskieren
quarrel	(activity)	Streit
(to) quit	(unit 5)	kündigen, aufhören
rather	(unit 4)	eher, lieber
ready-to-serve meal	(unit 11)	Fertiggericht
reason	(unit 3)	Grund, Ursache
(to) receive sth.	(unit 9)	etwas erhalten
receptionist	(unit 5)	Empfangsdame, Portier
recipe	(unit 8)	(Koch-)Rezept
(to) reduce	(unit 3)	reduzieren
reference	(activity)	Arbeitszeugnis
refusal	(unit 5)	Ablehnung
register	(unit 9)	Verzeichnis
regularly	(unit 12)	regelmäßig
relative	(unit 12)	Verwandte/r
(to) remain undiscovered	(unit 10)	unentdeckt bleiben
remark	(unit 7)	Bemerkung
remote control	(unit 9)	Fernbedienung
rental period	(unit 6)	Mietzeitraum
resident	(unit 8)	Bewohner/-in, Heiminsasse
responsibility	(unit 4)	Verantwortung
responsible	(unit 8)	verantwortlich

restless	(unit 12)	ruhelos, schlaflos
retailer	(unit 13)	Einzelhändler
retirement home	(unit 10)	Altenheim
(to) return	(unit 6)	wiedergeben, anzeigen; zurückbringen
revenge	(unit 12)	Rache
reverse	(activity)	umgekehrt
(to) roast briefly	(talking games)	kurz anbraten
roll-in shower	(unit 9)	mit Rollstuhl benutzbare Dusche
routine	(unit 2)	(Tages-)Ablauf
rubbish tip	(unit 2)	Müllhalde
rule	(unit 3)	Regel
sacrifice	(list. comp.)	Opfer
salary	(unit 9)	Einkommen
sales	(unit 3)	Schlussverkauf
sauté	(activity)	kurz Angebratenes
(to) save money	(unit 2)	Geld sparen
scientific	(unit 9)	wissenschaftlich
(to) scream	(unit 1)	schreien
(to) scrub	(unit 5)	schrubben
secular	(unit 9)	weltlich
secure	(unit 4)	sicher
segments	(activity)	Teilstücke
(to) select	(unit 11)	auswählen
self-awareness	(unit 4)	Selbstwahrnehmung
self-esteem	(unit 4)	Selbstwertgefühl, Selbstachtung
semi	(unit 6)	Halb-, Reihen-
semi-detached house	(unit 6)	Doppelhaushälfte
senior citizen	(unit 10)	Senior/-in
senseless	(unit 4)	sinnlos
(to) separate	(unit 3)	sich trennen, scheiden
(to) serve food	(unit 2)	Essen servieren
(to) shadow	(unit 1)	begleiten
shy	(unit 1)	schüchtern
(to) sigh	(unit 1)	seufzen
sights	(list. comp.)	Sehenswürdigkeiten

silk	(unit 3)	Seide
similarity	(activity)	Ähnlichkeit
sin	(unit 13)	Sünde
skirt	(unit 3)	Rock
slice of bread	(unit 12)	Brotscheibe
slim	(unit 11)	schlank
(to) soak	(unit 3)	einweichen
social allowance	(unit 2)	Sozialhilfe
soda bread	(activity)	mit Backsoda gebackenes Brot
(to) solve a problem	(unit 4)	ein Problem lösen
solvent	(unit 3)	Lösungsmittel
somewhere else	(unit 2)	woanders
sorrow	(unit 4)	Traurigkeit
(to) sound good	(unit 2)	gut klingen
source	(unit 11)	Quelle
spacious	(unit 6)	geräumig
sparingly	(unit 11)	sparsam
special needs	(unit 9)	Behinderung, besondere Bedürfnisse
species	(unit 13)	Arten, Spezies
(to) spend; spent; spent	(unit 5)	(Zeit) verbringen, auch: (Geld) ausgeben
spin drier speeds	(talking games)	Schleuderdrehzahlen
staff	(unit 5)	das Personal
staff entrance	(unit 5)	Personaleingang
stain	(unit 3)	Fleck
starchy foods	(unit 11)	stärkereiche Lebensmittel
(to) stare into space	(unit 1)	Löcher in die Luft starren (ugs.)
(to) stay awake	(unit 12)	wach bleiben
steam bath	(unit 7)	Dampfbad
steel-toe cap	(unit 3)	Stahlkappenschuh
(to) step down	(unit 10)	zurücktreten
sterile	(unit 10)	steril
(to) stir while cooking	(talking games)	während des Kochens umrühren
stockings	(list. comp.)	Strümpfe
stomach	(unit 12)	Magen
stout	(unit 7)	dunkles Starkbier

straightaway	(unit 4)	sofort
(to) straighten out	(unit 6)	gerade machen, strecken
(to) strengthen muscles	(unit 12)	Muskeln stärken
stripped floor	(unit 6)	Fußboden ohne Auslegeware
(to) stutter	(unit 9)	stottern
suburb	(unit 11)	Vorort
(to) succeed (in)	(unit 8)	Erfolg haben, gewinnen
success	(activity)	Erfolg
suggestion	(unit 9)	Empfehlung
suit	(unit 3)	Anzug
suitable	(activity)	passend
(to) summarise	(activity)	zusammenfassen
superior	(unit 13)	Vorgesetzte/r
support	(activity)	Unterstützung
(to) support	(unit 8)	unterstützen
(to) suppress	(unit 10)	unterdrücken
surgical ward	(unit 1)	chirurgische Station eines Krankenhauses
survey	(unit 3)	Untersuchung, Umfrage
sweaty palms	(unit 9)	schwitzende Hände
sweater	(unit 3)	Pullover
(to) sweep	(unit 5)	fegen
synthesizer	(unit 9)	Umwandler
syrup	(unit 12)	Sirup
table	(unit 6)	Tabelle
(to) take care of s.o.	(unit 1)	sich um jmd. kümmern
(to) take delight in	(list. comp.)	Vergnügen finden an
(to) take into account	(activity)	etwas berücksichtigen
(to) talk over	(unit 6)	darüber reden, durchsprechen
target	(unit 7)	Ziel
task	(activity)	Aufgabe
tasteful	(unit 12a)	geschmackvoll
team	(unit 2)	Mannschaft
(to) tell s.o. off	(unit 10)	jmd. ausschimpfen

temporarily	(unit 7)	zeitlich begrenzt
terraced houses	(unit 6)	Reihenhäuser
theatre	(unit 1)	Operationssaal (auch: Theater)
thumb	(unit 12)	Daumen
(to) tidy up	(unit 2)	aufräumen
tight clothes	(unit 11)	engsitzende Kleidung
tiled	(unit 6)	gefliest
tiles	(unit 6)	Fliesen, Kacheln
till	(list. comp.)	Kasse
tongue	(unit 12)	Zunge
tonsilitis	(unit 12)	Mandelentzündung
tooth (sg.), teeth (pl.)	(unit 8)	Zahn, Zähne
(to) toss and turn	(unit 12)	sich hin und herwälzen
tough	(unit 12)	rau, hart
towel	(unit 12)	Handtuch
tradesmen	(unit 6)	Handwerker
traffic jam	(unit 13)	Verkehrsstau
trainee	(unit 7)	Auszubildende/r
training	(unit 5)	Ausbildung
tray	(unit 2)	Tablett
tray	(unit 1)	Tablett
(to) treat	(unit 5)	jmd. behandeln
trolley	(unit 1)	Handwagen, Einkaufswagen
tub	(unit 3)	Wanne
tumble-dryer	(unit 3)	Wäschetrockner
tunic	(unit 3)	Kittel
turkey	(unit 7)	Truthahn
(to) turn down	(unit 6)	leiser drehen; auch: ablehnen

twice	(unit 4)	zweimal
unfortunately	(unit 7)	unglücklicherweise
uprising	(unit 10)	Aufstand
urgently	(unit 13)	dringend
vegetarian	(unit 11)	Vegetarier/-in
violence	(unit 10)	Gewalt
violent	(unit 10)	gewaltsam
vocational school	(unit 1)	berufsbildende Schule
vowel	(activity)	Vokal
wage	(unit 13)	Lohn
waistcoat	(unit 3)	Weste
wardrobe	(unit 3)	Kleiderschrank
waste	(unit 3)	Verschwendung, auch: Abfall
wealthy	(unit 11)	reich
week off	(unit 8)	eine Woche dienstfrei
weight	(unit 11)	Gewicht
wheelchair	(unit 9)	Rollstuhl
whole grain	(unit 11)	Vollkorn
widow (female), widower (male)	(unit 6)	Witwe; Witwer
window pane	(unit 6)	Fensterscheibe
wooden	(unit 5)	hölzern
(to) work on shifts	(unit 8)	im Schichtdienst arbeiten
work placement	(unit 1)	Praktikumsplatz
(to) worry	(unit 12)	sich Sorgen machen
(to) wrap	(unit 3)	einpacken
(to) yell	(unit 4)	schreien
youth hostel	(unit 6)	Jugendherberge

Bildnachweis

archiv-klar/Reto Klar: S. 88
Associated Press GmbH, Frankfurt am Main: S. 75/2
Bavaria Agentur, Hamburg: S. 129
Betonstein-Union GmbH, Hamburg: S. 135
Bilddatenbank NRW Staatskanzlei des Landes Nordrhein-Westfalen: S. 25/3
Michael Collins Centre, West Cork, Ireland: S. 99/3
DK Berufsmode: S. 27/1
dpa Picture-Alliance GmbH, Frankfurt a.M.: S. 10, 40, 57, 69/2,3,4; 71/5, 75/1, 76, 79/5, 87/3-5; 90/1, 91; 99/1, 102/1, 143/1
Ecolab, Forth Worth, Texas: S. 26/2
Ehmsen, Birgit, Kiel: S. 117, 120, 121
Fotolia Deutschland, Berlin - © www.fotolia.de: S. 5/3, 79/2 (marka Wariatkau), S. 6/2, 11, 79/1 (Jason), 15/1 (Andreas Wolf) , 15/2 (Supar Perfundo), 15/3, 4, 7, 59, 69/5, 84/1, 106 (Yuri Arcurs), 15/5 (Skikids-akiebler) ,15/6 (Popkonzert-G.Light), 15/8 (sterneleben), 15/9 (Uwe Annas), 16 (Scott Griessel), 20 (Esther Hildebrandt), 26/1 (Christian Schwier), 27/4 (Kayros Studio), 27/5 (reinobjektiv), 27/7 (foustontene), 27/8 (badhogfotolia), 27/10 (robinmac), 27/11 (Trud Design), 30 (Brigitte Bonaposta), 37/1 (vlorzor), 37/2 (mangostock), 38 (Klaus Eppele), 39 (by-studio), 43 (Mary), 34 (Angelika_Bentin), 65 (fotofrank), 66 (LVDESIGN), 69 (womue), 70/1 (haveseen), 70/2 (pixstore), 71/1 (Bergfee), 71/2 (jomare), 71/3 (Adam Gregor), 71/4 (photolens), 78, 84/2 (sterneleben), 91 (o.A.), 94 (Benny Weber), 99/2 (Olly), 101 (Oliver Flörke), 109 (o.A.), 115/1 (Alexey Lobur), 115/2 (o.A.), 115/3 (Christian Schwier), 115/4 (fotodesign-jegg.de), 115/5 (alma-sacra), 125/1 (ceteastock), 125/2 (Maria P.), 125/4 (Klaus-Peter Adler), 132/1 (Gernot Krautberger), 132/2 (Akhilesh Sharma), 133/1 (contrastwerkstatt), 133/2 (Giuseppe Parisi), 134 (mdworschak), Umschlagfoto (Yahia LOUKKAL)
Fritsche, Burkhard, Köln: S. 7
GaWo Berufsbekleidung: S. 27/2,9
Gay, Claude-Bernard, Hamburg: S. 77, 151, 152, 154
Getty Images, München: S. 5/2, 19, 41, 103/2
iStockphoto, Berlin: S. 5, 46/1, 79/4 (desperado)
Krankenhaus München Schwabing, München: S. 93; 111
Krüper, Werner, Steinhagen: S. 35, 79/3, 81, 125/3
MEYRA-ORTOPEDIA Vertriebsgesellschaft mbH, Kalletal-Kalldorf: S. 90/2
Senkingwerk GmbH, Hildesheim: S. 5/1
Simpfendörfer, D. (Hrsg.), Dr. E. Höll-Stüber, HAUSWIRTSCHAFT nach Lernfeldern, Ernähren und Verpflegen (HT 4202), Hamburg: S. 94
TransFair, Verein zur Förderung des Fairen Handels mit der „Dritten Welt" e.V., Köln: S. 143/2
Werkstatt Bremen, Eigenbetrieb der Stadtgemeinde Bremen: S. 87/1
wikimedia.org: S. 78/1
www.pressebox.de: S. 101/1
www.superstock.co.uk: S. 87/2

Sämtliche nicht im Bildquellenverzeichnis aufgeführten Zeichnungen: Liliane Oser, 22083 Hamburg